DEVELOPMENT INITIATIVES IN INDIA

DEVELOPMENT INITIATIVES IN INDIA

Editors

V. Narayana Reddy
Associate Professor of Anthropology
S. V. University, Tirupathi

D. Sunder Raj
Junior Faculty
Council for Social Development, Hyderabad

M. Romesh Singh
Dept. of Anthropology
University of Hyderabad, Hyderabad

SERIALS PUBLICATIONS
NEW DELHI (INDIA)

First Published-2008

ISBN: 978-81-8387-191-4

Published by

SERIALS PUBLICATIONS
4830/24, Prahlad Street, Ansari Road
Darya Ganj, New Delhi-110002 (India)
Phone : 23245225 Fax : 91-11-23272135
E-mail: serials@satyam.net.in

CONTENTS

Note: The papers, which are in italics font, are to be typed and processed. The other remaining papers are being sent in soft copy.

ACKNOWLEDGEMENT

We are thankful to K. S. Bhat, Regional Director, Council for Social Development for his support in bringing out this edited volume.

We are grateful to S. Vijaya Kumar, Chief Editor, Indian Journal of Social Development, for his constant encouragement in our academic endeavor. We are thankful to all our colleagues and friends for their timely suggestions and valuable contributions. All the authors from the academic fraternity, Scholars from the Research, Training and Development front who have shared their rich experience through their papers, we owe a lot for all them.

We thank Ms. K. Mahalakshmi, Shri P. Kumar and Shri. Y. S. S. Prasad who have readily extended their unstinted assistance.

We are grateful to Shri. S. K. Jha, Serials Publications, New Delhi for publishing this book in a nice way.

We thank all those who have helped and contributed directly and indirectly in our venture.

Hyderabad

V. Narayana Reddy
D. Sunder Raj
M. Romesh Singh

CONTRIBUTORS

P. N. Rao, Associate Professor, Dept. of Economics, Nagarjuna University, A. P. 522 510.

K. Prabhakar, Research Scholar, Department of Economics, S. K. University, Anantapur 515 003.

K. Satyanarayana Reddy, Associate Professor, Department of Economics, S. K. University, Anantapur 515 003.

M. Srinivasa Reddy, Research Associate, CESS, N.O Campus, Begumpet Hyderabad 500 016.

M. Lakshmi Narasaiah, Professor, P.G Centre, Sri Krishnadevaraya University, Kurnool.

L. Reddeppa, Faculty Member, Council for Social Development, Hyderabad–500 030.

P. Venkateswarlu, Department of Economics, Osmania Unversity, Hyderabad.

R. D. Singh, Reader, Department of Regional Planning and Economics Growth, Barkatullah University, Bhopal.

R. Venkata Ravi, Associate Fellow, Council for Social Development, Hyderabad-500 030.

V. Narayana Reddy, Associate Professor, Sri Venkateswara University, Tirupathi.

Awadhesh Kumar Singh, Faculty, MMEM Programme, Institute of Management Sciences, Lucknow University, Lucknow.

Satya Prakash Pandey, Visiting Faculty, Institute of Development Studies, Lucknow University, Lucknow.

N. Narayanasamy, Professor of Extension Education, Gandhigram Rural Institute, Gandhigram 624 302, Tamil Nadu.

M. P. Boraian, Reader in Extension Education, Gandhigram Rural Institute, Gandhigram 624 302, Tamil Nadu.

M. Perumal, Lecturer in Economics, Urumu Dhanalakshmi College, Tiruchirappalli.

K. Anil Kumar, Research Scholar, Dept. of Anthropology, University of Hyderabad, Hyderabad.

M. Romesh Singh, Faculty, Council for Social Development, Rajendranagar, Hyderabad-30.

I. Sundar, Lecturer in Economics, Directorate of Distance Education, Annamalai University, Chennai.

D. Pulla Rao, Associate Professor, Dept. of Cooperation & Applied Economics, Andhra University, Visakhapatnam-530 017.

Lakshmi Kulshetra, Head Dept. of Economics & Management, Dayalbagh Educational Institute (Deemed University), Agra.

Smitha Gupta, Senior Lecturer, Dept. of Economics & Management, Dayalbagh Educational Institute (Deemed University), Agra.

K. Sudha Rani, Associate Professor, Dept. of Adult Education, S.V. University, Tirupati-517 502.

G. Hussain Reddy, Project Assistants, Dept. of Adult Education, S.V. University, Tirupati-517 502.

K.G. Bharathi, Project Assistants, Dept. of Adult Education, S.V. University, Tirupati-517 502.

Lakshmi Thakur, Head & Associate Professor, M. D. S. University, Ajmer.

Neelam Bharadwaj, Associate Professor, Agricultural Communication, G. B. Pant University of Agricultre and Technology, Pant Nagar – 263 145, Uttaranchal.

S. K. Kashyap, Associate Professor, Agricultural Communication, G.B. Pant University of Agriculture and Technology, Pant Nagar-263 145, Uttaranchal.

D. Sunder Raj, Faculty, Council for Social Development, Hyderabad-500 030.

K. Vijaya Kumar, Associate Professor of Sociology, School of Distance Education, Andhra University.

P. H. Mohammad, Faculty, Council for Social Development, Rajendranagar, Hyderabad-30.

M. Venkataramana, Faculty, Council for Social Development, Hyderabad-500 030.

B. S. Vasudeva Rao, Associate Professor, Dept. of Adult & Continuing Education, Andhra University, Visakhapatnam-530 017.

M. V. S. S. Prakasa Rao, Researcher, Dept. of Adult Continuing Education, Andhra University, Visakhapatnam-530 017.

P. Hazarika, Faculty Member, Demow College, Demow, Sivasagar, Assam.

INTRODUCTION

Development continues to be a matter of concern both at the conceptual as well as the implementation levels. In fact, development is nearly a household word in the present society. Common adjectives to the word development include community, social, economic, area, regional and the like. Attempts to evolve a comprehensive and convincing definition of development have failed mainly due to persistent inadequacy of comprehensive about its ever-expanding role and subtleties of related specialization and march of multidisciplinary intricacies in the midst of changing political and systematic realties. Development is widely participatory process of directed change in a society, intended to bring about social, economic, political and cultural advancement for the people through greater control over their environment (Jag Mohan Singh Verma, 1998:39).

Scholars like Exman: 1996; Nagel: 1967; Weidner: 1970 and Chturvedi: 1978 strongly opined that development denotes the advancement of a society through progressive stages. Bringing out a society from latent or elementary condition will be regarded as a development. It is found in various fields with different aims. Sometimes, it is used to connote a process, whereas sometimes the product of a process. It is not merely an economic phenomenon, rather a societal phenomenon encompassing all aspects of human life. Moreover, development is the rational process of organizing and carrying out conceived and staffed programmes or projects and process of growth in the direction of nation building and socio-economic progress.

Belshaw (1977) described development as an increase in the capacities of the society to organize for its own objectives and to carry out its programmes more effectively. From this point of view, development is an organized activity and a multidimensional process to improve the social, cultural, economic and human conditions of the people for balanced growth of the society. Vidyarthi (1981) defines development as "growth" plus "change". It involves material and human factors. He clarifies this point saying that the economic approach of development is not acceptable because socio-cultural factors also are integral part of the dynamics of growth and that social change is not a simply a non-functional effect of planning. Therefore, development is a holistic phenomenon. Hence, development process has to be ultimately assessed for impact on quality of life and human well being. In this context, the human development index, developed and refined by the United Nations Development Programme (UNDP) over the last decades deserves special mention. It consists of a scale from zero to one ranking countries in terms of quality of life of its people, particularly the poorest. The index is computed from– gross domestic product per capita, adjusted for local purchasing power; life expectancy at birth; adult literacy; the number of persons enrolled in educational institutions. Originally developed by Mahbub ul-Haq, the index has been used since 1993 by the United Nations Human Development Program, which issues an annual report. Because of continual improvements in the statistical measures used to determine the score, comparisons of scores or ranks from reports in different years is problematic.

The term development involves all aspects of human activity. In still broader context, nations have been defined as develop or developing. But how can one justify that one is more developed than those who are to be developed. These questions have become very sensitive now-a-day when one finds under developed in some sphere everywhere. A society or nation may be more developed in economic front whereas; it may be underdeveloped in social front. So, one cannot define development in some aspects only, rather it should be viewed multi-dimensionally. The narrow concept of development prevalent in the fifties and early sixties has been seriously questions and has been widened to include non-economic aspects as well. The negative consequences and social injuries of rapid technological changes witnessed in the forms of widespread alienation increase in divorce rate, crime, social violence, drug addiction, AIDS and other patterns of social pathology, not to speak of pollution and depletion of resources, have brought the narrow economic conceptualisations under critical study. It is obvious that in our approach to economic development of a community, we must take into account many social, political, ecological, legal, religious co-efficient of economic factors, which interact one another in the social system of that community.

Development, in its varied dimensions, is a subject of intense and absorbing interest for social scientists in all the countries, whether developed or developing. Much has already been written and much more may be in the pipeline to further unravel and explore the multifaceted realties of development. In recent times, development thinking in the developing world has undergone a sea change giving rise to a serious search for alternative development paradigms. In India, development, definitionally and conceptually, denotes progress–social, economic, educational, cultural, scientific and technological change brought by planned and programmed efforts to inaugurate an era of orderly and peaceful transformation of a society in a constitutionally desired direction.

With the dawn of Independence and adoption of the constitutions of free India, new strategies, initiatives and approaches have come into, being based on past experiences and changing needs. Variety of approaches and strategies like top-down approach, regional planning, target group approach, integrated development, participatory development, joint forest management, poverty alleviation and family oriented programmes have formed part of the development initiatives. Of late, however, the prime emphasis and concentration has been paid to the people's participation in the development process at grass-roots level. Besides, various groups and NGOs are striving hard to increase the awareness and participation levels of rural people. The Panchayats and Co-operative bodies are in existence for five decades. According to Constitution, allocating more power to the Panchayats is a significant step for the development of rural people.

In this connection, the present book has made an attempt to document various experiments made by government and other organizations and also experiences gained in such process and its impact on life of the people. The book is classified into four sections– *Agriculture Development, Rural Development, Women Development and Social Development,* which can also provide holistic view of various development initiatives taken up for poor people in the country.

AGRICULTURE DEVELOPMENT

India has been and continues to be a predominantly rural country. According to 2001 census, 72.25 per cent of India population of (total population 1027 million lives in villages. Agriculture is a crucial component of the Indian economy and it accounts for two-third of the employment and it provides food, nutritional and employment security. Hence, agricultural development continues to remain as primary task among various development initiatives launched by the government. Simultaneously, initiated various steps to improve the agriculture practice in rural India. In this connection, this section brings out various agriculture development issues by presenting five seminal papers.

The first paper entitled *"Impact of Agricultural Credit on Productivity An Econometric Analysis"* by P.N. Rao, clearly indicates that with advent of green revolution and consequent agricultural development the demand for credit for agricultural production activity has increased. Financial support to farm households, in particular to small and marginal farmers will have direct impact on the production process. Though institutional arrangements made by central and state governments created large network of credit delivery system to agriculture, they are not able to meet the complete credit needs of small and marginal farmers while several studies have established that credit constraints can effect farmers' investment behaviour only a limited number of studies have empirically measured the effect of credit constraints on productivity. So there is an urgent need to examine the implications of institutional credit on productivity.

This paper further highlights the existing pattern of credit delivery system does not cover all categories of farm households in the region, where the thrust is to expand agricultural output. Therefore there should be some redirection in the existing credit policies with regard to the capital needs of small and marginal farmer.

A paper entitled "*Changes In The Productivity of Groundnut And Sugarcane. During Pre And Post Green Revolution Periods In Andhra Pradesh*" by K. Prabhakar, K. Satyanarayana Reddy and M. Srinivasa Reddy, explained that growth and stability in the production of groundnut and sugarcane were complementary to each other rather than competitive in irrigated regions. Though significant and positive growth in the production of groundnut and sugarcane has emerged as a common feature in all the three regions of the state, its magnitude is not uniform across the regions. Instability in area and production of these two crops are relatively quite prominent at regional level while stability is quite prominent at state level. Yield variability is equal to average instability at three regions in both the period II and I i.e. pre and post Green Revolution period. Area instability is the major source of production instability. Therefore, concerted efforts should be made to safeguard the farmers against instability. This calls for adequate measure to improve location-specific production technology, through research, development and extension efforts and also through ensured input supply mechanism. It is possible that most of the fluctuations are due to pricing and payment policies of the two crops. This is an area that needs further investigated.

It is well known fact that irrigated agriculture is up against an enormous challenge. India's population continues to grow at a tremendous rate. Over the next 10 years, there will be more extra mouths to feed. Water is becoming increasingly scare for agriculture, with conflicting demands being made on limited supplies by the domestic and industrial sectors. The most attractive irrigation sites have already been exploited. Yet, irrigated agriculture will have to deliver average output increases of at least 3.5 per cent year if future food demands are to be met in India. In this background, a critical essay entitled *"Irrigation Management–Facing the Challenge"* by Lakshmi Narasaiah brings out the importance of proper irrigation management in the country. This paper highlighted that forty years ago in the 1950s and 1960s, India has worried about its capacity to produce sufficient food to feed its growing population. Episodes of food scarcity were not uncommon. It was dreaded that millions would die of hunger. Then dawned the miracle of the "green revolution". Cereal production increased by leaps and bounds, boosted by expanded irrigation, increased fertilizer application and modern crop varieties. The vigorous response in mobilizing financing towards boosting agricultural production paid off. Moreover, given the importance of irrigation to the India's food supply and the vast resources expanded on irrigation development, it is tragic that the actual performance of irrigation systems is so disappointingly low. In the post-green revolution era, it has become increasingly evident that the performance of irrigation systems, especially in large-scale systems, is sub-optimal whether measures in terms of achieving planned area targets or in terms of production potentials created by the physical works. In many irrigation systems, the actual area irrigated is much lesser than the command area. Sharp inequities in water supplies between farmers in the head reaches of irrigation systems and those located downstream are another manifestation of poor performance. Investigations in the Tungabhadra Irrigation Scheme reveal the tail-end of a major distributory commanding 25% of the total area, received approximately 20-40% of the targets discharge while the upper reaches got more than their share.

This paper further pointed out that lack of maintenance has caused many systems to fall into disrepair, further inhibiting performance. Over time, distribution canals have become silted up, increasing the likelihood of breaching, damage to outlets and leading to salt build-up in the soil.

In the similar line, L. Reddeppa's paper *"Bore Well Irrigation in Drought Areas: A Study in Andhra Pradesh"*, also critically examined the impact of bore well irrigation on cropping pattern, productivity, incremental income and its effects on socio-economic development of the small and marginal farmers in Andhra Pradesh. This paper is based on the primary data collected from the small and marginal farmers who received assistance under the bore well irrigation scheme. This study clearly indicated that the bore well irrigation has made them to shift from domestic consumption crops to cash crops. This paper brings out the positive impact of introducing bore well irrigation scheme in the study areas. For instance, it has not only ensured food security for them but also purchased valuable assets to the family. Their social status has also been improved in terms of good marriage proposals to their children and gained recognition in the society and relatives after bore well irrigation.

The last paper of this section *"Price Elasticity of Acreage under Cotton Crop: A Case Study of Telangana Region"* by P.V. Venkateshwarlu describes the changes in prices lagged year have been planning a vital role in agricultural sector. In order to study the impact of the prices on the area under cultivation, various empirical exercises have been carried out in India. As far as Andhra Pradesh state is concerned, most of the empirical studies on acreage response to the changes in lagged prices have been confined mainly to food crops. Therefore, this article calls for serious attention from concern authority to generate empirical information on the responsiveness of acreage to the changes in lagged prices of commercial crops such as cotton. This crop in Telangana region of Andhra Pradesh has attracted the attention of the policymakers as most of the farmers cultivating this crop have attempted suicides.

This paper makes an attempt to examine the impact of lagged prices on the acreage under cotton crop in selected districts of Telangana region and clearly shows that both lagged prices of cotton and yield found to be significant in all the districts influencing the decision of the farmers in allocating the area under cotton. Therefore, suitable price policy to augment the area under cotton crop in Telangana districts is required to bring a break through in overall production.

RURAL DEVELOPMENT

Rural development is not merely development of rural areas but it should also result in the fortification of living standards among the rural masses into self-reliant and self-sustaining communalities. It implies the development of area and people in the rural economy and society. This is highly essential for the integrity, unity and development of the nation. Therefore, rural development is a subject widely discussed in many platforms in terms of inter related social, economical and political issue of development. This section included papers, which turn on to various rural development discourse, perspective and experiences by depicting seven papers.

The first paper of this section begins with R.D. Singh's paper entitled *"Sustainable Community Based Regional Development: A Case of BIMARAU Region"*. This paper investigates the institutional and structural problems of underdevelopment of these regions. The socio political conflicts and the demand for social justice and the socio-political rigidities ignoring the planned economic development by the central and regional governments have resulted in serious socio-economic conflicts in these regions. This paper explores the issues of sustainable development in backward regions, the historical process of colonial control on peripheral agrarian and forest habitat, the pattern of regional eco-degradation and vicious circle of under development in BIMARAU region and provides a strategic model for sustainable community based regional development and information system required for it.

In the late 90s, the grassroot level governance assumes much significance in the process of decentralised development, as a lot depends on the efficacy of local level government in the process of planning for development programmes and managing the same. In the context of local level governance, primarily move includes methods and means by which the higher level of institutions devolving responsibilities and authorities to the lower institutions for managing public resources to solve local level problems and fulfill the needs of the local community. The PRIs are to perform a role of decentralized governance for the participatory development at the grassroot level. A paper entitled *"Participatory Planning at Village Level: A Case Study on Initiatives"* by R. Venkata Ravi, V. Narayana Reddy rightly claimed that the participatory development, in true sense, need to be initiated by the Gram Panchayat by involving the local community in the process of planning and managing the development programmes. Needless to state that only such development plans would reflect the aspirations and felt-needs of the local community. Moreover, decentralized rural development has been a paramount concern of both the Government and Non-Government Organizations for many decades. A series of approaches, strategies and activities have been developed to initiate decentralized development that have made different amount of dent on the development of people in the society. The experiences gained show that the people are unable to absorb the development benefits owing to the various factors, particularly lack of participation. So, the strategies shifted towards participatory development by focusing on the capacity building of the people in terms of increasing competence to get control over the process of decision-making and participation.

It further suggests that any development agency working for the development of Model Village or Gram Panchayat need to prepare a wide-ranging participatory micro level plans covering all sectors and focusing on all sections of the village community. In such a perspective plan, role of Gram Panchayat, CBOs and NGO can be identified. It is also necessary to involve the upper tier Panchayat Raj Institutions while going in for such an exercise to ensure some amount of funds to take up the action plans prepared under the micro level planning document. It would help the Gram Panchayat to tap the people participation the planning process. Moreover, it would also help to gradually build the basic facilities in the village. Involving the people involvement through the CBOs in the process of planning is not sufficient but also required to be involved in contributing for taking up few activities with funds available with them. It is required to tap the un-used resources available with CBOs– like Water Users Association, Forest Management Committee and Self Help Groups. It is equally necessary to make the community to understand that when they are asking for certain facilities from the Gram Panchayat, they have to regularly need to pay what is due to the Panchayat from them.

Discourse on rural marketing occupied an important placed in the current rural development initiatives in India. To bring more light into the issue, Awadesh Kumar Singh and Satya Prakash Pandey's paper entitled *"Rural Marketing and Post Liberalized Era: Emerging Perspectives and Issues"* highlighted the potential on rural marketing in post-liberalized era and also to review the corporate response to the emerging changes in rural markets. The rural scheme is now undergoing a sea change, resulting from the multi-pronged activities undertaken for the overall development of rural areas. There have been significant improvements in the rural sector in respect of agricultural production, spread of education, banking facilities, electrification, transportation, communication, etc., with the increased purchasing power, access to communication and awareness about modern lifestyles, the rural sector needs a better marketing thrust. The growth of the corporate sector means increased production, and this in turn, requires identification and penetration into high growth potential markets. In this context, rural markets have good prospects for most of the goods and services of this liberalized economy. This paper suggested that it is crucial for a company to redesign its marketing-mix, because not much is left in the urban market, which is heading towards saturation. Contrary to this, the rural market has not been tapped scientifically by majority of the companies. In the changing scenario, the corporate houses need strategies for exploitation of potential of rural markets in India.

In Course of time, rural development has traversed from 'government driven community development' to collective effort based 'participatory development and currently, it stands at 'community-driven development'. Participatory development process thus stands neutral to the erstwhile "supply driven" development and the contemporary 'demand–driven' development. In this background, *N. Narayanasamy and M.P. Boraian's paper" Primacy of Participatory Methods in Rural Impact Assessment"* endorsed that Participatory Rural Appraisal (PRA) is an innovative methodology, which aids in locating problems, analysing resources, evolving solutions, formulating projects, monitoring and assessment of the impact on the community. PRA has therefore been professed by Donor agencies, practiced by NGOs, preferred by the government, probed by research institutions and preached by universities like Gandhigram. Indian Council for Social Science Research sponsored research (ICSSR) study, at Gandhigram, which studied the efficacy of PRA methods among the NGOs, concluded that PRA methods are better than the conventional survey research methods in harvesting rural information which would be useful in the tasks of project planning, resource analysis, project implementation, monitoring and impact assessment. It has emerged as an innovative tool of development research methodology with wider application in rural areas, PRA has been found to be better than survey methods in respect of accuracy of data, rapidity of data collection, cost effectiveness and community participation in the process of collecting information from the rural communities. Comparative study of these two methods in a micro setting revealed that the PRA took less time togather, analyse and report the data, less costly, as accurate as the data collected under survey method and people's participation was high in the data gathering process.

Their paper also suggested that PRA could be used as an effective method as well as a tool in the process of impact assessment of agriculture and rural development programmes. With participatory evaluation gaining popularity, greater emphasis is laid on stakeholders' participation in the process of evaluation. People's conception of the development intervention described in words, maps, pictures, etc., matter more in impact assessment. Participatory impact assessment is thus, made a learning process wherein the participants increase their awareness and understanding about the factors effecting their situation and thereby increases their control over the development process.

For the success of any development programme, people's participation is most important. Since the community development programme is a programme of the people and for the people, their roles for its success cannot be overlooked. They are the main basis on whom depends all development. Without the will and participation of the people, development programme will be a forced liability and will not succeed. Considering its importance, M. Perumal's paper entitled *"Sustainable Rural Development through People's Participation"* clearly pointed out that Sustainable Rural Development is the need of the hour and both the central and state governments have launched various programmes for the betterment of the living conditions of the rural mass. This requires people's participation. This paper mainly focuses the participation in the concept of rural development. People's participation at different stages and programmes are also discussed in the paper.

Local/indigenous knowledge encompasses the body of knowledge, which indigenous people have accumulated over generations concerning their environment. It includes knowledge on identification, utilization and management of resources built through observation, experimentation and innovation. Although it is passed on from generation to generation it is not static. It is this knowledge that has guided men through ages in living within their environment. The paper entitled *"Local and Sustainable Development: A Case of Konda Reddi Tribes"* by K. Anil Kumar describes that many indigenous communities, they are wholly or partly dependent on the forest to eke out their livelihood. Their belief systems, social, economic and ritual activities are intricately interwoven around the forest and hills. Indigenous people and forests are ecologically and economically inseparable. They have co-existed since times immemorial and will continue to co-exist in a mutually reinforcing relationship. The indigenous people hold this symbiotic relationship in great esteem and they regard various species of forest as their kith and kin. In recent years, alarmingly high rate of deforestation in many developing countries has been a matter of concern for the people living there and for the development administration. The process of deforestation certainly affects the economy of the state concerned, but more than that it affects the forest dependent communities, as it is closely linked with their subsistence. There are many forest communities, who still depend upon forest exclusively for their food. In view of the indigenous wisdom available among the indigenous groups, there is an urgent need to document properly the indigenous knowledge systems of the various indigenous groups in the country and also promote such life sustaining aspects of culture of various indigenous communities in India.

Therefore, it would be wise to protect and promote indigenous knowledge and wisdom widely in order to reduce poverty among indigenous people. Thus, the above information is highly valuable as it has development among the indigenous communities over generations. So, it is time for academicians, scientists, planners and NGOs, to take care to practice and to intimate proper documentation of indigenous knowledge systems in a more scientific way.

Over five decades of independence witnessed the arrival of various committee reports dealing with socio-economic situation of the tribal population, and evaluation of functioning of development agencies and their policies. Based on this reports new strategies, initiatives and approaches came into existence for the development of tribals. Consequently, efforts were made in successive five year plans to uplift the poor tribal living in our country. Continuous efforts have been made to ameliorate the living condition of the poor tribals. However, it has been percolated to few elite groups and deprived the deserving people. As result, it leads to disparity of development progress in the tribal society. It is mainly due to improper implementation of the programmes, lack of awareness etc. In this backdrops, M. Romesh Singh's paper *"Refection of Tribal Development Programmes: A Case of Manipur"* examined the various reasons for imbalance of development progress in tribal areas of Manipur through micro level study and its possible remedies to fill the gap in planning and policy.

The paper concluded that the planning and development strategy for the tribal development in Manipur is common for both the hill and plain areas. There is no separate planning and development strategies for tribals who are living in the hill areas. Majority of the tribals are living in the hill areas whereas very few populations live in the plain areas. They have different kinds of lifestyles, which cannot be treated as common with regard to their development activities. Moreover, tribals living in plain areas are more advanced and well educated, which do not require much attention like hill people. Even though, the plain people were more benefited from many development programmes carried out by the government agencies that were basically meant for the poor tribals. Hence, the common planning and development strategies also led to the deprivation of majority of the tribals living in hill areas.

WOMEN DEVELOPMENT

To accelerate overall growth and prosperity of the nation, it is very important to create opportunities for socio-economic development of women in India as they constitute half of the population and play a vital role in development of the family and society. The subject of development of women is multidimensional, multisectoral and multidisciplinary in its nature. Since independence, government is taking special attention to empower the women by implementing various programmes. To provide in-depth understanding of women development issues in the country, this section presents seven papers, which are dealing with core issues like self help groups, education and employment and agribusiness etc.

The pace of economic development of the Indian economy to an extent depends upon the development of the rural sector. In this connection banking institutions have been engaged themselves in the implementation of anti-poverty programmes through various approaches. Among the approaches of inplementing anti-poverty Programmes, financing women self-help groups is an important aspect of development strategy in rural India, because economic empowerment is a major focus in the overall empowerment of women. Economic empowerment could be envisaged as a great access to financial resources outside the household. Significant increase in women's own income and power to retain such income and use it at her own discretion, equal access and control over resources at the household level alongwith financial reliance on women. Consequently, a paper entitled *"Inter State Inter Regional Variations in Performance of Banking Institutional Finance Women Self-Help Groups."* By I Sundar, analyses the performance of banking institutions in financing women self-help groups, taking indicators relating to the number of groups concerned, amount sanctioned, peer group credit based on state wise and region wise analysis. This paper suggested that government should allocate more funds for rural development particularly bank credit for the benefit of poor women in the backward and isolated areas.

D. Pulla Rao's paper *"Deprivation of Women in Education And Employement In India:* An *Historical Perspective"* clearly brings out the historical trends of depriving women in education and employment. This paper described that women constitute about 50 per cent in the total population in India. But, they are not given equal opportunities either in education or in employment and hence they are left far behind their male counterparts in all most all the fields of life. They are deprived in the social, economic and political sectors. The over all rate of growth of women employment was recorded less than one per cent during the period 1993-94 to 1999-2000. Lack of equal access to education and employment deprived them equal access to the legislatives both at state level and at the central level. For example, in the present Lok Sabha women constitute only 8.16 per cent to the total members of the Lok Sabha. After Independence, the government of India has designed several strategies for promotion of girls education. Separate institutions for girls/women education were opened. Special incentives to attract the girls/women into the academic institutions were introduced. As a result, the female literacy rate has gone up from 7.93 per cent in 1951 to 54.16 per cent by 2001. In the field of higher education also the share of girls enrollment into various faculties has increased very substantially. The increase in women enrollment in the educational institutions has its impact on the women employment in educational institutions The annual compound growth rates suggest that employment of female teachers has been increasing at a faster rate than that of the male teachers. The employment reservation policy of some state government in favour of women had its impact on higher employment of women teachers in the educational institutions. Yet, in spite of all these favourable Policies and programmes for women, women could not get their due share in employment. Unless some more new strategies are evolved, the women in India will not get their due share and hence the management of gender diversity will become a major issue for future India.

Policy makers have the tendency to define women exclusively in terms of their social roles and to ignore their economic roles. They have simply assumed that what men do is publicly important, measurable and subject to the influence of government policy. Recently, policy makers are becoming more aware that ignoring women's productive role is a serious distortion of reality, which reduces the efficiency as well as the equity of government programmes. Laxmi R. Kulshrestha and Sunita Gupta's paper "A *Study of value addition* by *the Housewives to the family income through Extended SNA Activities"* made a humble effort to devise a method to not only make visible but also to highlight the enormous amount of unpaid work that women do and subsidizes all other kinds of work. This paper further argued that though there are difficulties in valuation of domestic services, but they are not impossible to deal with women must receive due place in economic and social sphere.

K. Sudharani,G. Hussain Reddy and K. G. Bharathi 's paper *"Influence of Literacy and SHG Participation on Social*

Sustainability" examines the influence of literacy and SHG participation on the three aspects namely, communication skills, decision-making capacity and awareness on health, legal and developmental programmes which are the basic components for attaining social sustainability. The present paper is based on the study conducted in the Tirupati Rural and Tirupati Urban Mandals of Chitoor District in Andhra Pradesh. It also proved that literacy and SHG participation shows positive impact on the awareness-decision making and communication kills of the respondents. The literacy alongwith collective strength (SHG Participation) contributed much in promoting competence among the respondents. However, it was low among SHG participation without literacy and literates without SHG participation.

India has unplanned population growth due to mass illiteracy, conservative traditions and customs. Nearly half of the population of our country is below the age of 18 year. If we do not prepare them with the adequate knowledge through population education and awareness, we shall be defeating the purpose of our population policy. Which is based on the democratic principle of voluntary participation of the individual in the population control programmes. The young minds are receptive to such ideas so that they can easily develop a healthy and favourable attitude for a small family. It becomes our duty to aware the people about population phenomena. Like all other problems, the problem of population growth begins in the human minds and the seeds of its solution must also be sown. In this background, Laxmi Thakur's paper *"Population Awareness of Secondary School Teachers: A Case Study of Ajmer City"* clearly spelt out that awareness is a process where the person comes to know about the new ideas or practices. The term "Population Awareness" refers to factual knowledge about population dynamics required understanding the nature and magnitude of the burden impose by rapid population growth. Population awareness can develop an informed society. The key concept is, responsibility and rational decision-making involved further knowledge and understanding of the consequences of one's action, which in turn links individual to the society, then to the nation and next to the world. Hence, an individual becomes an important element in the entire developmental process.

Family planning experts have also recognised that it is very difficult task to make aware the adult couples, because they are slow learners with the rigid values and beliefs. So, it becomes our moral duty to aware the people about this daunting problem. If a teacher is aware about the phenomenon, he or she can make aware students at very early stage of their educational life, as the young mins are more receptive to the new ideas. This paper pointed out that if population awareness programme is to be succeeding one has to lay great emphasis on processes where real learning takes place by bringing about a change in a learner in his understanding, values and attitudes. This involves adoption of very effective methods and subtle means and techniques by a skilled and a dedicated person.

Neelam Bhardwaj and SK Kashyap's paper *"Participatory Communication in Agribusiness: A Development for Hill Women of Uttaranchal"* highlighted that information is the key component in the development process. Information is not only used as input for scientific research but also a national resource for entrepreneurial decision-making. Information management aims at harmonization of development goals, human resources and technologies. Hill women, who live in fragile ecoregions and exposure and other information sources. The trainer should develop training modules, manuals and other materials suitable for both the literate and illiterate women involved in agri business operations. In operations, the women contribute more in the hill area. The hope of generating prosperity in the hill area agribusiness largely depends upon making their contributions more viable through strong linkage with the training organizations, banking and cooperates sectors. Training organizations should also ensure additional support for credits, expert guidance for marketing information and media organizations for the commercial advantage. Participatory communication can become a inspiring force for development in a significant way.

Poverty alleviation has been the primary concern of development planners since long. Poverty alleviation efforts mainly through state driven credit intervention produced only sub-optional results. The real break-through came when efforts to fight poverty emanated from within with in civil society. The new people centered paradigm has broadened the scope of anti-poverty policies and gave a special role to credit, particularly micro finance in the overall poverty eradication process. Lack of institutional credit has been considered as one of the major constraints to the poor to come out of the vicious circle of poverty. D Sunder Raj's paper *"Self-Help Groups And Poverty Alleviation"* highlights that even after 50 years of independence there is no proper banking system to meet the credit needs of the poor. At the government level attempts like introduction of cooperatives followed by nationalization of commercial banks and opening up of regional rural banks were made with a view to reach the institutional credit to the weaker sections particularly the poor. However, all these efforts hardly helped the poor to have better access to institutional credit. Mainly because, the credit needs of the poor are small and urgent. Providing affordable credit to the poor has been recognized as a prime component of development strategy from a long time. Many schemes and resources have thus been devoted to the provision of credit targeted at the poor especially in the rural areas. The Self-Help Groups (SHGs) or the Thrift and Credit Groups are mostly informal groups whose members pool savings and re-Iend within the group on rotational or need basis. Self-help groups are organized in the selected villages for economic and social development of the rural poor and women in particular. These groups have a common perception of need and impulse towards collective action. Several development agencies have promoted and inspired formation of different kinds of thrift and credit groups in Andhra Pradesh to channelise the various poverty alleviation and social development programmes.

SOCIAL DEVELOPMENT

The problem that most of the countries face to day is not that of lack of economic development but that of a problem of distorted development. Distorted development has occurred primarily because economic growth has not been accompanied by concomited improvement in social development. The proponents of social development, therefore, argue that economic growth that has benefited only segment of society is meaningless (Midglay, 1995: 158). Development continued to be viewed primarily in economic terms and economic development model remained unchanged until 1990s. The scenario seems to be somewhat different after world submit for social development (1995) which reaffirmed that the idea of economic development cannot solve the critical social problems facing humanity. Social development is central to the needs and aspirations of the people throughout the world, and to the responsibility of the government and all sector of the civil society. Like "development", 'social development' too has several connotations and is often used very broadly to refer to improvements in human well being. In this section, five papers depicting some of the important issues which are part of social development.

"Population Explosion Vs. Environmental Degradation" by K. Vijaya Kumar described that the relationship between population growth and environmental degradation is felt worldwide. Though various efforts are being made for better progress and development of the society in all fields of life, the rapidly growing population is nullifying some. Unless the 'population bomb' is diffused, all efforts are useless and norm less society will prevail in future. Hence, every citizen should be taught about the negative reflections on rapid growth of population in the degradation of environmental quality leading to physical, social and economic problems and health hazards.

The concern for the plight of child labourers is one such area that attained a galvanised global action through various regional and international deliberations. As a result of these trends demonstrating tremendous appeal for the child cause, India has been identified as a country harbouring the largest number of child labourers of the world. However, the phenomenon of child labour in Indian context has been perceived mostly as an economic problem. Several studies have relegated the economic actors- such as poverty, income etc- as the causes for rampant child labourers in India. Thus, they have neglected focussing on the anthropological/sociological reasons, which are mostly required in a study like child labour in Indian context. In this connection, an essay entitled *"Child Labour In India: An Anthropological Perspective"* by P H Mohammad pointing to lack of such attempts paid to understand child labour from the anthropological/sociological perspective, highlights certain social institutions existed in traditional Indian society which have streamlined the activity of employing children into work force and thus to allow the child labour phenomena to exits in institutional form, in Indian society. The Jajmani system, hereditary specialisation of occupation, socialisation process/ training etc. existed as part of the traditional occupational social structure in India are highlighted as the vehicles which facilitated Indian society to harbour the largest number of child labourers through the child history.

After Independence, we have completed 50 years of planned development process. Since the top to down approach has failed in getting the expected results, more emphasis was laid on micro level planning. The Government observed looking into the results it that people's participation should be the prime concern and mere concentration of economic growth will not help in obtaining the desired results in development. The planned development has both success and failures. During this period, we also witness the emergence of end number of NGOs working in various aspects for the development of the nation. M. Venkataramana's paper *"Non Government Organisations in India: Some Observations"* emphasizes that NGOs are growing as third sector of development their role is very important for the people of our country. This paper richly presented the holistic scenario of the NGOs functioning across the country. The paper also suggested that NGOs should clearly know their roles much before starting the programme and while implementing the programme. Otherwise, it leads to suspicion in the public, which leads to problems even for the existence of the NGO. Moreover, updating the knowledge, training in latest developments, involving in Conferences, Seminars, etc., publicity of the work done either in the form of brochure, report or media will also help the NGOs in strongly establishing themselves by which they can perform well in their activity.

The test of good governance lies in the goals and objectives of a government. In its policies and programmes, in the manner of their execution in the results achieved and above all, the general perception of the people about the quality of functioning of its various agencies towards the public, their sincerity, honesty and commitments towards public duties. It is also important to see that there is on undue concentration of power. B S Vasudeva Rao and Prakash Rao's paper *"Value* of *Good Governance: role* of *Governance and NGOs" suggests* that for achieving value based governance, there is need to rectify certain areas in both government and non-government organizations like corruption, enlisting the support of non-officials bodies, need to implement ideas generated on administrative reforms, need to change political climate, need to democratise and vitalize, Panchayat Raj Institutions. The committed involvement of functionaries and active participation of masses only gives value for good governance.

The world of child labourers is a world of large-scale violation of human rights and in unorganised sectors of the economy. These sections of children are the victims of ruthless torture and exploitation. UN adopted Convention on the Rights of the Child (CRC) 1989 is a healing approach to ameliorate the sufferance of the child labourers in Asian countries, including India where child labour is a predominant phenomenon. *P Hazarika' paper "Adoption* of *UN Convention on the Rights* of *the Child,* 1989 *and Child Labour in India"* pointed out that India has adopted the convention under unavoidable circumstances but its execution still remains to be poor. Many countries of the world have adopted certain welfare measures, other than CRC, either on the government initiatives or in coordination with

NGOs, for abolition of the child labour practices. This paper further claimed that Indian has not succeeded to execute such programmes, but she could abolish the child labour system implementing the plan of actions through the NGOs, VOs and Panchayats.

The foregoing discussions provide a comprehensive understanding on various development issues in India. It also clearly shows that development planning in the country has attempted several strategies and initiatives for the upliftment of poor over the years. However, most of the papers reflected that there is a long way to go for achieving the desired results. In this volume, 24 seminal papers explored the various loopholes exist in the process of development planning and implementations of programmes. Moreover, offered fruitful suggestions and remedies, which can be used for driving the development initiatives in right direction for making a prosperous nation in near future.

REFERENCES

Belshaw, C. (1977), *"The Contribution* of *Anthropology to Development"* in H.M.Mathur (ed) Anthropology in the Development Process, New Delhi, Vikas Publishing Company.

Chaturvedi, T.N. (1978), *"Development. The Dynamics* of *Thorns and Thistles"* in Sharma, S.K. (ed) Dynamics of Development: An International Perspective, Vo1.2, New Delhi, Concept Publication.

Exman, M.T. (1966), *"The Politics* of *Developmenf"* in Montgowerey and Siffin (ed) Approach to Development: Politics, Administration and Challenge. New York, Mc. Graw Hill.

Jag Mohan Singh Verma. (1988), *"Models* of *Development:* A *Critique"* in Srivastava S P (ed). The Development Debate: Critical Perspective, Jaipur , Rawat Publications.

Midglay J . (1995), *"Social Development* as a *Political Philosophy"* in Daniel S Sanders (ed). The Developmental Perspective in Social Welfare, Manoa, University of Haivai Press.

Nagel (1967), *"Determinism and Development"* in B. B. Harris (ed) The Concept of Development: An Issue in Study of Human Behaviour, Mennesopolis, University of Minnesefa Press.

Rao, P.V. (2001), "*Reflections on Tribal Development*" in *Journal* of *Rural Development, Vol.20(1), pp.87-97.*

Vidyarthi, L.P. 1981 "*Tribal Development and its Administration*", New Delhi, Concept Publishing House.

Weidner, E.W. (1970), "*The Elements* of *Development Administration*" in Weidner (ed). Development Administration in Asia. Durcham, Duke University Press.

SECTION I

AGRICULTURE DEVELOPMENT

1

IMPACT OF AGRICULTURAL CREDIT ON PRODUCTIVITY: AN ECONOMETRIC ANALYSIS

P. N. Rao

With advent of green revolution and consequent agricultural development the demand for credit for in Agricultural Production activity has increased. The new agricultural technology is capital intensive and envisages the use of modern inputs like chemical fertilizers, pesticides, HYV seeds irrigation alongwith machines in farm operations. The backwardness of Indian agriculture characterized by low productivity may be attributed to inadequate use of this modern inputs. The deficiency of capital may be another reason for the backwardness of the agriculture in many backward regions. The Indian Agricultural sector dominated by small and managerial farmers, nearly 70% of the farm households are small and marginal farmers. The marketed surplus of there small and marginal farmers being very low, deficiency of capital has become major constraint in the use of modern technology for the small and marginal farmers. The external financial support plays an contributory role for the availability of new agricultural technology and then by increases productivity.

The institutional credit delivery system is such that all borrowers cannot be provided sufficient credit, lenders favour

* Associate Professor, Dept. of Economics, Nagarjuna University, Guntur, AP-522 510

those who can present collateral towards the loans they take. Such people pose less risk because they provide better guarantees in case of default and their incentives contribute to a lower default risk. Farmers with smaller holdings cannot offer collateral security such as land and other assets and they are compelled to borrow from informal sources like moneylenders and traders who charge high rates of interest in the absence institutional credit when they are not access to institutional credit. In developing countries where there are large inequalities in ownership of assets, the costs of credit would be higher for the asset-poor, and consequently the distribution of credit would also be unequal.

Financial support to farm households in particular to small and marginal farmers will have direct impact on the production process. The direct impact is through purchase of quality inputs at an appropriate time at a place where the inputs are offered at less cost. But the farmers who do not have either capital or access to Bank credit, purchase the inputs from the dealers who supply inputs on credit without any bargaining at high price. Adequate financial resources enable the farmer to plan the farm operations at an appropriate time. This in turn reduce the cost, risk and uncertainty associated with farm productivity. The farmers who are able to get bank finance are expected to be more dynamic and use level of modern inputs are also expected to be high when compared to those farmers who are not able to get bank finance. Agricultural credit with less cost therefore encourage the farmers to take up more remunerative crop enterprise.

Agricultural credit, facilitate the small and marginal farmers to plan the different agricultural operations and enables him to use intensive use of modern inputs coupled with change in the composition of crops, is likely to result in high revenue from cultivation. It is expected that credit made available at low cost can intensify the use of basic inputs such as fertilizers and pesticide and enable the farmers timely completion of different operations alongwith the approximate mix of the basic inputs which raises the productivity of land and other inputs. This upward shift in the production function made it possible to obtain additional output per unit of land with same amount of other inputs or in other wards with lesser amount of these inputs, it became possible to get the same level of output per acre.

Andhra Pradesh is the major rice producing state in India. The state of Andhra Pradesh in country's total rice production is about 30 per cent. Hence, rice production has become the one of the determinants of growth state economy. The average yield of paddy per acre is below the national average. The low productivity is attributed to low level adoption of new technologies as compared to the other states and other countries where productivity is higher. Rice economy of the state is in the hands of small and marginal farmers. The major obstacle for the small and marginal farmers is the deficiency of capital and deficiency of institutional support. Low productivity small marketed surplus of small and marginal farmers force them to depend on institutional credit in the absence of other sources of credit at reasonable terms. Therefore small and marginal farmers need financial support to increase the marketable surplus, so as to increase their income through optimum use of available resources. Though institutional arrangements made by central and state governments created large network of credit delivery system to agriculture, they are not able to meet the complete credit needs of small and marginal farmers.

While several studies have established the credit constraints can affect farmers' investments behaviour, only a limited number of studies have empirically measured the effect of credit constraints on productivity. The few recent studies that have looked at this relationship have found evidence against the widely held belief that institutional credit is an essential part of development measure in the growth of agricultural production. So there is need to examine the implications credit on rice productivity. So it is proposed to investigate the impact of credit on farm productivity in the Krishna delta of Andhra Pradesh in India.

METHODOLOGY

The measurement of the impact of credit can be done in two ways *i.e.* cross-section comparison of farms with credit and without credit. The reference period for these studies is generally one agricultural year. And the other way is comparison is changes in farms before and after credit facility. A limitation of the cross-section comparison is that it is difficult to select a sample of farm households that are homogeneous in all respects. Farms with credit may differ from farms without credit, in respect of farm size, crops grown, accessibility to modern inputs, extension services and capital, etc. They generally expected to use higher levels of inputs and better seeds. Notable differences also can be expected in the quality of management of these two categories of farms. Because of these dissimilarities between the farms with credit and without credit, cross-section comparison studies face conceptual problems in isolating and quantifying the impact of credit.

The comparison of changes in the farms before and after the availability of credit, though this type of studies do not suffer from the deficiencies arising out of heterogeneity in the cultivating farm holdings, encounter different types of problems. The reliability of the position relating to pre-credit period depends on the ability of the farmer to recollect and report necessary details with accuracy. This would be a serious problem if availability of credit facilities have been for several years.

It was therefore, thought that a cross section comparison of farms carefully selected, is a better alternative. To ensure near homogeneity, in farm holdings, with and without credit were selected from the same village as irrigation, soil, ecological conditions and cropping pattern would be broadly similar in a village.

SAMPLING DESIGN

Data used has been obtained through a sample survey conducted in the study area for the agricultural year 2002-03. The technique adopted in the sample survey is multi-stage stratified random sampling. A sample of 230 farm holdings are selected to cover a wider area and in the first stage 10 villages are selected at random from the list of all the villages in the study area.

In the second stage, a census schedule has been canvassed among the cultivator households of the selected villages to elicit information on farm size and level of credit. All these households of each village are divided into two categories namely farms using institutional credit and farms not using institutional credit and they are termed as credit and non-credit farm holdings and they are arranged in an ascending order of the size of the holdings. Twenty three households from each village are selected and the households are distributed in the two categories basing on the principle of probability proportional sampling. The households in each category are stratified into four categories basing on the farm size, viz. marginal (less than 2.50), small (2.51 to 5.00), medium (5.01 to 10.00) and large (above 10 acres) farms and the sample households are distributed among these categories basing on the principle of probability proportion of each size group and sample households are selected at random. The sample so selected consist of 150 farm households with credit facility and 80 farm households without credit facility.

Data relating to cropping pattern, value of output, value of by product, value of inputs used such as seeds, manures, fertilizers, pesticides, irrigation, human labour (family and casual labour), bullock labour and machine labour used is collected from each of the selected cultivators for paddy crop by personal interview.

DECOMPOSITION ANALYSIS

It is expected that the availability of institutional credit triggers a process by which the land productivity will increase significantly. But these are only preliminary inferences about the complex relationship between land productivity and credit facility. Also credit will result changes in the input use pattern, which in turn may effect land productivity. Thus it can be inferred that the increase in land productivity is not only through credit but also due to changes in the use of other factors of production. Therefore, it is essential to decompose the total increase in production per acre into increase due to credit and increase due to the changes in the use of other inputs. Total change in output per acre due to credit facility has been calculated by comparing the outputs on the farms with credit and farms without credit. The production conditions of agricultural farms are characterized by constant returns to scale. This imply that scale effects are absent and farm level Cobb-Douglas production function can be expressed in per acre terms. It is also true that institutional credit facility will brought about a structural change in general and the technological parameters of the production function of the farms with access to credit are different than those of non-credit farms. Hence the Cobb-Doughas production function expressed in per acre terms for both categories farms can be expressed in the following form.

$$\text{In } Y = \text{In } A + a_1\text{In}X_1 + a_2\text{In}X_2 + a_3\text{In}X_3 + a_4\text{In}X_4 \quad ....(1)$$

$$\text{In } Y' = \text{In } A' + b_1 \text{ In } X'_1 + b_2 \text{ In } X'_2 + b_3\text{In}X'_3 + b_4\text{In}X'_4 \quad ....(2)$$

Y = output per acre on the farms with credit

Y' = output per acre on without credit

X_1 = value of fertilizers used per acre on the farms with credit

X_2 = value of pesticides per acre on the farms with credit

X_3 = value of seeds per acre on the farms with credit

X_4 = value of human labour per acre on the farms with credit

X'_1 = value of fertilizers and manures per acre on the farms without credit

X'_2 = value of pesticides per acre on the farms without credit

X'_3 = value of seeds per acre on the farms without credit

X'_4 = value of human labour per acre on the farms without credit.

(a1, a2, a3, a4) are the output elasticity coefficients of fertilizers, pesticides, seeds and human labour on the farms with credit whereas (b1, b2, b3, b4) are the corresponding elasticity coefficients for the farms without credit.

Taking the difference between the equations (1) and (2) and adding some terms and subtracting the same terms.

$$\ln Y - \ln Y' = (\ln A - \ln A') + (a_1 \ln X_1 - b_1 \ln X'_1 + a_1 \ln X'_1 - a_1 \ln X'_1) + (a_2 \ln X_2 - b_2 \ln X'_2 + a_2 \ln X'_2 - a_2 \ln X'_2) + (a_3 \ln X_3 - b_3 \ln X'_3 - a_3 \ln X'_3) + (a_4 \ln X_4 - b_4 \ln X'_4 + a_4 \ln X'_4 - a_4 \ln X'_4) \quad ....(3)$$

Rearranging the terms in equation (3)

$$(\ln Y - \ln Y') = (\ln A - \ln A') + [(a_1 - b_1) \ln X'_1 + (a_2 - b_2) \ln X'_2 + (a_3 - b_3) \ln X'_3 + (a_4 - b_4) \ln X'_4] + [a_1 (\ln X_1 - \ln X'_1) + a_2 (\ln X_2 - \ln X'_2 + a_3(\ln X_3 - \ln X'_3) + a_4 (\ln X_4 - \ln X'_4)] \quad ....(4)$$

Equation (7.4) can be written as

$$\ln [Y/Y'] = [(\ln (A/A')] + [(a_1 - b_1) \ln X'_1 + (a_2 - b_2) \ln X'_2 + (a_3 - b_3) \ln X'_3 + (a_4 - b_4) \ln X'_4] + [a_1 \ln (X_1/X'_1) + a_2 \ln (X_2/X'_2) + a_3 \ln (X_3 / X'_3) + a_4 \ln (X_4 / X'_4)] \quad ....(5)$$

The above equation permits to decompose the total difference in output per acre between credit used farms and the farms which do not have access to credit, into credit component and other input components. It decomposes the natural logarithm of the ratio of per acre output on credit farms and per acre output on non-credit farms which is approximately an aggregate percentage change in output per acre with the availability of institutional credit. The impact of credit can be observed by looking at the changes in the intercept term and slope parameters. The first two bracketed expressions in equation–5 measures the change in output per acre due to change in the intercept term and changes in the slope parameters as a consequence of credit facility.

The second bracketed expression, the sum of arithmetic changes in output elasticity's weighted by the logarithm of value of that input used, is a measure of change in output due to shift in slope parameters of the production function. The third bracketed expression is the sum of logarithms of the ratios for each input of credit to non-credit each weighted by the output elasticity of that input. This expression is a measure of change in output due to difference in the per acre values of fertilizers, pesticides, seeds and human labour inputs used, given the output elasticity's of these inputs with credit.

The estimated values of the least square regression coefficients or elasticity's for credit and non-credit farms are reported in table 1. Here, the dependent variable is the value of gross output per acre (main and by-product) in natural logarithms. The estimated Cobb-Douglas production function appear to be better fit as the variation explained in yield by different farm inputs put together varies between 88 and 98 per cent in paddy production. Further, most of the elasticity coefficient have registered the expected signs with a prior economic logic and found to be significant at probability levels

Table 1
Per Acre Ols Estimates of the Production Function Hall (All Farms)

Variable	*Parameter*	*Estimated Value*	*T-value*	*R2*
	Credit Farms			
Constant	Log A	3.0225*	7.85s	0.88
Fertilizers	a1	0.3570*	6.92s	
Pesticides	a2	0.1931*	5.21s	
Seeds	a3	0.2762**	2.62s	
Human Labour	a4	0.1182***	1.79s	
	Non-credit Farms			
Constant	Log A′	3.3798*	15.20s	
Fertilizers	b1	0.3449*	5.02s	0.95
Pesticides	b2	0.1391*	6.18s	
Seeds	b3	0.2229	4.68s	
Human Labour	b4	0.1808*	3.92s	

Note: Dependent Variable Is Value of (Rs) Output Per Cropped Acre
*Significant At One Per cent Level
**Significant At Five Per cent Level
***Significant At Ten Per cent Level

ranging from one to ten per cent. The results of the estimated production functions reveal that fertilizer is the most important input to which output is highly responsive. Elasticity of output with respect to fertilizer is positive and significant at one per cent probability level.

From the results it can also be observed that another important input to which output is highly responsive is expenditure on pesticides. The coefficients associated with pesticides is found to be positive and significant at 5 per cent probability level in case of non-credit farms. On the other hand in credit farms, though this coefficient turned to be negative, it is found to be not significant even at ten per cent probability level. It could also be observed that the elasticity coefficient of output with respect to fertilizers and pesticides is higher on credit farms as compared to non-credit farms with few exceptions.

The elasticity coefficient of seeds is positive and significant. The output elasticity coefficient of seeds is high in credit farms when compared to non-credit farms. Thus credit has raised the output elasticity coefficient of seeds. The output elasticity coefficient with respect to human labour is positive and significant in both categories of farms. Here the output elasticity with respect to human labour is higher in credit farms than that on non-credit farms.

Table 1.1
Per Acre Ols Estimates of the Production Function
(Marginal Farms)

Variable	*Parameter*	*Estimated Value*	*t-value*	*R2*
	Credit Farms			
Constant	Log A	2.0034*	2.86	
Fertilizers	a1	0.3984**	2.10	0.87
Pesticides	a2	0.1764*	4.72	
Seeds	a3	- 0.1805	1.35	
Human Labour	a4	0.2701**	2.34	
	Non-credit Farms			
Constant	A'	3.9460*	5.51	
Fertilizers	b1	0.2079	1.45	0.77
Pesticides	b2	0.1042**	- 2.51	
Seeds	b3	- 0.0050**	2.13	
Human Labour	b4	0.1792**	2.05s	

Note: Dependent Variable Is Value of (Rs) Output Per Cropped Acre.
* Significant At One Per cent Level
** Significant At Five Per cent Level

In order to ascertain the impact of farm size on credit the analysis is carried out for different size groups of farms. The results of the estimated production functions of different size groups of farm are furnished in table 2. The results of the estimated regression equation reveals that the coefficients associated with different explanatory variables have registered the expected signs and found to be significant at probability levels ranging from one to ten per cent. Here also in most of the cases the magnitude of elasticity coefficients associated with fertilizers and pesticides is found to be higher in farms with credit category, while the elasticity coefficient those associated with seeds and human labour are higher in the farms without credit category as compared to the other category.

Table 2

Per Acre Ols Estimates of the Production Function (Small Farms)

Variable	*Parameter*	*Estimated Value*	*t-value*	*R2*
	Credit Farms			
Constant	A	1.4149*	4.31	0.95
Fertilizers	a1	0.3938*	4.12	
Pesticides	a2	- 0.2479**	1.96	
Seeds	a3	0.1768**	2.53	
Human Labour	a4	0.3942*	5.10	
	Non-credit Farms			
Constant	A′	3.5977*	6.74	
Fertilizers	b1	0.2588*	2.80	0.84
Pesticides	b2	0.1391*	2.22	
Seeds	b3	0.1638***	1.79	
Human Labour	b4	0.2858**	2.58	

Note: Dependent Variable is Value of (Rs) Output Per Cropped Acre
*Significant At One Per cent Level
**Significant At Five Per cent Level
***Significant At Ten Per cent Level

In order to evaluate the net impact of credit and other inputs, the results of decomposition analysis is presented in table-3. The percentage change in the value of output (rupees per acre) taken together has been decomposed into the percentage change in output due to credit and percentage change in output due to change in per acre use of other inputs. The total estimated change in the value of output table 3 with an access to credit worked out to 15.34 per cent which is marginally less than the observed change in output (15.48 per cent).

Table 3
Per Acre Ols Estimates of the Production Function
(Medium And Large Farms)

Variable	*Parameter*	*Estimated Value*	*t-value*	*R2*
	Credit Farms			
Constant	A	4.300*	2.62	
Fertilizers	a1	0.2945***	1.75	0.87
Pesticides	a2	0.2359*	2.97	
Seeds	a3	0.3085	1.11	
Human Labour	a4	0.0764	0.65	
	Non-credit Farms			
Constant	A'	2.999*	7.32	
Fertilizers	b1	0.3322*	3.83	0.84
Pesticides	b2	0.2533*	4.44	
Seeds	b3	0.2006	0.40	
Human Labour	b4	0.0198	0.38	

Note: Dependent Variable is Value of (Rs) Output Per Cropped Acre
*Significant At One Per cent Level
**Significant At Five Per cent Level
***Significant At Ten Per cent Level

The difference between the observed and estimated change in output may be because of the non-inclusion of certain factors either due to the problem of quantification or due to the non-availability of adequate data. The net impact of credit can be captured by adding the first two bracketed expressions of equation 5. Credit alone is estimated to have increased the output by about 6.18 per cent. From this, it is evident that with the same level of use of fertilizers, pesticides, seeds and human labour, the farmers with an access to credit have obtained 6 per cent more output per acre than those who do not have access to credit. The difference in the use of fertilizers, pesticides, capital and human labour have increased the output per acre by 6.24, 3.52, -0.29 and (-) 0.31 per cent respectively. Changes in the use of all these inputs put together have increased the output by about nine per cent.

Table 3
Decomposition Analysis of Total Difference in Output (Value in Rs.) Per Acre Between Credit And Non-credit Farms (All Farms)

	Item	*Percentage attributable*
Total observed difference in output		15.48
1.	Credit	6.18
2.	Changes in inputs	
a.	Fertilizer	6.24
b.	Pesticides	3.52
c.	Seeds	- 0.29
d.	Human Labour	- 0.31
	All inputs	9.16

Total Estimated Changes due to all Sources

Among different size groups the observed difference in output value between credit and non-credit farms (Table 4) is found to be the highest on small farms (26.49 per cent) and lowest on large farms (11.65 per cent). The estimated change due to credit and changes in the use of different inputs put together also moves in the same direction. The impact of credit on farm productivity is found to be the highest on small farms (15.03 per cent) and this is followed by large farms (7.12 per cent) and marginal farms (5.97 per cent). As the combined effect of different farm inputs is considered, its effect on productivity shows an inverse relationship with farm size. The same pattern can be discernable with respect to individual input factors.

Table 4
Decomposition Analysis of Total Difference in Output (Value in Rs.) Per Acre Between Credit And Non-credit Farms of Size Groups

Item		*Percentage attributable*		
		Marginal Farms	*Small Farms*	*Large & Medium Farms*
Total observed difference in output		16.90	26.49	11.65
1.	Credit	5.97	15.03	7.12
2.	Changes in inputs			
a.	Fertilizer	10.06	9.16	4.59
b.	Pesticides	3.53	- 2.98	2.63
c.	Seeds	3.33	1.18	3.12
d.	Human Labour	1.20	2.22	0.04
	All inputs	11.47	9.58	4.14
Total estimated changes due to all sources		17.44	24.61	11.26

VALUE OF THE INPUTS SAVED AND EXTRA OUTPUTS PRODUCED

To evaluate the value of inputs saved and quantity of extra output produced with the availability of credit, the following method is used

Y = Output per acre on farms with credit

Y′ = Output per acre on farms without credit

R = Value of fertilizers, pesticides, seeds and human labour required to produce Y_M on farms with credit

R′ = Value of fertilizers, pesticides, seeds and human labour required to produce Y_N on farms without credit.

r = Percentage change in output per acre with credit but with input use level of fertilizers, pesticides, seeds and human labour of farms without credit.

SR = value (in Rupees) per acre of fertilizers, pesticides, seeds and human labour saved with the use credit.

From the above definition

$R' = [1 - r/100]\ R$

$SR = SR = R\text{-}R' = [r/100]\ R$

The value of extra output produced with the introduction of credit can also be calculated using the input levels of non-credit farms in the following manner.

Let

$Y = Y - Y'$ = Total change in output per acre

rY = Value of extra output produced per acre due to the access to credit.

The value (in rupees) of inputs saved per acre with the use of bank credit is given in table 5. Use of bank credit alone has saved about Rs. 269.77 per acre. Thus availability of bank credit enabled the farmers to save inputs significantly in the production of paddy. The intra size group analysis of the value (in rupees) of inputs saved per acre with the use of bank credit is presented in table 6. It can be observed from the table that use of bank credit in small farms has saved Rs. 700, while it is Rs. 210 and Rs. 308 in marginal farmers to save the inputs significantly.

Table 5
Value of Inputs (Rs.) Saved Per Acre Due to Credit (All Farms)

Item	*Amount*
R	4400.32
R′	4670.06
r	6.18
S	269.77

Table 6
Value of Input (Rs.) Saved Per Acre Due to Credit : Size-wise

Item	*Amount*
	Marginal
R	4268.73
R′	4478.75
r	4.92
S	210.02
	Small
R	4708.96
R′	4408.71
r	14.86
S	699.75
	Large and Medium
R	4322.97
R′	4630.76
r	7.12
S	307.79

Table 7
Value of Extra Output (Rs.) Produced
Per Acre Due to Credit (All Farms)

Item	*Amount*
Y	13277.17
Y′	11946.42
Y = Y-Y′	1330.75
r	6.18
r/100*Y	82.24

Table 8
Value of Extra Output (Rs.) Produced Per Acre Due To Credit (All Farms)

Item	*Amount*
	Marginal
Y	13668.90
Y'	11168.51
Y = Y-Y'	1500.39
r	4.33
r/100*Y	64.97
	Small
Y	14371.52
Y'	11957.10
Y = Y-Y'	2414.42
r	14.86
r/100*Y	358.78
	Large and Medium
Y	12875.12
Y'	11898.90
Y = Y-Y'	976.22
r	7.12
r/100*Y	69.50

The value of extra output produced per acre with the availability of credit is reported in Table 7. In paddy production the additional revenue per acre due to the availability of credit alone is Rs. 82.24. The value of extra output produced per acre among different size groups with availability of credit is given in table 8. The value of additional output produced is Rs. 449 which is the highest in small farms when compared to other size groups. Thus small and marginal farms are more benefited due to the availability of credit.

CONCLUSIONS

Availability of credit in the study area has substantially raised overall productivity per cropped acre of land. Paddy are the major crop of the area, have registered improvement in the output per acre with the availability of credit. The results of the estimated production function reveals that fertilizers and pesticides are most important inputs to which output is highly responsive. From this analysis, it is found that output elasticities of fertilizers and pesticides are higher on farms with credit compared to that on the farms without credit. It is also observed that credit has raised the output elasticity coefficients of seeds and human labour. Intra size group analysis also supports this conclusion.

The value of output per acre paddy production is observed to have increased by nearly 15.5 per cent. Output decomposition equation also estimated nearly 15.35 per cent increase in output per acre of which 6 per cent is exclusively attributed to credit and the remaining 9 per cent to change in the use of fertilizers, pesticides, seeds and human labour. The intra-size group analysis indicates that the impact of changes in the use of different farm inputs on productivity changes is relatively high on marginal and small farms compared to large farms. It is also noted that output impact of different inputs on paddy productivity changes is higher on marginal and small farms compared to that on large farms. Availability of credit enabled the farmers to save inputs. The value of inputs saved due to credit is higher on small and marginal farms compared to that on large farms.

POLICY IMPLICATIONS

Modernization of agriculture is a worldwide trend. Modernization and capital inputs are highly interrelated. In the adoption of technological innovations, credit is perhaps the most critical one. Unfortunately, the history of agricultural policy in many developing countries, including India, failed to fill up the credit needs of the small and marginal farmers. In recent years, scientific studies about the impact of institutional credit to small and marginal farmers are able to pinpoint with a great deal of accuracy the desirable consequences and welcome features of credit. If anything, the present study highlights the more positive aspects of institutional credit. The arguments that have been made in the present study regarding the social costs and benefits of the existing pattern of credit lead to the conclusion that net social benefits are positive. Analysis of data from the present study indicates that the existing pattern of credit delivery system does not cover all categories of farm households in the region, where the thrust is to expand agricultural output. As credit help to save resources, they enable to increase the output by raising crop intensity and yield per acre. Institutional finance to be socially more beneficial in the context of shortages and high prices of agricultural inputs. Being in an age of technology, we simply cannot ignore the beneficial fallout from institutional support to small and marginal farms.

One clear implication for public policy is that it is necessary to weigh carefully, which types of credit delivery system to small and marginal farm households that is desirable to meet national production targets and which need to be implemented at any given point of time for ensuring high productivity that can compete in the global market. For the formulation and implementation of suitable credit policies it will be necessary for the government to evolve complementary fiscal and administrative measures so as to influence the decisions of individual farmers. It is important to recognize that government policies and farmers decisions correspond more closely so that they sub-serve national needs and priorities.

Therefore, there should be some redirection in the existing credit policies with regard to the capital needs of the small and marginal farmers. So far, government policies in this regard have served credit needs of large farms. Needless to say that these policies need suitable alterations to enable a more acceptable distribution of the benefits accruing from them. The credit should be cost-effective so that even small and marginal farmers gain access to them and get benefited. The target groups should not exclude the small and marginal tenant farm households under tenancy if they come under some cooperative arrangements

REFERENCES

Adams, Dale W. and Delbert A. Fitchett, eds. 1992, Informal Finance in Low-Income Countries Boulder, Colo.: Westview Press.

Aleem, Irfan, 1990, "Imperfect Information, Screening, and the Costs of Informal Lending : A Study of a Rural Credit Market in Pakistan", World Bank Economic Review 4(3) : 32949.

AERC (Applied Economics Research Centre) 1998, "Borrowers' Transaction Cost Study", Final Report : Rural Financial Market Study (Phase II), University of Karachi, Karachi, Pakistan.

Binswanger, Hans P., and Shahidur R. Khandker, 1995, "The Impact of Formal Finance on the Rural Economy of India", The Journal of Development Studies, Vol. 32, No. 2 : 23462.

Binswanger, Hans P., and Mark R. Rosenweig, 1986, "The Behavioural and Material Determinants of Production Relations in Agriculture", The Journal of Development Studies, Vol. 32 (October) : 50339.

Braverman, Avishay, and J. Luis Guasch, 1989, "Rural Credit in LDCs : Issues and Evidences", Journal of Economic Development (Korea), Vol. 14 (June) : 734.

Brugger, Ernst and Sarath Rajpatirana eds. 1995, New Perspectives on Financing Small Business in Developing Countries, San Francisco : ICS Press.

Carter, Michael R. Keith D. Weibe, 1990, "Access to Capital and its Impact on Agrarian Structure and Productivity in Kenya", American Journal of Agricultural Economics, Vol. 72 : 114650.

Carter, Michael, R. 1988, "Equilibrium Credit Rationing of Small Farm Agriculture", Journal of Development Economics, Vol. 28 :83103.

Feder, Gershon, Lawrence J. Lau, Justin Y. Lin, and Xiaopeng Luo, 1990, "The Relationship between Credit and Productivity in Chinese Agriculture: A Macroeconomic Model of Disequilibrium", American Journal of Agricultural Economics, Vol. 72 : 115357.

Ghate, Prabhu, 1992, Informal Finance : Some Findings from Asia, Oxford University Press.

Malik, Sohial J., Mohammad Mushtaq and Manzoor A. Gill, 1991, "The Role of Institutional Credit in the Agricultural Development of Pakistan" Pakistan Development Review, Vol. 30 : 103948.

Von Braun, Joachim, Sohail Malik and Mafred Zeller, 1993, "Credit Markets, Input Support Policies and the Poor; Insight from Africa and Asia", International Food Policy Research Institute, Washington, DC.

World Bank, 1993, "A Review of Bank Lending for Agricultural Credit and Rural Finance, 194892", Washington, DC.

Yaron, Jacob, 1992, "Successful Rural Financial Institutions", World Bank Discussion Paper No. 150, Washington, DC.

Zeller, Manfred, 1993, "Credit for the Rural Poor in Sub-Saharan Africa", International Food Policy Research Institute, Washington, DC.

Zuberi, Habib, 1989, "Production Function, Institutional Credit and Agricultural Development in Pakistan", Pakistan Development Review, Vol. 28, 43-56.

2

CHANGES IN THE PRODUCTIVITY OF GROUNDNUT AND SUGARCANE DURING PRE AND POST GREEN REVOLUTION PERIODS IN ANDHRA PRADESH

*K. Prabhakar & K. Satyanarayan Reddy**

M. Srinivasa Reddy

Andhra Pradesh commands the maximum area under groundnut crop. The state ranks first having 32.64 per cent of total groundnut acreage (2000-01) though it contributes only 20.3 per cent of the total production. But the situation is not the same in case of sugarcane production. There have been year-to-year fluctuations in groundnut and sugarcane production in Andhra Pradesh after the Green Revolution Period. These fluctuations adversely affected the production, employment and income distribution. A knowledge of the past trends in area, production and productivity, both aggregated at the state level and disaggregated at the regional level helps the planner in deciding the growth rate for different regions and for the state as a whole and in devising suitable strategies such as the kind and degree of incentives to be offered to the growers to achieve the targeted growth rate. Further, besides the growth rate, the problem of instability in sugarcane and groundnut production

* Research, Scholar and Associate Professor respectively. Dept. of Economics, Sri Krishnadevaraya University, Anantapur - 515 003, AP.

* Research Associate, Centre for Economic and Social Studies, N. O. Campus, Begumpet, Hyderabad - 500 016.

has attracted the attention of scientists and planner in the recent past. The instability in groundnut and sugarcane production is mainly attributed to the uncertainty in supply of raw materials. In view of the above observation, it is felt necessary to carry-out empirical investigation that can reveal the growth rate and instability in sugarcane and groundnut production in different regions of Andhra Pradesh. And it is also essential to identify the risk inducing factors in crop production, which will promote the economic development. The present study is therefore, an attempt in this direction. The specific objective of the study is to examine the sources of growth and instability in the production of groundnut and sugarcane crops and changes in their pattern after the Green Revolution Period.

DATA AND METHODOLOGY

The present study has made use of Time Series Data on Area, Production and Productivity of Groundnut and Sugarcane Crops for Rayalaseema region, Coastal Andhra region and Telangana region as well as for the state with the reference to the two periods viz. Period I (1960-1971, Pre Green Revolution Period) and Period II (1971-2001, Post-Green Revolution Period). Secondary data also used for analytical purposes. Semi-log equations were fitted to estimate compound growth rates in area. Production and Productivity of groundnut and sugarcane crops. Instability in area, production and productivity was measured through co-efficient of variation analysis using detrended data.

RESULTS

Growth Rate Analysis

Growth Rate in Area, Production and Productivity of groundnut and sugarcane crops in different regions of Andhra Pradesh are given in Table 1 and Table 2 respectively.

Table 1 indicates that the area under groundnut registered a significant and positive growth rate in all the regions of the state, as well as at the state level as a whole, during the period I (pre-green revolution period), but in period II (post-green

Table 1

Growth Rates in Area, Production and Productivity of Groundnut in Different Regions of Andhra Pradesh

Particulars	*Regions*							
	Rayalaseema		*Coastal Andhra*		*Telangana*		*Andhra Pradesh*	
	Period I	*Period II*	*Period I*	*Period II*	*Period I*	*Period II*	*Period I*	*Period II*
Area								
Coefficient	1.05116*	1.02876*	1.06183*	1.00188	1.12885*	1.02188	1.06862*	1.01962*
Standard error	0.0079	0.00311	0.0045	0.00570	0.0116	0.01915	0.0063	0.00371
R^2	0.82	0.75	0.95	0.00	0.92	0.04	0.92	0.50
Growth Rate	5.12	2.88	6.18	0.19	12.88	2.19	6.86	1.96
Production								
Coefficient	1.05246*	1.027722*	1.05443*	1.012220*	1.13247*	1.016487*	1.06686*	1.022204*
Standard error	0.0188	0.012136	0.0048	0.006668	0.0216	0.005749	0.0141	0.006343
R^2	0.45	0.15	0.93	0.11	0.79	0.22	0.70	0.30
Growth Rate	5.25	2.77	5.44	1.22	13.25	1.65	6.69	2.22
Productivity								
Coefficient	1.0012	0.997458	0.9930	1.010313*	1.0032	1.010128*	0.9984	1.002606
Standard error	0.0125	0.005299	0.0066	0.001896	0.0225	0.003734	0.0143	0.003809
R^2	0.00	0.01	0.11	0.51	0.00	0.21	0.00	0.02
Growth Rate	0.12	-0.25	-0.70	1.03	0.32	1.01	-0.16	0.26

*Significant at 5 per cent level of significance

Note: Period I is pre-green revolution (1960-1971)
Period II is post-green revolution (1971-2001)

revolution period) only Rayalaseema region has registered a positive and significant growth, and the other two regions; Coastal Andhra and Telangana regions have registered very insignificant growth, while at the state level, the growth rate is positive and significant. The highest growth rate in groundnut are is observed in Telangana region and lowest in Rayalaseema region in period I. The groundnut acreage registered a compound growth rate of 6.86 per cent per annum at the state level. In the period II, the highest growth rate in groundnut area is observed in Rayalaseema region and lowest in Coastal Andhra region. 1.96 per cent per annum growth rate of groundnut area was observed at the state level.

Groundnut production registered a positive significant growth in all the three regions during both period I and II respectively. The highest growth rate is observed in Telangana region followed by Coastal Andhra, Rayalaseema regions, and the state as a whole registered 6.69 per cent growth per annum in period I. In period II, the highest growth rate is observed in Rayalaseema, followed by Telangana, Coastal Andhra regions. In period III, 2.22 per cent per annum growth rate was recorded at the state as a whole.

During period I, groundnut productivity registered a positive but insignificant growth rates in Telangana and Rayalaseema regions and a negative growth rate is recorded in Coastal Andhra region. The state as a whole registered a negative growth rate of 0.16 per cent per annum in period I. During the period II, the highest growth rate was in Telangana region followed by Coastal Andhra region. In Rayalaseema region, a negative growth in productivity was recorded while 0.26 per cent per annum growth rate was recorded at the state level in period II.

Table 2, indicates that the area under sugarcane registered significant and positive growth rates in Rayalaseema, Coastal Andhra regions and a positive but insignificant growth was recorded in Telangana region in period I. In this period 5.26 per cent positive significant growth rate was observed at the State level. The same trend was observed in period II also (1.51

Table 2

Growth Rates in Area, Production and Productivity of Sugarcane in Different Regions of Andhra Pradesh

Particulars	*Regions*							
	Rayalaseema		*Coastal Andhra*		*Telangana*		*Andhra Pradesh*	
	Period I	*Period II*	*Period I*	*Period II*	*Period I*	*Period II*	*Period I*	*Period II*
Area								
Coefficient	1.0502*	1.01648*	1.0526*	1.01767*	1.0099	1.00686	1.0526*	1.01506*
Standard error	0.0223	0.00345	0.0138	0.00383	0.0200	0.00606	0.0217	0.00353
R^2	0.35	044	0.61	0.43	0.03	0.04	0.38	0.39
Growth Rate	5.02	1.65	5.26	1.77	0.99	0.69	5.26	1.51
Production								
Coefficient	1.03735*	1.01728*	1.04377*	1.01043*	0.98998	0.99876	1.02564*	1.00869*
Standard error	0.0217	0.00446	0.0137	0.00413	0.0210	0.00703	0.0141	0.00419
R^2	0.24	0.35	0.52	0.18	0.02	0.00	0.26	0.13
Growth Rate	3.74	1.73	4.38	1.04	-1.00	-0.12	2.56	0.87
Productivity								
Coefficient	0.98736*	1.00081	0.99349	0.99289*	0.97972	0.99200	0.98510*	0.99414
Standard error	0.0044	0.00415	0.0055	0.00326	0.0286	0.00708	0.0048	0.00398
R^2	0.48	0.00	0.14	0.15	0.05	0.04	0.52	0.07
Growth Rate	-1.26	0.08	-0.65	-0.71	-2.03	-0.80	- 1.49	- 0.59

* Significant at 5 per cent level of significance

Note: Period I is pre-green revolution (1960-1971)

Period II is post-green revolution (1971-2001)

per cent growth rate per annum was recorded at state level in period II).

Sugarcane production registered a positive and significant growth in Coastal Andhra and Rayalaseema regions, and a negative growth rate in Telangana was recorded during both the period II and I. At the state level it records 2.56 and 0.87 per cent growth in sugarcane production in both periods respectively.

In the case of yield growth rate of sugarcane, it is negative in all the three regions, but it is insignificant in Rayalaseema region. At the state level also it registered a negative but insignificant growth trend, i.e. 1.49 per cent was decreasing per annum at state level in period I. In period II, Rayalaseema region is only registered positive but insignificant yield growth rate. In Coastal Andhra region it was observed as negative but significant and in Telangana region negative growth per annum was registered. At the state level as a whole, 0.59 per cent of yield was decreasing per annum.

INSTABILITY

The instability in area, production and productivity of Groundnut and sugarcane at both regional level (Rayalaseema, Coastal Andhra and Telangana regions) and state level was determined through coefficient of variation and the results are presented in Table 3 and Table 4 respectively.

The variability of the coefficients were worked out using detrended data. In period I, Telangana region registered relatively higher variability in groundnut followed by Coastal Andhra region while Rayalaseema registered the lowest. The variability of Groundnut production was again maximum the regions of Telangana followed by Rayalaseema, while Coastal Andhra registered the lowest yield variability. Thus among the three regions of the state, instability in area, production and productivity of groundnut is relatively quite prominent in the Telangana region; Instability in production and productivity is the lowest in the Coastal Andhra region while Rayalaseema registered the lowest area instability.

During period II, Rayalaseema registered highest variability in groundnut area followed by Telangana while Coastal Andhra

Table 3

Regional Variability in Groundnut Area, Production and Productivity

Particulars	Regions							
	Rayalaseema		*Coastal Andhra*		*Telangana*		*Andhra Pradesh*	
	Period I	*Period II*	*Period I*	*Period II*	*Period I*	*Period II*	*Period I*	*Period II*
Area	18.29	25.21	19.67	2.83	37.93	7.33	22.2	17.2
Production	22.61	24.96	18.05	10.93	42.81	14.27	25.57	19.89
Productivity	11.93	1.31	7.12	9.13	20.9	8.39	12.96	2.79

Table 4

Regional Variability in Groundnut Area, Production and Productivity

Particulars	Regions							
	Rayalaseema		*Coastal Andhra*		*Telangana*		*Andhra Pradesh*	
	Period I	*Period II*	*Period I*	*Period II*	*Period I*	*Period II*	*Period I*	*Period II*
Area	26.53	15.98	21.57	16.53	20.51	4.63	23.97	13.78
Production	23.7	17.87	18.71	10	22.35	3.41	16.33	8.53
Productivity	5.96	1.68	5.73	6.42	25.36	8.05	6.78	5.22

registered the lowest. The variability in Groundnut production trend was also same as area variability trend. Yield variability is higher in the regions of Coastal Andhra followed by Telangana while the Rayalaseema is the lowest. Thus among the three regions area, production is highest in Rayalaseema region, but this region is lowest in case of productivity variability among the three regions. Telangana region is second highest in area and production variability followed by Coastal Andhra region.

In period I the variability for sugarcane estimates shows that the Rayalaseema region registered highest area variability, followed by Coastal Andhra region and Telangana region is at the lowest.

The variability of sugarcane production was also highest in Rayalaseema region followed by Telangana and Coastal Andhra regions respectively. Yield variability was highest in Telangana region; the lowest was recorded in Coastal Andhra region. Instability in area and production in Telangana region is the highest and instability in production and productivity in Coastal Andhra is the lowest, while Telangana registered the lowest area instability.

During the period II, the variability in area is highest in Coastal Andhra region; followed by Rayalaseema region while the Telangana region is the lowest. Variability in production is highest in Rayalaseema region and the lowest in Telangana region, but in case of yield variability it is reversed to production variability, i.e. highest variability was recorded in Telangana region and lowest is in Rayalaseema region. Thus among the three regions of the state, instability in area and production is relatively quite prominent in Rayalaseema region, but the same region is lowest in productivity variability. As for instability in area and production is concerned Telangana registered the lowest.

CONCLUSIONS

From the above findings, it can be concluded that the growth and stability in the production of groundnut and sugarcane were complementary to each other rather than competitive in irrigated regions. Though significant and positive growth in the production of groundnut and sugarcane has emerged as a common feature in all the three regions of the state, its magnitude is not uniform across the regions. Instability in area and production of these two crops are relatively quite prominent at regional level while stability is quite prominent at state level. Yield variability is equal to average instability at three regions in both the period I and II i.e, pre and post Green Revolution periods. Area instability is the major source of production instability. Therefore, concerted efforts should be made to safeguard the farmers against instability. This calls for adequate measure to improve location-specific production technology, through research, development and extension efforts and also through ensured input supply mechanism. It is possible that most of the fluctuations are due to pricing and payment policies of the two crops. This is an area that needs further investigated.

REFERENCES

Suresh Pal and Sirohi A.S., *"Sources of Growth and Instability in the production of commercial crops in India", Indian Journal of Agricultural Economics,* Vol. 43, No. 3, July-Sept., 1988, pp. 456-463.

P.B.R. Hazell, *"Instability in Indian Food Grain Production"*, Research Report No. 30, *International Food Policy Research Institute,* Washington, D.C., 1982.

Archana Singh and R.S.L. Srivastava, *"Growth and Instability in Sugarcane Production in Uttar Pradesh : A Regional Study", Indian Journal of Agricultural Economics,* Vol. 58, No. 2, April-June, 2003.

Parthasarathy G, *"Agricultural Production – Andhra Pradesh Growth Rates and Fluctuations of Agricultural Production – A District wise Analysis in Andhra Pradesh", Economic and Political Weekly,* Issue-26, Vol. XIX, 1984, pp. A-74.

Sen S.R., *"Growth and Instability in Indian Agriculture", An address to the twentieth Conference of the Indian Society of Agriculture Statistics,* Jan 10-12, 1967.

Data Source, *"Statistical Abstract and Seasons and Crop Reports of Andhra Pradesh", Bureau of Economics and Statistics of Andhra Pradesh,* Hyderabad from 1960-2001 (yearly issues).

3

IRRIGATION MANAGEMENT–FACING THE CHALLENGE

M. Lakshmi Narasaiah

Irrigated agriculture is up against an enormous challenge. India's population continues to grow at a tremendous rate. Over the next 10 years, there will be more extra mouths to feed. Water is becoming increasingly scare for agriculture, with conflicting demands being made on limited supplies by the domestic and industrial sectors. The most attractive irrigation sites have already been exploited. Yet, irrigated agriculture will have to deliver average output increases of at least 3.5 per cent per year if future food demands are to be met in India.

Forty years ago in the 1950s and 1960s, India has worried about its capacity to produce sufficient food to feed its growing population. Episodes of food scarcity were not uncommon. It was dreaded that millions would die of hunger. Then dawned the miracle of the "green revolution". Cereal production increased by leaps and bounds, boosted by expanded irrigation, increased fertilizer application and modern crop varieties. The vigorous response in mobilizing financing towards boosting agricultural production paid off.

Given the importance of irrigation to the India's food supply and the vast resources expanded on irrigation development, it is tragic that the actual performance of irrigation systems is so

* Professor of Economics, Sri Krishnadevaraya University Post-Graduate Centre, Kurnool- 518 002

disappointingly low. In the post-green revolution era, it has become increasingly evident that the performance of irrigation systems, especially large-scale systems, is sub-optimal whether measures in terms of achieving planned area targets or in terms of production potentials created by the physical works.

In many irrigation systems, the actual area irrigated is much less than the command area. Sharp inequities in water supplies between farmers in the head reaches of irrigation systems and those located downstream is another manifestation of poor performance. Investigations in the Tungabhadra Irrigation Scheme reveal the tail-end of a major distributory commanding 25% of the total area, received approximately 20-40% of the targets discharge while the upper reaches got more than their share.

Lack of maintenance has caused many systems to fall into disrepair, further inhibiting performance. Over time, distribution canals have become silted up, increasing the likelihood of breaching, damage to outlets and leading to salt build-up in the soil.

SUCCESSFUL FARMER-MANAGED IRRIGATION SYSTEMS

Farmers have long demonstrated their potential capability to manage irrigation systems efficiently. Farmer-managed irrigation systems (FMIS) also known as traditional, indigenous, communal or peoples' systems, are often classified "minor" or "small-scale" irrigation systems, although they may be found in command areas of 15,000-20,000 hectares.

Many successful farmer-managed irrigated systems, which have been functioning effectively for hundreds of years, represent a valuable, accumulated investment. They are also reservoirs of largely untapped irrigation management experience.

Research has revealed that FMIS contribute to the production of a significant portion of the subsistence food supply. Ground water irrigation systems, often found in areas affected by drought, play a strategic role in promoting food security. In India ground-water development which is increasing in importance is predominantly farmer-managed. In this country an estimated 2C millions hectares are already under ground-water irrigation. When mismanaged though, ground-water irrigation could impact negatively on the environment.

In addition to the hectarage under farmer-managed ground water irrigation, farmer-managed tank irrigation systems cover about 8.5 million hectares in this country. Farmer-managed irrigation systems have also allowed intensification of agriculture to partially meet the food needs of rapidly growing populations.

LITTLE AWARENESS

Yet, despite the widespread interest in irrigation management turnover through India there is very little documentation about the processes used and the results obtained from irrigation management turnover. Many policy-makers do not know how to turn over management of their irrigation institutions in an effective way. They typically have very little, if any, awareness of the range of organizational options, which may be suitable under different conditions. There is an urgent need, therefore, for a systematic, comparative assessment of the range of approaches being used, constraints to implementation and the impact on performance of transferring management to non-governmental or farmers' organizations.

Successful irrigation in the future will be that which supports much higher levels of agricultural productivity, enhances responsiveness to more diversified and dynamic crop markets, stimulates more profitable irrigated agriculture for wide numbers of rural poor, substantially improves water use efficiency and supports the sustainable use of scarce land, biomass and water resources.

In the coming years the irrigation sector will be in ferment, with decision makers, agency managers and farmers needing better information and strategic processes to make intelligent choices in the management of irrigated agriculture.

4

BORE WELL IRRIGATION IN DROUGHT PRONE AREAS– EXPERIENCE OF ANDHRA PRADESH

*L. Reddeppa**

INTRODUCTION

Knowledge base backed by high investments on modern agricultural inputs in many developed countries has made them to achieve a higher level of productivity in agriculture sector. Such a growth in productivity of agriculture is attributed to the improvement of the farmers capacities in the water use efficiencies and cropping intensities; selection of appropriate crops suitable to the soils; scientific use of modern inputs like high yielding variety seeds, fertilizers, pesticides; and substitution of labour with new technologies for various agricultural operations. Here, the individual efforts of the farmers apart, government backing in the promotion of agriculture is also much high through provision of subsidies and incentives to the farmers for application of modern inputs including technologies at cheaper rate; extension services for optimum use of inputs depending on the nature of soils; implementation of insurance measures to safeguard the farmers from the risks and uncertainties of the crop failures; and support for storage, processing and marketing facilities to their produce. The farmers are organised in such a way to shift from low productive to high productive crops and also

* Faculty Member, Council for Social Development, Hyderabad.

quick to the adjustments of demand and supply conditions of the market.

The Indian agriculture is in a correction phase in recent years that the farming community at large are facing a growing risk of crop uncertainties for multiplicity of reasons. The major problems culminating to the farmers are inadequate irrigation facilities, and frequent droughts; no guarantee for the quality of inputs – seed, fertilizers and pesticides available in the market; frequent attacks of new diseases and pests to the crops; inadequate access to credit facility and insurance cover to the crops; and high cost of inputs and fluctuations in the prices of agricultural produce. The agriculture sector is over crowded with labour force that more than 60 per cent of the labour force depending on agriculture producing less than 30 per cent of the Gross National Produce, which is also coming largely from the irrigated crops. The main stumbling block in the growth of Indian agriculture is that a large section of the farmers are having a land holding size of less than a hectare, which is uneconomical to adopt modern methods of cultivation to improve the productivity of the crops.

ISSUES AND CHALLENGES OF INDIAN AGRICULTURE ARE AS FOLLOWS

- Salinity, Alkalinity are serious problems particularly in command areas.
- Knowledge, extension services and new technologies are not transferring to the farmers in general and small and marginal farmers in particular.
- Application of organic manures and use of pesticides are much less in the country.
- Average landholding size is much less compared to the developed countries, which is not economical for creation of irrigation sources, adoption of new technologies and application of modern agricultural inputs.
- Subsidies available to the agricultural sector are much less compared to the few developed countries. At the same time, which are also not reaching properly to the

target group, due to leakages and involvement of middlemen at various stages.

- The coverage of crop insurance for several crops is much less and the crop uncertainties are very high.
- The damage to the output is much high, particularly in the case of vegetables and food products due to lack of adequate storage and processing facilities in the country.
- Farmers are in distressed condition due to high cost of inputs and supply of spurious seeds, pesticides, etc.
- Soil, water and resource conservation measures are not up to the mark due to lack of awareness to the farmers and lack of conscious efforts from the government side.
- The fate of Indian farmers clearly described by M.V.Rao[1] :

"More Produce More Loss
Less Produce Less Loss
No Produce No Loss "

The present study is an attempt to analyse the rural development through irrigation; trends in the growth of irrigation under different sources; promotion of equity and distributive justice in the utilization of ground water sources particularly bore well irrigation; impact of borewell irrigation on cropping pattern, productivity, incremental income and its effects on socio-economic development of the small and marginal farmers in Andhra Pradesh. This study is based on the primary data collected from the small and marginal farmers received assistance under the bore well irrigation scheme of Andhra Pradesh Backward Classes Cooperative Corporation ltd., implemented for a period of 4 years between 1998-99 and 2001-2002. The primary data has been collected through specially designed schedule (questionnaire) from 5 backward districts in the state of Andhra Pradesh. The backward districts are identified based on the predominance of drought prone area. Accordingly, the districts chosen for the study are Nalgonda, Prakasam, Anantapur, Chittoor and Mahabubnagar. The bore wells for the study are 40 selected in each district out of 200 to

300 bore wells sinking under the scheme. The bore wells are mostly covered in 8 to 9 Mandals, which are geographically spread in all the regions of the district. In all, the primary data have been collected from 204 families benefited under bore well scheme in the five districts. The primary data relating to the cropping pattern, yield, income, etc., are pertains to be the cross section year 2002-2003.

ROLE OF IRRIGATION FOR RURAL DEVELOPMENT

Irrigation plays a crucial role in the growth of production and productivity of agriculture. The modern agricultural inputs like High Yielding Varieties (HYV) of seeds, fertilizers and pesticides and new technologies will be more effective only on the availability of irrigation. It was observed that "the impact of irrigation is seen to operate through higher yields, increasing intensity of crop cultivation, widening of the choice of crops to include more lucrative crops through stabilising output variations by reducing dependence on the uncertain and fickle weather"[2]. The contribution of irrigation facility to the attainment of development objectives of food security, poverty alleviation and quality of life of rural population is well documented in several studies. The Planners and Agricultural Scientists in the early years of planning have committed to put their sincere efforts with a vision to achieve self-reliance in the production of food grains through increasing irrigation potential.

The improvement in irrigation facilities and use of modern agricultural inputs of green revolution had made the country to become self-reliant in the production of food grains more than three decades ago. However the benefits of growth in the earlier years of green revolution had not percolated to the backward and drought prone areas, particularly to the small and marginal farmers due to lack of adequate irrigation facilities, poor access to institutional credit, high cost of inputs and inadequate supplies of modern agricultural inputs, and small size of landholdings for a large section of rural population. The resultant effect was that the imbalances in the growth and development of agriculture have been widened among regions-irrigated/developed Vs drought prone/backward areas vis-à-vis with the big farmers Vs small and marginal farmers.

Realising this, a series of measures have been initiated since early seventies to mitigate the imbalances in the development of agriculture among regions and farmers. The programmes like Drought Prone Area Programme (DPAP), Small and Marginal Farmers Development Agencies (SFDA's), Watershed Management Programmes (WMP), Minimum Needs Programme (MNP), Integrated Rural Development Programme (IRDP), Rural Landless Employment Guarantee Programme (RLEGP) and Million Wells Programme (MWP) etc., have been operative in the country to increase the crop production of small and marginal farmers and well being of landless living under conditions of poverty, particularly in backward and drought prone areas. The package of assistance made available to the small and marginal farmers in backward and drought areas include the provision of irrigation, supply of modern agricultural inputs, extension services, etc., besides provision of subsidised loans to take up income generating activities in agriculture and allied activities like dairying, poultry, farming, sheep rearing, etc. However, the defusion process started to spread backward areas and also drought prone areas after initiation of area- specific and target oriented programmes from mid seventy's[3].

PROMOTION OF BORE WELL IRRIGATION IN ANDHRA PRADESH

The investment required for creation of large and medium irrigation projects and minor irrigation tanks has been mobilised by the government in the country and the farmers are used to pay the irrigation cess / tax as fixed to them. The expenditure to the farmers for utilisation of water to the crops under command areas is much less, mostly subsidised. On the other hand, the tank irrigation is mostly cost free to the farmers. However it is lost its charm in recent years that the area irrigated under tanks declined year after year due to encroachment of farmers under foreshore areas and siltation of tanks. The data indicate that the area under tank irrigation was 6.63 lakh hectares in 1987-88 declined to 5.67 lakh hectares in 2001-2002 in the State of Andhra Pradesh. It is imperative that the farmers are relying on ground water sources to meet the growing demand for irrigation.

The farmers rely on ground water sources is different from the farmers of canal system that the farmers depending on ground water sources have to mobilise financial resources on their own for sinking dug or bore wells, and also for bailing equipment. Apart from these, the farmers have incur expenditure on electricity or diesel cost, interest on finances mobilised for creation of the irrigation source and also the cost of maintenance of bailing equipment. The resultant effect was that the ground water sources were not affordable to the small and marginal farmers, which have been mostly exploited by the landlords and big farmers up to the end of the seventies. The small and marginal farmers, and landless labour were used to depend on the big farmers and landlords for their livelihood through cultivation of lands of big farmers on lease basis or working as a wage labour. Realising this, several protective measures have been taken to promote agriculture of small and marginal farmers since middle of the eighties. The area under tank irrigation was about 10 lakh hectares in 1987-88 increased to 45.50 lakh hectares by 2001-02.

The dug well irrigation was popularised in the backward areas during the Eighty's after implementation of Million Wells Programme of the Government of India. Apart from these, the state government was also implemented several programmes and weaker sections like SCs and STs and Backward Castes. The resultant effect is that the area under dug well irrigation was about 10 lakh hectares in 1987-88 increased to 45 lakh hectares in 2001-02, a net growth of 355 per cent. Within a span of 15 to 20 years, the dug well irrigation was also not able to meet the needs of the farmers due to the population growth and new dependency on ground water sources, and prevalence of drought conditions in the country. Vagaries of monsoons and increase in ground water draft in recent years have been resulted in decline of ground water levels. The farmers are forced to go in for deeper zones so as to protect their crops. The area under tube well irrigation was increased from 2.30 lakh hectares to 26.30 lakh hectares between 1987-1988 and 2001-2002, a net growth of 1043 per cent. It shows that the dependency of the farmers on tube well irrigation has increased in recent years. The cumulative effect of low rainfall and excess drawing of ground water sources has increased the incidence of failures of the dug wells as well as bore wells in providing irrigation to the farmers, particularly in the drought prone areas.

The ground water sources are mostly exploiting by the semi-medium, medium and large farmers, because they can mobilize investments more easily by virtue of their higher landholding size and a higher economic status. At the same time, they can spent more on agricultural inputs to utilise irrigation sources more productively by distributing their land to different crops on economies of scale depending on the availability of water. However, the small and marginal farmers could not mobilise investment for creation and maintenance of the irrigation sources on their own for various reasons. Realising this, the Andhra Pradesh Backward Classes Cooperative Finance Corporation Ltd., (APBCCFC) has been implementing bore well irrigation scheme for the benefit of small and marginal farmers of the weaker sections in the state of Andhra Pradesh. This scheme was specially designed and has been implementing for the benefit of small and marginal farmers living below poverty line. About 4000 bore wells with a cost of Rs. 20 crores, @ Rs. 50,000 each given to the target group. The package of assistance under these programmes includes the term loan, margin money and subsidy for creation of bore well irrigation. Hence, an attempt is made to study the impact of bore well irrigation on change in cropping pattern, land productivity, incremental income, etc. and its combined effect on socio-economic development of small and marginal farmers in the state of Andhra Pradesh.

DEPTH OF THE BORE WELLS

The farmers in drought prone areas are cultivating a large portion of their lands under rainfed conditions and small portion of their lands under minor irrigation sources like small tanks, dug wells and bore wells. The extent of area irrigated would depend on the rainfall, water storage facilities, ground water feasibility and water use efficiencies of the farmers in the area. However, the area irrigated might not be increased if there is any huge rainfall deficiency continuously for two to three years in a row. It is obvious that the drought conditions would made them to suffer more in terms of additional expenditure on sinking new or old dug or bore wells further deep to protect their crops. The circumstances would force them to take the risk and uncertainties of additional expenditure on irrigation sources due to lack of other skills and alternative sources of income. Sometimes, these may lead to either total loss or minimise the income from the crops under unfavourable conditions, which are more so in the case of small and marginal farmers.

As per the guidelines of the Scheme, a minimum land of 3.5 acres is required for getting assistance from the Corporation. The assistance from the Corporation can be availed by the small and marginal farmers either individually 'or' two to three farmers jointly on partnership basis. The data reveals that majority of wells are given to farmers on partnership (60 per cent) basis. Such cases were substantially high at 76 per cent in Prakasam, followed by 73 per cent in Anantapur and 59 per cent in Mahabubnagar and these type of wells are less in Nalgonda (45 per cent) and Chittoor (46 per cent). It is noteworthy that there were no disputes among the beneficiaries in the utilisation of the bore wells (except one case in Nalgonda district), because most of the partnership bore wells were sanctioned either in the name of the brothers of the divided family `or' in the name of father and son to promote irrigation among the small and marginal farmers in the study districts at the time of application. Though the scheme was initiated to provide irrigation to the individual farmers, the implementing authorities have made efforts to improve the partnerships of small and marginal farmers under the bore well scheme. However, the partnership between two different communities and non-relatives were hardly 2 per cent in each district.

The expenditure or investment on each dug or bore well depends on the depth in which the water level is available in the ground level; extent of land owned under the source; expected area to be irrigated; type of bailing equipment and its horse power; length of the pipe line to be required for the source; and willingness and capacity of the farmer to invest on the irrigation source. The willingness and capacity of the farmer again depends on the availability of funds from own sources and mobilising capacity of funds from other private and public sources, and expected outcome from the source of irrigation in the future. Sometimes, the depth of the bore well beyond 250 feet would be infructuous in some areas and is required to go into a depth of more than 400 feet in certain areas. The required investment for sinking of bore well would be more, which is beyond the affordability of the small and marginal farmers. For this, the farmers needs techno-economic feasibility report from a reputed geologist to know the type of the soil, rock structure and water potential in the ground water level, and the estimated budget required for sinking of the bore well. Otherwise, it is difficult for the farmers to take risk and initiatives for creation of a bore well.

Table 1
District wise Depth of the Bore Well

S. No	*District*	*Distribution of the Depth (in Feets)*					
		Up to 180	*181-200*	*201-250*	*251-300*	*301 & above*	*Total*
1.	Nalgonda	27 (68)	11 (27)	2 (5)	-	-	40 (100)
2.	Prakasam	12 (29)	17 (41)	6 (15)	5 (12)	1 (2)	41 (100)
3.	Anantapur	19 (47)	12 (29)	10 (24)	-	-	41 (100)
4.	Chittoor	1 (2)	2 (5)	6 (15)	8 (20)	24 (48)	41 (100)
5.	Mahabubnagar	12 (29)	26 (63)	3 (7)	-	-	41 (100)
	Total	71 (35)	68 (33)	27 (13)	13 (6)	25 (12)	204 (100)

It was observed from the study that the depth of the bore well was up to 200 feet in 68 per cent of cases in all the five districts taken together. This may be perhaps due to the availability of water below the depth of 200 feet as suggested by the Geologists. Accordingly, the eligible loan was also sufficient to dig the bore well up to a depth of 200 feet, without involvement of any own investment. However, the situation was different in Chittoor district that the depth of the bore wells was more than 300 feet in 48 per cent of the cases. Such cases were 2 per cent in Prakasam and nil in other districts (Table 1).

Own investment on the bore well over and above of the government assistance has been varied from Rs. 5,000 to Rs. 10,000 in more than 30 per cent of the cases; Rs. 10,001 to Rs. 20,000 in 24 per cent of the cases; and it was more than Rs. 20,000 in 24.5 per cent of the cases. The additional cost incurred to them is mainly for digging additional depth of the bore well more than that of the eligible loan limit; getting power supply; laying of additional pipe line to cover irrigation for the total land under the source; and taking up of systematic land development (land levelling), etc., For details with regard to the district-wise own investment of the beneficiaries in the creation of bore well asset, see Table 2.

Table 2
Own Investment on Bore Well Irrigation

S. No.	*District*	*Size of Own Investment (Amount in Rupees)*				
		Up to 5000	*5001-10000*	*10C01-20000*	*20001 and above*	*Total*
1.	Nalgonda	9 (22.5)	12 (30.0)	6 (15.0)	13 (22.5)	40 (100)
2.	Prakasam	10 (24.4)	17 (41.5)	9 (22.0)	5 (12.2)	41 (100)
3.	Anantapur	3 (7.3)	12 (29.3)	18 (43.9)	8 (19.5)	41 (100)
4.	Chittoor	6 (14.6)	2 (4.9)	12 (29.3)	21 (51.2)	41 (100)
5.	Mahabubnagar	13 (31.7)	21 (51.2)	4 (9.8)	3 (7.3)	41 (100)
	Total	41 (20.1)	64 (31.4)	49 (24.0)	50 (24.5)	204 (100)

One common feature observed in the study is that the farmers were going deeper zones every three to four years depending on the availability of water and capital investment. There is a competition among the farmers adjacent to their lands. Some of them failed to get water even after digging two to three fresh bore points. Here, the farmers could not recover the cost and it is a wasteful expenditure on the expectation of prospects from the bore well. Such risks and uncertainties are high in agricultural sector; particularly the small and marginal farmers would be more vulnerable to the situations.

CHANGE IN THE CROPPING PATTERN OF SMALL AND MARGINAL FARMERS

The land owned under 204 sample bore wells was 966.10 acres in all the five study districts, with an average area of 4.74 acres. The actual area irrigated under these 204 bore wells was 596.60 acres, an average of 2.92 acres under each bore well. The proportion of actual area irrigated to the area owned was 61.75 per cent. It shows that the performance of the bore wells in providing irrigation to the farmers even after 3 to 4 years of their existence was quite encouraging.

The bore wells were classified into five categories according to the area irrigated viz., Nil, 0.01 – 1.00, 1.01 – 2.00, 2.01 – 3.00, 3.01 and above acres. It was observed from the study that the bore wells failed to provide any irrigation were 26 (13 per cent) in the total bore wells. Such wells were substantially high at 10 (24.4 per cent) in Prakasam, followed by 7 (17.1 per cent) in Anantapur, 4 each (10 per cent each) in Nalgonda and Mahabubnagar and lowest at 1(2.4 per cent) in Chittoor district.

Table 3
Distribution of Area Irrigated

S. No.	*Area Irrigated (Acres)*	*Single Crop (Nos.)*	*Two Crops (Nos.)*
1.	Nil	26 (12.7)	104 (51.0
2.	0.01-1.00	16 (7.8)	11 (5.4)
3.	1.01-2.000	42 (20.6)	28 (13.7)
4.	2.01-3.00	38 (18.6)	28 (13.7)
5.	3.01 & above	82 (40.2)	33 (16.2)
Total		204 (100)	204 (100)

Note: Figures in Parentheses indicate the percentage to the totals

Further, it was also observed that the bore wells not provided any irrigation to the second crop were substantially high at 71 per cent in Mahabubnagar and it was followed by 58 per cent each in Nalgonda and Prakasam and 46 per cent in Anantapur district. Such bore wells were lowest at 22 per cent in Chittoor district, which shows that the bore wells in Chittoor district have been providing iirigation for the second crop, particularly the long run crop, sugarcane. The bore wells in Chittoor district are comparatively better than that of the other districts in providing irrigation to the area. For details with regard to the area irrigated, 0.01 – 1.00, 1.01 – 2.00, 2.01 – 3.00 and more than 3 acres by the bore wells both single crop as well as second crop, see Table 3.

Table 4
Crop-wise distribution of area (Area in Acres)

Sl. No.	*Crops*	*Distribution of Area*	
		Before Bore Well	*After Bore Well*
1.	Jowar	70.5 (30)	21.00 (10)
2.	Cotton	60.0 (23)	53.50 (23)
3.	Paddy	92.0 (42)	284.25 (136)
4.	Groundnut	340.2 (86)	99.80 (40)
5.	Sugarcane	6.5 (5)	59.00 (21)
6.	Maize	14.0 (8)	3.0 (3)
7.	Mirchi	15.5 (8)	37.5 (28)
8.	Redgram	109.5 (43)	41.5 (20)
9.	Greengram	7.0 (5)	5.5 (5)
10.	Vegetables	4.0 (4)	31.5 (29)
11	Others	31.5 (16)	152.2 (67)
	Total	750.7 (204)	788.75 (204)

It was observed from the study that the small and marginal farmers have been shifted from rain-fed crops to irrigated crops like Paddy, Sugarcane, Vegetables, Orchid crops like Bathai, Lemon and Poppai, Mango, etc. after bore well irrigation. The area under Paddy was increased more strikingly from 92 acres to 284 acres; area under Sugarcane was increased from 6.5 acres to 59 acres (mostly in Chittoor district); area under Orchid crops was went up from 31.5 acres to 152 acres; and area under vegetables was increased from 4.0 acres to 32 acres. On the other hand, the area distributed among rain-fed crops like Jowar, Groundnut, Redgram, and Maize was declined after bore well irrigation. More specifically, the decline of area was from 71 acres to 21 in Jowar, from 340 to 100 acres under groundnut, from 109 acres to 42 acres under Redgram, and from 14 acres to

3 acres under Maize after providing bore well irrigation facility. The increase in area was substantially under Paddy in Prakasam (530 per cent) and Nalgonda (350 per cent). Area under Orchid crops in Prakasam and Anantapur districts and Sugarcane in Chittoor district. The farmers have also been cultivating rain-fed crops in most of the areas due to the source of bore wells either dried up or inadequate supply of water under the source. The details with regard to the change in the cropping pattern before and after bore well irrigation are given in Table 4.

GROWTH IN PRODUCTION AND PRODUCTIVITY OF CROPS AFTER BORE WELL IRRIGATION

The impact of the bore well has been seen in terms of growth in production of crops like Paddy, Sugarcane, Mirchi, Groundnut, Vegetables, Cotton and Orchids under the source of bore well irrigation. The data reveals that there is a spurt in the growth of total crop production from 924 quintals to 3,669 quintals under Paddy and it was from 80 quintals to 1,033 quintals under Jaggery; from 81 quintals to 159 quintals under Cotton; from 43 quintals to 185 quintals under Mirchi; from Nil to 762 quintals under Vegetables (mostly Tomato), etc., besides protection of their Orchids (Bathai, Poppai and Lemon) crops in the five districts. The data reveals that farmers have also been cultivating small portion of their lands under irrigated crops other than the bore well irrigation sources like tanks and dug wells prior to the bore well. However, the farmers have increased their areas under irrigated conditions after bore well. The productivity levels in terms of per acre yield have been increased in all the crops. For details, see Table 5. However, the per acre yield under each crop after bore well irrigation was substantially higher than that of the respective per acre yield of each crop before bore well irrigation.

NET INCOME

The irrigation impact can be assessed based on net income generated from crops to the family (total value of production – total cost of production), which can be compared to the net income generated prior to the bore well irrigation. The data show that the net income from agriculture has been less than Rs. 10,000 in 80 per cent of the beneficiaries prior to the bore well declined to 31 per cent. On the other hand, it was more than Rs. 10,000 in 20 per cent of the beneficiaries prior to the bore well increased to 70 per cent after irrigation. More specifically, the net income was Rs. 20,001 and above in 1 per cent of the beneficiaries prior to the bore well increased to 41.2 per cent after bore well (Table 6), which shows that the bore well irrigation have a positive impact on net income generated to the beneficiaries even in the drought year.

Table 5
Crop-wise per acre yield before and after Bore well Irrigation
Yield in Quintals

Sl. No.	*Crops*	*Per acre Yield* *Before Bore Well*	*After Bore Well*
1.	Jowar	2.17	1.95
2.	Cotton	1.35	2.97
3.	Paddy	10.04	12.91
4.	Groundnut	2.88	7.39
5.	Sugarcane	12.31	17.51
6.	Maize	2.71	10.00
7.	Mirchi	2.77	4.93
8.	Redgram	0.98	1.64
9.	Greengram	1.57	1.27
10.	Vegetables	-	24.19
11	Others	3.42	8.92

Table 6
Distribution of Net Income Generated to the Beneficiaries

Sl. No.	*Income Range (Rs.)*	*Total* *Before*	*After*
1.	Nil	24(11.8)	12(5.9)
2.	Up to 5000	54(26.5)	16(7.9)
3.	5001 - 10000	86(42.2)	34(16.7)
4.	10001 - 20000	39(19.1)	58(28.4)
5.	20001 - 30000	1(0.5)	55(27.0)
6.	30001 & above	-	29(14.2)
Total		204 (100)	204 (100)

INCREMENTAL INCOME

The incremental income is derived by deducting the net income before bore well from the net income after bore well irrigation (current year), which is nothing but over and above of the net income generated after bore well irrigation. The results show that incremental income was Nil in 20 per cent of the beneficiaries for the reasons like deficiency 'or' no water from the source and defunct of the electric motor, the incremental income of the farmers is in the range of Rs. 10,001 to Rs. 20,000 in 31 per cent, above Rs. 20,000 in 20 per cent, and Nil in 20 per cent of the beneficiaries (Table 7). It shows that more than 50 per cent of the beneficiaries have generated an incremental income of more than Rs. 10,000. The horticulture crops are under various stages of growth and the farmers are expecting a good income from the crop for a longer period, which will be commenced with a span of 2 to 4 years. Such farmers are 20 to 30 per cent in Prakasam and Anantapur; 5 to 10 per cent in Chittoor district and are not even 5 per cent in the other two districts of Nalgonda and Mahabubnagar.

Table 7
Distribution of Beneficiaries according to the size of Incremental Income after Bore Well Irrigation

Range of Income (Rs.)	*Total Beneficiaries*
Nil	40 (19.6)
Up to 5000	14 (6.9)
5001 - 10000	44 (21.6)
10001-20000	63 (30.9)
20001-30000	27 (13.2)
30001 & above	14 (6.9)
Total	204 (100)

SOCIO-ECONOMIC DEVELOPMENT OF SMALL AND MARGINAL FARMERS

For greater understanding of the subject, the beneficiaries perceptions were recorded in terms of improvement of their credit worthiness; recognition of the family in the society and relatives; clearance of old debts; and performance of social functions in the family after bore well irrigation. It was observed from the beneficiaries that the credit worthiness of the farmers have improved in majority of the beneficiary farmers (57 per cent), because they are mobilising funds even from the private sources to meet their expenditure on emergencies; needs of agricultural investment; and required expenditure to perform social functions. Their socio-economic status and recognition in the society and relatives have also improved in majority of the families (60 per cent) after bore well irrigation in all the districts. It was also observed that majority of the beneficiaries (70 per cent) have cleared their old debts after bore well irrigation.

It is most expensive and burdensome for payment of dowry in terms of cash, jewellery, and other expenditure to perform marriage in the farmer's communities in general and marginal and small farmers in particular. However, they performed marriages to their children and also family members with lesser burden in a sizeable number of families (44 per cent). At the same time, they expressed that they have arranged good matches for their children/family members. They have taken reasonably good amount of dowry in terms of cash and jewellery in the case of sons and also given the same treatment in getting bridegrooms to their daughters and family members. On the whole, Majority of farmers expressed that bore well scheme not only providing employment, food and social security for the present but also for their children. The growth in the income have a positive effect on their qualitative and quantitative changes achieved with regard to children education, family planning, health, and purchase of lands, gold and silver items after the bore well irrigation.

CONCLUSION

Access to irrigation is most crucial to the development of the agriculture in general and rural development in particular. The modern agricultural inputs are effective only on the availability of irrigation. Realizing this, much emphasis has been given for promotion of irrigation in the country through public investment on canal and tank irrigation in the early years of planning. The irrigation facilities and modern agricultural inputs have made the developed and irrigated areas more flourished. The resultant effect is that the imbalances in growth and development of agriculture have been widened among regions and farmers after green revolution. A series of measures have been taken up to mitigate the imbalances and to achieve equity and distributive justice among regions and farmers. Among these measures, promotion of public investment on exploitation of ground water sources of irrigation in backward and drought prone areas is more vital to the development of agriculture. The implementation of the Bore well Irrigation Scheme of APBCCFC is one among the initiatives in the promotion of agriculture of small and marginal farmers living below poverty line. The results from the study clearly indicate that the bore well irrigation has made them to shift from food to non-food crops and also to horticulture crops depending on the climate, soil conditions and water availability from the source. A sizeable proportion of the farmers have been generating substantial income from the bore well even in the severe drought year 2003. Majority of them expressed that the bore well irrigation has not only ensured food security for them but also purchased valuable assets to the family. Apart from this, their social status has also been improved in terms of good marriage proposals to their children and gained recognition in the society and relatives after bore well irrigation.

REFERENCES

Rao, M.V., Valedictory Speech given in the National Seminar on "Sustainable Development in India" organised by the Department of Economics, Osmania University, Hyderabad on 28th March 2005

Bharadwaj Krishna, "Irrigation in India – Alternative Prospectives", Research in Economics : Second Survey, Monograph-3, ICSSR, New Delhi, 1990.

Rao, CH. H., Agricultural Growth, Rural Poverty and Environmental Degradation in India, Oxford University Press, New Delhi, 1994.

5

PRICE ELASTICITY OF ACREAGE UNDER COTTON CROP: A CASE STUDY OF TELANGANA REGION

*P. Venkateswarlu**

INTRODUCTION

It is well known fact that the changes in prices in lagged year have been playing a vital role in Agricultural Sector. The farmers behaviour and action in allocating the area under the crops have been influenced by the lagged prices of the Agricultural commodities. In order to study the impact of the prices on the area under cultivation various empirical exercises have been carried out in India. The results of these studies diverge from crop to crop and region to region. As far as Andhra Pradesh state is concerned, most of the empirical studies on acreage response to the changes in lagged prices have been confined mainly to food crops. Therefore, there is need to generate empirical information on the responsiveness of acreage to the changes in lagged prices of commercial crops such as cotton. This crop in the Telangana region or Andhra Pradesh has been attracted the attention of the policy makers as most of the farmers cultivating this crop have attempted suicides. Therefore, the proposed study makes an attempt to examine the impact of lagged prices on the acreage under cotton crop in selected districts of Telangana region.

* Field Investigator, Dept. of Economics, Osmania University, Hyderabad-500 007

There have been a bulky number of empirical studies on supply response to the changes in lagged prices of different crops in Andhra Pradesh. The review of some of the empirical studies that have been carried out by different authors on responsiveness of acreage to the changes in lagged pries of different crops in Andhra Pradesh has obviously illustrates the most of the empirical studies on supply response function have been confined to other than cotton crop in Telangana region which is a backward area in Andhra Pradesh. Therefore, there is a need to generate empirical information on supply response of cotton in Telangana region. In view of this, the present study examines the responsiveness of the acreage under cotton to the changes in lagged prices in selected districts of Telangana Region of Andhra Pradesh state discrepancy.

OBJECTIVES OF THE STUDY

More explicitly the present study has been carried out with the following objectives:

(1) To examine the responsiveness of acreage to the changes in lagged prices of cotton crop, and
(2) to examine the speed of adjustment or extent of discrepancy between actual change in the area and desired change in the area under cotton crop.

Thus, the study examines the impact of lagged prices in terms of price elasticity on both in short-run and long-run and speed of adjustment between actual change in the area and desired change in the area under cotton crop in selected districts of Telangana Region of Andhra Pradesh.

Keeping the above objectives in view, the empirical strength of the following hypothesis has been tested as well:

The responsiveness of acreage under cotton crop in current year to the changes in lagged year prices of the cotton is moderately lower in short run as compared to long-run.

DATA BASE AND TIME PERIOD

Since the study is based on secondary time series data, the required data on acreage, production, yield, irrigated area under cotton crop, rainfall and prices of cotton crop has been collected from the season and Crop Reports of Andhra Pradesh and Statistical Abstracts of Andhra Pradesh and other reports for the period 1955-56 to 2002-03.

SUPPLY RESPONSE FUNCTION FOR EMPIRICAL ANALYSIS

In order to examine the above objectives and test the empirical strength of the hypothesis the following form of relationship is hypothesized.

$$A_t = f\,(A_{t-1}.\ P_{t-1}.\ Y_{t-1}.\ R_t,\ I_t)$$

Where

A_t = The area under cotton crop in 't' year

A_{t-1} = The area under cotton crop in last year (t-1)

P_{t-1} = The harvest price of cotton crop in last year (t-1)

Y_{t-1} = The yield of cotton crop in last year (t-1)

R_t = Rainfall in 't' year

I_t = Irrigated Area in 't' year

EMPIRICAL METHODOLOGY

Study Area

As the present study is based on secondary time series annual data, the required secondary time series data has been collected for the eight districts viz., Adilabad, Khammam, Karimnagar, Mahabubnagar, Medak, Nalgonda, Nizamabad and Warangal.

Data Collection

The secondary time series data on area, production, yield, irrigated area under cotton crop, rainfall and prices have been collected from the season crop reports, statistical abstracts of Andhra Pradesh and other reports published by the Directorate of Economics and Statistics. Government of Andhra Pradesh and Annual Administrative Reports published by Commissioner of Marketing Department, Government of Andhra Pradesh.

Time Period

As the study is concerned with the estimation of price elasticity of acreage under cotton crop in the selected districts of Telangana region of Andhra Pradesh state, the required data on area, production, yield, irrigated area, rainfall and prices have been collected for the period 1955-56 to 2002-03.

Empirical Supply Response Function

For the purpose of generating empirical information on price elasticity of supply response of cotton crop in selected districts of Telangana region, both (A) linear and (B) log-linear forms of equations have been considered. The model is considered by hypothesizing that the desired area depends mainly on lagged prices of the crop.

(A) $A^*_t = b_0 + b_0 P_{t-1}$ (1)

A^*_t = Desired area under cotton crop in hectares in 't' year

P_{t-1} = Average price of cotton crop per in t-1 year

Since desired area under cotton crop is not observed, the following Nerlovian's Partial Adjustment Mechanism is followed to estimate the above function.

$$A_t - A_{t-1} = \delta (A^*_t - A_{t-1}) \quad (2)$$

Where,

δ = Coefficient of adjustment whose value will by and large be less than unity

A_{t-1} = Area under cotton crop in t-1 year

A_t = Area under cotton crop in 't' year

By substituting Equation (1) in Equation (2), the following equation is obtained

$$A_t = A_{t-1} = \delta (b_0 + b_1 P_{t-1} - A_{t-1})$$
$$A_t = \delta (b_0 + b_1 P_{t-1} - A_{t-1}) + A_{t-1}$$
$$A_t = \delta b_0 + \delta b_1 P_{t-1} - \delta A_{t-1} + A_{t-1}$$
$$A_t = \delta b_0 + b_1 P_{t-1} + (1-\delta) A_{t-1}$$
$$A_t = b_0^* + b_1^* P_{t-1} + (B_2^{*\prime}) A_{t-1}$$

Where,

$b_0^* \;=\; \delta b_0$
$b_{1^*}^* \;=\; \delta\, b_1$
$b_2 \;=\; 1=\delta$
$1\text{-}b_2^* = \;\delta < 1$

Average Price Elasticity in short-run $= \delta A_t / \delta P_{t-1} * P_{t-1} / A_t$
$= b_1^* .\cdot P_{t-1} \,/\, \sqrt{\bar{A}t}$

Average Price Elasticity in long-run $= SRE/\delta = b_1\, P_{t-1}/A_t/\delta$

(B) $\log A_t^* = \log b_0 + b_1 \log P_{t-1}$ (3)

Since A*t is not observable, the following non-linear partial adjustment mechanism suggested by Nerlovian is followed to estimate the above function.

$\log A_t - \log A_{t-1} = \delta\,(\log A_t^* - \log A_{t-1})$ (4)

By substituting Equation (3) in Equation (4), the following is obtained.

$\log A_t - \log A_{t-1} = \delta\,(\log b_0 + b_1 \log P_{t-1} - \log A_{t-1})$
$\log A_t = \delta\,(\log b_0 + b_1 \log P_{t-1} - \log A_{t-1}) + \log A_{t-1}$
$\log A_t = \delta \log b_0 + \delta\, {}_* b_1 \log P_{t-1} - \delta \log A_{t-1} + \log A_{t-1}$
$\log A_t = \log b_0^* + b_1^* \log P_{t-1} + (1\text{-}\delta) \log A_{t-1}$
$\log A_t = \log b_0^* + b_1 \log P_{t-1} + b_2^* \log A_{t-1}$

Where,

$\log b_0^* \;= \delta \log b_0$
$b_1^* \;= \delta\, b_1$
$b_2 \;= \delta\, b_2$

Price Elasticity in Short-Run $= \delta \log A_t / \delta \log P_{t-1} = b_1$
Price Elasticity in Long-Run $= SRE/\delta$

Both the linear and log linear forms of equations have been fitted to the time series data. On the basis of economic, statistical and econometric criteria, an appropriate form of equation has been selected to examine the price elasticity of acreage under cotton crop in selected districts of Telangana Region. The districts selected for the study are Adilabad, Karimnagar, Khammam, Mahabubnagar, Medak Nizamabad, Nalgonda and Warangal.

It ought to noted that though there is no methodological enhancement, the results of the present empirical study, based on the latest time series data, will be useful in understanding the impact of factors such as lagged price, lagged-yield, rainfall and irrigated area in allocating the area under cotton crop by the farmers in selected districts of Telangana region. The empirical estimates of short-run and long-run price elasticities based on latest data append to the existing stock of literature on acreage response function.

SUPPLY RESPONSE FUNCTION-EMPIRICAL FINDINGS

The empirical findings and analysis relating to the price elasticities of acreage under cotton crop in selected districts of Telangana region of Andhra Pradesh have been presented here. Table 1 provides the results relating to price elasticities of acreage under crop in Adilabad district of Telangana region for the period 1955-56 to 2002-03.

Table 1

Price Elasticity of Acreage under Cotton Crop in Adilabad District of Telangana Region (1955-56 to 2002-03)

$$\text{Log } A_t = \log 5.118 + 0.14 \log Y_{t-1}^* - 0.42 \log I_t^* + 6.72 \log R_t^* + 0.650 \log P_{t-1}^* + 0.47 \log A_{t-1}$$

(2.597) (0.05) (-0.102) (0.839) (0.234) (0.11)

$R^2 = 0.76$

$\bar{R}^2 = 0.73$

Notes: 1. Figures in the brackets are standard errors
2. * Significant at five per cent level

It can be seen from the above table that the lagged yield, the irrigated area under cotton crop, rainfall and the lagged average annual price are significantly influencing the decisions of the farmers in allocating the area under cotton crop in 't' year in Adilabad district. The regression coefficients of the lagged yield, rainfall and lagged price have positive sign. However, the sign of the regression coefficient of the variable under irrigated area under the crop is negative which is bewildering. These estimates are trustworthy as the standard errors of the regression coefficients of different variables are found to be less than half of the regression coefficients.

Table 2 presents the regression results pertaining to acreage response function for cotton crop for Karimnagar district.

Table 2

Price Elasticity of Acreage under Cotton Crop in Karimnagar District of Telangana Region (1955-56 to 2002-03)

$$A = \underset{(2168.322)}{7893.655} + \underset{(10.62)}{30.323}\, Y_{t-1}^{*} + \underset{(3.729)}{27.713}\, P_{t-1}^{*} + \underset{(0.03)}{0.22}\, A_{t-1}$$

$$R^2 = 0.924$$

$$\bar{R}^2 = 0.9188$$

Notes: 1. Figures in the brackets are standard errors
2. * Significant at five per cent level

The results show that the regression coefficients of yield and acreage and prices of cotton crop in lagged year are found to be reliable in influencing the decisions of the farmers in allocating the area under cotton crop in Karimnagar district. The insignificant variables have been deleted from the function as they are found to be trivial. The linear acreage response function is considered for the analysis. The percentage of variation explained by the yield and acreage price is very high.

Table 3 presents the regression results pertaining to acreage response function for cotton crop for Khammam district.

Table 3

Price Elasticity of Acreage under Cotton Crop in Khammam District of Telangana Region (1955-56 to 2002-03)

$$\text{Log } A_t = \log \underset{(0.558)}{3.604} + \underset{(0.212)}{0.625} \log Y_{t-1}^{*} + \underset{(0.289)}{1.975} \log P_{t-1}^{*} + \underset{(0.017)}{0.16} \log A_{t-1}^{*}$$

$$R^2 = 0.888$$

$$\bar{R}^2 = 0.8804$$

Notes: 1. Figures in the brackets are standard errors
2. *Significant at five per cent level

Table 3 presents the regression results pertaining to acreage response function of the cotton crop for Khammam district.

Though, both linear and log linear acreage response functions have been fitted to the data, the log linear acreage response function has been selected for the analysis. It is found that the regression coefficients of the lagged yield and lagged pries, constant elasticities of acreage under cotton crop in current year with respect to lagged yield and lagged prices are significantly influencing the area under cotton in t period.

The numerical values given in the table show that the elasticity of acreage in current year with respect to lagged yield is less than unity and the elasticity of acreage in current year with respect to lagged yield more than unity evincing the fact that farmers are more responsive in taking a decision while allocating the area under cotton crop to the changes in lagged prices. The farmers' responsiveness to the changes in yield is found to be relatively inelastic.

Table 4 gives the regression results pertaining to acreage response function for cotton crop for Mahabubnagar district.

Table 4
Price Elasticity of Acreage under Cotton Crop in Mahabubnagar District of Telangana Region (1955-56 to 2002-03)

$$\text{Log } A_t = \log 2.085 + 0.515 \log Y_{t-1}^* - 0.086 \log I_t^* + 1.222 \log P_{t-1}^* + 0.32 \log A_{t-1}$$

(0.594) (0.13) (-0.003) (0.304) (0.12)

R^2 = 0.671

$\bar{R}^2$ = 0.645

Notes: 1. Figures in the brackets are standard errors
2. *Significant at five per cent level

In case of Mahabubnagar district the regression results pertaining to supply response function for cotton crop show that the regression coefficients of price and yield are statistically significant showing that these variables are influencing the area under cotton crop in Mahabubnagar district. Since the estimated supply function is in log linear form the regression coefficient of price is the constant elasticity of area under cotton crop with respect to lagged prices showing that at a one per cent increase in the lagged price of cotton crop will lead to increase the area under cotton crop by 1.2 per cent immediately. Thus the farmers belonging to Mahabubnagar district are more responsive in taking a decision in allocating the area under cotton crop to the changes in the lagged prices of the cotton crop.

Table 5
Price Elasticity of Acreage under Cotton Crop in Medak District of Telangana Region (1955-56 to 2002-03)

$$\text{Log } A_t = \log 1.824 + 0.054 \log Y_{t-1}^* + 0.098 \log I_t^* - 0.296 \log R_t^* + 0.798 \log P_{t-1}^* + 0.32 \log A_{t-1}$$

(1.093) (0.008) (0.003) (-0.134) (0.325) (0.03)

$R^2 = 0.573$

$\bar{R}^2 = 0.522$

Notes: 1. Figures in the brackets are standard errors
2. *Significant at five per cent level

The regression results presented in Table-4 for Medak district show that the regression coefficients of lagged price, irrigated area together, rainfall and lagged yield are found to be statistically significant showing the positive impact on acreage under cotton crop in current year. The regression coefficient of lagged price which is constant price elasticity of acreage in short run explaining that one percent increase in lagged price will lead to increase the area under the cotton crop by 0.80 per cent per annum.

Table 6 givers the regression results pertaining to acreage response function for cotton crop for Nizamabad district.

Table 6
Price Elasticity of Acreage under Cotton Crop in Nizamabad District of Telangana Region (1955-56 to 2002-03)

$$\text{Log } A_t = \log 1.600 + 0.418 \log Y_{t-1}^* + 0.107 \log I_t^* + 0.525 \log P_{t-1}^* + 0.53 \log A^*_{t-1}$$

(0.604) (0.154) (0.032) (0.199) (0.032)

$R^2 = 0.556$

$\bar{R}^2 = 0.5148$

Notes: 1. Figures in the brackets are standard errors
2. *Significant at five per cent level

The regression results show that the regression coefficient of lagged price is found to be statistically significant showing that price has been vital in influencing the decisions of the farmers in allocating the area under the cotton crop in Nizamabad District. The estimated price elasticity in short run shows that a one percent increases in lagged price leads to increase the area under cotton crop in Nizamabad district by 0.53 per cent. The price of elasticity is relatively inelastic showing sluggish responsiveness of farmers to the changes in lagged prices.

Table 7 shows the regression results relating to acreage response function for cotton crop for Nalgonda district.

Table 7

Price Elasticity of Acreage under Cotton Crop in Nalgonda District of Telangana Region (1955-56 to 2002-03)

$$\text{Log } A_t = \log 0.164 + 0.157 \log Y_{t-1}^{*} + 0.316 \log I_t^{*} + 0.119 \log R_t^{*} + 1.421 \log P_{t-1} + 0.281 \log A_{t-1}$$

(1.903) (0.003) (0.135) (0.032) (0.351) (0.103)

$R^2 = 0.655$

$\bar{R}^2 = 0.614$

Notes: 1. Figures in the brackets are standard errors
2. *Significant at five per cent level

The regression results furnished in the above table show that the variables such as lagged prices, lagged yield, rainfall and irrigated area are found to be reliable in influencing the decisions of the farmers in allocating the area under cotton crop as estimated standard errors are less than half of the corresponding regression coefficients. The constant elasticity of acreage under cotton crop with respect to lagged prices is found to be somewhat more than unity.

Table 8 presents the regression results pertaining to acreage response function for cotton crop for Warangal district.

The estimated supply response function for cotton crop for Warangal district shows that the coefficients of lagged prices and lagged yield are statistically significant showing the positive impact. Since the estimated supply response is in log linear form, the regression coefficients of price and yield in lagged year are constant elasticities. Though they are significantly positive they are less than unity showing the inelastic nature.

Table 8
Price Elasticity of Acreage under Cotton Crop in Warangal District of Telangana Region (1955-56 to 2002-03)

$$\text{Log } A_t = \log 0.770 + \underset{(0.485)}{0.924} \log Y_{t-1}^{*} + \underset{(0.337)}{0.990} \log P_{t-1}^{*} + \underset{(0.207)}{0.48} \log A_{t-1} \quad (0.230)$$

$$R^2 = 0.855$$

$$\bar{R}^2 = 0.837$$

Notes: 1. Figures in the brackets are standard errors
2. *Significant at five per cent level

Table 9 shows the short-run and Long-run Price Elasticities with Speed of Adjustment in the selected districts of Telangana region.

Table 9
Short-run and Long-run Price Elasticities with Speed of Adjustment in the Selected Districts of Telangana Region (1955-56 to 2002-03)

District	*SRPE*	*LRPE*	*Speed of Adjustment*
Adilabad	0.650	1.14	0.57
Karimnagar*	1.20	1.54	0.78
Khammam	1.975	2.35	0.84
Mahabubnagar	1.22	1.979	0.68
Medak	0.798	1.173	0.68
Nizamabad	0.525	1.211	0.47
Nalgonda	1.421	1.976	0.72
Warangal	0.99	1.90	0.52

Notes: SRPE : Short-run Price Elasticities
LRPE : Long-run Price Elasticities
* : SRE evaluated at average values.

SHORT-RUN AND LONG-RUN PRICE ELASTICITIES AND SPEED OF ADJUSTMENT

The elasticities of acreage under cotton crop with respect to lagged prices in short-run are found to be relatively lesser as compared to the corresponding price elasticities in long-run in all the districts. In Karimnagar, Khammam, Mahabubnagar and

Nizamabad districts, the short-run elasticities of acreage with respect to lagged prices are more than unity evincing the immediate impact of lagged prices on acreage in current year is more elastic and less elastic in other districts. The long-run price elasticities are not only high but also more than unity in all the district evincing the fact that an increase in lagged prices would stimulate the farmers to bring more area under cotton crop in the long-run. So far is the speed of adjustment is concerned, the discrepancy between actual change and the desired change in the area under cotton can be eliminated by more than 50 per cent in a year. In Medak district, 0.47 per cent of discrepancy can be eliminated between actual change and desired change in the area under cotton crop in a year. The speed of adjustment between actual change and desired change in Khammam district is very lofty evincing that the discrepancy between actual change and desired change can be speedily eliminated in a year. In other words, the cotton growers in Khammam district are speedily responding to the changes in lagged prices, all else equal.

CONCLUSION

Thus the empirical results based on the estimates of the regression coefficients evince the fact that both lagged prices of cotton and yield found to be significant in all the districts influencing the decision of the farmers in allocating the area under cotton. Therefore, suitable price policy to augment the area under cotton crop in Telangana districts is required. To bring a break through in over all production. Further, the results show that the elasticities of area under the cotton crop with respect to lagged prices are moderately higher in the long run showing the fact that farmers respond to the changes in the last year price in allocating the area under cotton crop. Further, the speed of adjustment between actual change and desired change in the area under cotton crop is found to be more than fifty per cent in all the districts except for Nizamabad district showing that more than fifty per cent of the discrepancy can be eliminated every year. It should be noted that the results of the present study, subject to limitations of the data, would be useful in understanding the impact, inter-alia, of lagged prices on the area under cotton crop.

REFERENCES

J.R. Behman, Supply Response in Inderdeveloped Agriculture : A Case Study of Four Major Annual Crops in Thailand, 1937-1963, North Holland Publishing Company, Amsterdam, 1968.

Batra, M.M., Price Variations in Groundnut and Groundnut oil, A Study : 1952-53 to 1967-68, Economic Times, 26 March 1969.

Batra M.M., Supply Response of a Subsistence Crop under Traditional and New Technologies, Indian Economic Review, Vol. XI (New Series), No. 2, October 1976.

Dasgupta, Sipra, Agriculture : Producer's Rationality and Technical Change, Asia Publishing House, Bombay, 1970.

Jai Krishna Rao, M.A., Dynamics of Acreage Allocation for Wheat in Uttar Pradesh, A Study in Supply Response, Indian Journal of Agricultural Economics, Vol. XXII, No. 1, January-March 1967, pp. 37-52.

Dharma Narain, The Impact of Price Movements on Areas under selected crops in India 1900-1939, Cambridge University Press, 1965.

Kaul, J.L., A Study of Supply Response to Price of Punjab Crops, The Indian Journal of Economics, XIVII, P.1. 1967.

Kaul, J.L. & D.S. Sindhu, Acreage Response to Prices for Major Crops in Punjab – An Econometric Study, IJAE, XXVI (4), 1971.

Jai Krishna, Price Expectation and Acreage Response for Wheat in Uttar Pradesh, IJAE, Vol. 20, No. 1, January-March 1965, pp. 19-23.

Madhan Mohan Batra, Agriculture Production : Prices and Technology, Allied Publishers Pvt. Ltd., New Delhi, 1978.

Raj Krishna, Farm Supply Response in India Pakistan : A Case Study of the Punjab Region. The Economic Journal, LXXIII, September 1963, pp. 477-487.

Rao, M.S. & Jai Krishna, Price Expectation and Acreage Response for Wheat in Uttar Pradesh, Indian Journal of Agricultural Economics, Vol. XX, No. 1, Jan-March, 1965, pp. 20-25.

Raj Krishna, Farm Supply Response in India Pakistan : A Case Study of the Punjab Region, The Economic Journal, Vol. 73, No. 291, September 1963, pp. 477-487.

Shashikala Sawant, Supply Behaviour in Agriculture, Himalaya Publishing House, Bombay, 1978.

Sidhu, D.A. Price Policy for Wheat in India, Chand S. Co. Ltd., New Delhi, 1999.

Tyagi D.S., Farmers Expectations of Future Prices and their Impact on Acreage Allocation, A Case Study in Supply Response in Western Uttar Pradesh, Ph.D., Thesis, Sardar Patel University, Vallabh Vidyanagar, 1971.

SECTION II

RURAL DEVELOPMENT

6

SUSTAINABLE COMMUNITY BASED REGIONAL DEVELOPMENT: A CASE OF BIMARAU REGION

*R. D. Singh**

INTRODUCTION

Regional economies in India are closely related to the ecology. The geo-ecologic relations which have evolved in historical perspective have a deterministic impact on the regional economic and social relations. Such relations may be analysed in two ways-

1. Horizontal ecologic and economic relations in intra-regional and inter-regional systems,
2. Vertical ecologic and economic relations in spatial framework.

The ecological and economic changes in the regional framework have resulted due to increasing internal demand for resources by the communities and the exogenus factors such as external political and economic control over the resources and economic activities. Before the British colonial political and economic control in India, the ecologic and economic changes were determined by the increased food demand and extensive agriculture by transforming the landuse pattern in the forest regions in favourable zones.

In horizontal space, the regional ecosystem and economic system evolved in uniques characteristics of environmental and

* R. D. Singh is Reader, Department of Regional Planning and Economic Growth, Barkatullah University, Bhopal Madhya Pradesh, India.

resource endowment, thus evolving plants and animal communities in close association with human communities in different ecologic regions of India. This can be very clearly identified in pastureland, forestry, agro-forestry, agriculture and fishing practices starting from mountain and plateau regions to plains and coastal regions of India, creating pattern of inter-related habitats, such as, forestry habitats, agricultural habitats and coastal habitats etc. having close linkages in inter-regional ecologic and economic systems.

Table 1
A Comparative Analysis of Regional Variation in Rural Habitation in India (1991)

	No. of Villages	
State	*Inhabited*	*Uninhabited*
India	587,226	47,095
Bihar	67,513	10,184
Madhya Pradesh	71,526	4,694
Rajasthan	37,889	1,921
Uttar Pradesh	112,803	11,147
Punjab	12,428	367
Haryana	6,759	229
Maharashtra	40,412	2,613
Tamil Nadu	15,822	958
West Bengal	37,910	2,979

Source: Statistical Profile of India, 1991

Table 2
A Comparative Analysis of Net Migration by Place of Birth (1991)

	Net Migration		
State/U.T.	Person	Male	Female
Bihar	-1,911,086	-1360,586	-550,502
Madhya Pradesh	+1,280,209	+672,238	+607,971
Rajasthan	-363,493	-276,164	-87,329
Uttar Pradesh	-3,813,318	-2,493,674	-1,687,833
Punjab	+298,485	170,552	127,933
Haryana	+465,635	-241,001	224,634
Maharashtra	+2,647,700	1,673,652	974,048
Tamil Nadu	-323,876	-214,550	109,326
West Bengal	4,027,447	2,339,614	1687,833
Kerala	-687,032	-373,246	313,786

Source: Statistical Profile of India, 1991, Registrar General of India Govt. of India, New Delhi.

The vertical linkages of regional economies were determined by the surplus productions around trade and distribution centres of the agro-based and forest-based products. Thus, the urban centres were the centres of trade, administration and culture as can be observed in river basins, coastal areas and such favourable zones suited for agriculture.

Forest and agriculture economies in agrarian system have been community controlled and environmentally determined and with close ethnic and occupational relations. However, the control of land, forest and minerals, during the British colonial rule, to meet the trade and industrial demands seriously affected the occupational and resources use pattern and quality of life of many occupational communities. The communities dependent on forest, agro-forestry, dairy, horticulture etc. were forced to migrate from their habitats to agricultural habitats as landless labourers in large number. The zamindari system developed by British rule resulted forced extraction of agricultural produce from agricultural communities. Thus, the agrarian and tribal communities suffered during colonial rule causing unemployment, poverty and exploitation by extractive forestry, mining and agricultural practices in exogenously controlled system through exploitation of resources. It may be inferred that the control, the process of resources use and their different social, economic and spatial linkages as destination are important institutional parameters to determine the implication on regional ecosystems.

IMPLICATIONS OF HISTORICAL COLONIAL DEVELOPMENT STRATEGY

It is necessary to analyse regional economies in India in historical perspectives and their ecologic relations with the local and regional occupational communities in spatial framework. The human communities in agrarian system were organised in close geo-ecologic relations which determined their organismic association with natural resources in evolutionary growth process of agrarian economies. The river basin and coastal regions became centres for production, exchange and culture. The population distribution were ecologically determined and space economies organised in concentric pattern resulting in tribal economy, agro-forestry, agriculture and marketing. The increased demand for food products resulted in extensive agriculture in forest region, but in close relations with ecology and communities.

Table 3
A Comparative Analysis of Population below Poverty Line in India (1983-1993)

States	*1983*	*1987-88*	*1993-94*
Bihar	52.22	52.13	54.96
Rajasthan	34.40	35.15	27.41
Madhya Pradesh	49.78	43.07	42.52
Uttar Pradesh	47.07	41.46	40.85
Punjab	16.18	13.20	11.77
Haryana	21.37	16.64	22.05
Maharashtra	43.44	40.41	36.86
West Bengal	54.85	44.72	35.66
Tamil Nadu	51.66	43.39	35.66
Kerala	40.42	31.79	25.43
All India	44.48	38.86	35.97

Source: Planning Commission

The British colonial interests evolved extractive agriculture system of exploitation of resources from agriculture and tribal habitats in zamindari system through deforestration and mining. Infrastructural system-administrative and transport evolved to facilitate more extraction of minerals, forest produce and agricultural cash crops. As a result, serious ecologic and economic crisis in forest and agricultural regions developed breaking down the occupational linkages in forestry, agro-forestry, dairy, horticulture and agriculture etc. and forced the large number of communities to depend on slave relations in agriculture. The historical accounts of tribal unrest and peasants protest against the colonial rule are the testimony of growing ecological conflicts in these regions.

The demographic and economic implications particularly in eastern India have been very serious. The population density in river basins particularly in Gangatic basin of U.P., Bihar, and Bengal has increased alarmingly. This was caused due to continued ecologic degradation in the mountainous regions, resulting in socio-political and socio-economic conflicts.

After independence, the colonial interests continued with modernisation and industrialisation political economic idealogy in centralised system and exploitation of forests and minerals continued from the coal-iron belt of India. The modernisational ideals with heavy industrialisation seriously affected community based economic activities like agriculture, animal husbandry and industries in many parts of the country particularly in BIMARAU region.

Table 4
A Comparative View of Literacy Rate of BIMARAU Region with other States in India (1981-1997)

States	*1981*	*1991*	*1997*
Bihar	26.20	38.48	49
Rajasthan	24.38	38.55	55
Uttar Pradesh	27.16	41.6	56
Madhya Pradesh	27.17	44.2	56
Punjab	40.86	58.51	67
Haryana	36.14	55.85	65
Maharashtra	47.18	64.87	74
West Bengal	40.94	57.7	72
Tamil Nadu	46.76	62.66	70
Kerala	70.42	89.81	93
All India	36.23	52.21	62

Source: Planning Commission

For convenience of analysis, the regional ecologic-economic systems may be divided in eastern, western, northern and southern regions, each regulated by a metropolitan centre. Because of the serious ecological degradation in eastern region, community life have been seriously affected. They northern region particularly due to lack of mineral resources didn't suffer serious degradation. The adoption of mineral based industrialisation strategy through nationalisation of forest and minerals resources continued the exploitation of the peripheral regions of Bihar, Orissa and Chhatisgarh to meet the trade and industrial raw material demands at metropolitan centres of Calcutta, Bombay and others.

Due to very close relation of forest ecology with surrounding agricultural ecology, the degradation and depletion of forest has resulted in degraded agro-ecological relation due to disturbances in drainage pattern and climatic condition resulting in drought.

Table 5
A Comparative Analysis of Annual Rate of Growth of Per Capita SDP between 1993-94 and 1997-98

	1983-84 to 1993-94 (Per cent Per Annum)	*1993-94 to 1997-98 (Per cent Per Annum)*
Bihar	0.78	2.14
Rajasthan	1.78	5.94
Uttar Pradesh	1.76	1.69
Orissa	1.37	2.61
Madhya Pradesh	2.38	2.71
Andhra Pradesh	3.49	2.40
Tamil Nadu	4.69	4.47
Kerala	4.11	3.70
Karnataka	3.76	3.42
West Bengal	2.69	5.45
Gujarat	2.50	7.62
Haryana	3.39	3.16
Maharashtra	4.96	3.90
Punjab	3.30	2.60
All 14 States	3.16	3.87

Source: Montek S. Ahluwalia, E.P.W., Vol. xxxxv, No. 19, May 2000 pp. 1637 to 1648.

The colonial control of resources– land, forest and minerals has resulted in serious unemployment, poverty and socio-political conflicts particularly in forest and agriculture regions. After independence, the continued feudal control of resources has resulted in caste based politics particularly in eco-degraded agricultural region in the country. The lack of decentralised regional planning and development strategy has resulted in serious caste based social and political conflicts, particularly in

Bihar and U.P. These conflicts are either caste based which is horizontal in social space and community based particularly in tribal regions. The caste based conflicts in agricultural regions are more sharp due to unequal distribution of land resources and virtual absence of regional economic and environmental planning due to vested political and administrative interest. The most serious problem in Bihar, is represented by serious eco-degradation in this state due to continued mining and deforestration.

The process still continues with globalisation policy in liberalised system and privatisation. The foreign investments are not moving to backward regions with very low level urbanisation. However, increased demand for power and other raw material resources would further increase mining and deforestration in the ecologically degrading regions.

PATTERN OF ECO-DEGRADATION AND IMPACT ON COMMUNITIES

The exogenous colonial interests have more serious effects in mineral and forest rich regions and regions more represented by feudal leisure class behaviour, particularly in Rajasthan, M.P., U.P., and Bihar. The less affected regions are the linguistic and cultural communities having cohesive social relations.

The variables used as indicator of eco-degradation and lack of community development are represented by decadal data on uninhabited villages, population below poverty line, low level of literacy, net migration by place of birth and annual rate of growth of per capita state domestic products etc. These are used as proxy variables to analyse the impact of eco-degradation as a cumulative causation of eco-degradation on communities, particularly in BIMARAU regions. Through BIMARAU regions are contiguous states, they are part of different regional geo-ecosystems.

The data on uninhabited villages by 1991 census alarmingly reflects that almost more than 11 thousand from U.P. and 10 thousand villages in Bihar are reported uninhabited. This reflects serious eco-degradation of human habitat and ecology.

The percentage of population under poverty is highest in Bihar, followed by U.P., M.P. and Rajasthan. Not only more than half of the population is below poverty line, this has increased between 1983-93 from 55.22 per cent to 54.96 per cent.

In terms of net migration by place of birth, alarmingly more than 38 lakh persons in Uttar Pradesh are reported to have moved out of the state, followed by Bihar having 19 lakh persons.

The literacy level only at 49 per cent by 1997 in Bihar is the lowest, the other three states in BIMARAU region have reached the level of almost 56 per cent.

Annual rate of growth of per capita SDP reflects an increase between 1983-84 to 1993-94 and 1997-98. Though the growth rate has increased in the end period, they are low except in Rajasthan. In U.P., it has declined from 1.76 to 1.69.

The above variables represent a vicious circle of underdevelopment explained by cumulative causation of resources flow from these regions and their peripheral location in metropolitan regional economies. These also explain the failures of regional governments to initiate community based development programme due to conflicting political and social interests.

STRATEGIC MODEL FOR SUSTAINABLE COMMUNITY BASED REGIONAL DEVELOPMENT AND INFORMATION SYSTEM

As discussed in the foregoing sections, strategic models may be evolved on the basis of the existing theoretical framework and empirical evidences. *Von Thunen's* concentric pattern theory of rural land use represents the concentric pattern of communities association with resources and activities around market centres represented by the regions in India.

Le Play provided a theoretical model for eco-balance in the regional economy and ecology through a geographical landscape planning model to evolve synergetic relations between people, activities and environment.

Place	←	Work	←	Folk
(Environment)	→	(Function)	→	(Organisation)

Le Play formula express the life process in space continum as environment acting through function upon organism and organism acting through function upon environment and these constitute interdependent elements of a Singh process, acting, reacting and interacting. Petric Geddes extended the Le Play's formula and through an example of Vally Section, explained the functional organisation in association with environment and organisms representing synergy between geography, economics, sociology and politics.

These two structural models represents regional ecosystem and economic system in close association of the communities. Though regional theories have dominated in later half of 20th century, the developmental models either have remined mechanistic and materialistic without development.

Gunar Myrdal in Asian Drama has frequently quoted the state policies and corruption as the important reasons of under-development and abstract ideologies with poor implementation in India. Myrdal's commulative causation theory and Hirschman's core-peripheral theory clearly explains the polarisation of development and backwash effects on peripheral regions. However these theories didn't clearly explain how these underdevelopment and dicholomy can be removed.

Tinbergen's spatial sectoral classification of local, national and international sectors indirectly provides a spatial planning model, however, fails to explain the communities participation in the development process.

Swaminathan, M.S. in his recent paper on population stabilisation and human resource development has emphasised on strategic shift to human resource development through environmental, health, education and nutrition security by involving communities through identification of their aspiration and priorities. A hierarchy of unmet needs can be spelt out starting from most pressing needs. Plan implementation and finances can concentrate on meeting the needs in phased manner.

Bose, A.N. identified antagonistic people's participation in community and rural development programmes, due to conflicting interests of landlords and landless labourers in the agrarian relation. On the basis of relative regional data on poverty, disaggregated according to income classes, he identified capital based and eco-degradation technology responsible for poverty and loss of reliance. As alternative, he suggested people based sustainable development model through land reforms and co-operative and strong people's unions to achieve the objectives of removal of poverty, eco-stability or sustainance of life support system and self-reliance or sustainance of political independence.

The growth model in regional science and economics have largely emphasised on infrastructural models following industrial growth strategies. The sectoral growth strategies and communities development programmes are largely failure in backward regions because these are not based on needs, priorities and aspirations of the people.

The recent literature on human ecologies and sustainable development have received a little attention in regional development literature. Moreover, information on regional ecosystem relation, occupational and socio-economic status and production relations in different communities in backward regions are not available either through Census or economic survey. An attempt is being made to use macro economic models in regional economies ignoring economic and ecologic relations. It is desirable to update the information on regional ecosystem relations and profile of different communities in terms of their occupation, access to resources and economic linkages. The census data on different communities' social and economic status is not available as also the traditional economic and occupational base in different regions.

The regionwise income data on communities based income indicators need to be prepared so as to initiate community based regional development programme.

The strategic model may be based upon following priorities.

1. Restoration of community controls over environmental resources like land, water, forest etc.
2. The institutional reform and legislation relating to local and regional land, forest and minerals in resource

regions need to be clearly made between the state, trade and local communities interests.

3. Massive conservation and development of degradation forest and wasteland through the local communities control and stoppage of trade interests controlling agricultural and forest wasteland.
4. Expansion of communities based agricultural and rural development programme to absorb the surplus labour in agriculture, horticulture, dairy, agro-forestry and rural and community based industries in co-operatives.
5. Identification of communities based small-scale and cottage industries at nodal centres based on local resources and absorb rural surplus labour.
6. Chanellising the private saving of landowners for productive small-scale industrial development to break the leisure class behaviour through training and entrepreneurial development.
7. Massive skill and entrepreneurial development programme in sustainable developmental activities at local and regional levels.
8. Identifying communities occupational and economic linkages in vertically linking activities like mining, industry, trade and services.
9. Community based resource conservation and development programmes like water, land and forest conservation and initiation of massive sustainable development programmes through community participation as area development through integrated social and environmental forestry, dairy, horticulture, fisheries, agriculture and developing the product linkages to the market removing the vested trade interests.

REFERENCES

Conkling, Edgar C. and Maurice Yates, (1976), "Mans economic environment", Mcgraw-Hill Book Company, New York.

Geddes, Sir P., (1949), "Cities in Evolution".

Myrdal, G. "Asian Drama".

Richardson, H.W., (1973), " Regional Growth Theory", The Macmillan Press Ltd., New York.

Swaminanthan, M.S. "Yojana", Vol. 44, No. 8, August 2000.

Bose, A.N. "People's participation for Rural Development: Two antagonistic prospectives," IJRS, Vol. XIX No. 1, 1987, pp. 40-48.

_______ "In search for an alternative direction for development", IJRS, Vol. XVIV, No. 2, 1992, pp. 9-20.

7

PARTICIPATORY PLANNING AT VILLAGE LEVEL A CASE STUDY ON INITIATIVES

R. Venkata Ravi and V. Narayana Reddy

INTRODUCTION

Decentralised rural development has been a paramount concern of both the Government and Non-Government Organizations for many decades. A series of approaches, strategies and activities have been developed to initiate decentralised development that have made different amount of dent on the development of people in the society. The experiences gained show that the people are unable to absorb the development benefits owing to the various factors, particularly lack of participation. So, the strategies shifted towards participatory development by focusing on the capacity building of the people in terms of increasing competence to get control over the process of decision-making and participation.

Panchayat Raj Institutions (PRIs) has been considered as most suited medium for the rural transformation and development. The PRIs is meant for institutionalization of participation, democratic and bottom-up model of development (Kaushik, 2005). In India, as part of the decentralisation process, series of structural changes have been initiated; new Panchayat Raj System is one of the significant efforts made towards ensuring a participatory rural development. Another important aspect in the decentralisation process is the expanding role of

NGOs as development organizations at grassroot level. The NGOs not only proved to be effective in the process of social mobilization, but also in organizing the community initiatives. This has resulted in emerge of Community Based Organizations (CBOs) at village level. Thus, the current state of affairs at village level is featured with various types of organizations working for the purpose of sustainable rural development. They are; Gram Panchayat (GP) - as local self-government; NGOs - as catalyst and development agency and Community Based Organizations.

The grassroot level governance assumes much significance in the process of decentralised development, as a lot depends on the efficacy of local level government in the process of planning for development programmes and managing the same. In the context of local level governance, primarily move includes methods and means by which the higher level of institutions devolving responsibilities and authorities to the lower institutions for managing public resources to solve local level problems and fulfill the needs of the local community. The PRIs are to perform a role of decentralised governance for the participatory development at the grassroot level. The participatory development, in true sense, need to be initiated by the Gram Panchayat by involving the local community in the process of planning and managing the development programmes. Needless to state that only such development plans would reflect the aspirations and felt-needs of the local community.

Currently, the NGOs are closely working in the Gram Panchayats both as "Partner" for collaborative development and as "Trainer" or "Resource Persons" for the Gram Panchayats. The development organizations are promoting efforts of the NGOs at the grassroot level in the process of strengthening Panchayats as institutional framework for participatory rural development. The NGOs are working with the Communities and Panchayats for effective democratic decentralisation and participatory development. The Gram Panchayats as local self government have to prepare Micro Plans for the socio-economic development with social justice which is main goal of the Constitutional Status provide to the Panchayats.

NEED FOR MICRO LEVEL PLANNING

Hence, an initiative has been made on "Pilot Basis" to prepare "Micro Plans" for a selected Gram Panchayat in partnership with local NGO, CBOs and Community. The main purpose of such attempt is to make the Gram Panchayat to mobilize resources to execute the development programmes. Moreover, in the process of planning, it is possible to assess the training needs of the various functionaries at gram Panchayat level in aspects of planning and related aspects; in long run, it helpful for building the capacity of Gram Panchayats.

Preparation of Micro-Plans at Gram Panchayat with other stakeholders has paved way for participatory development initiatives within the framework of democratic decentralization. Moreover, the functionaries in the GP have exhibited their capabilities in this process and also further it has also facilitate to identify the area for building their capacity to work a local self-government at village level.

The NGO is working in the village, as the development agency for implementing various programme and projects. The NGO has another important role as the Trainer of the GP functionaries and also building the capacity of the community for local self-governance. The Governance for Development at Grassroots should really aim at all round development of the village by using every available agency. Total potential of the village society need to be effectively utilized for positive gains. Every stakeholder needs to have a sense of participation in the development of local area ands community. The local level governance implies in proper coordination, motivation and regulation of development efforts by the various stakeholders and partners (Agarwal, 2005).

STAKEHOLDERS AND THEIR ROLE

Hence, an attempt has been made on *Pilot Basis* to have Micro Level Plan prepared for a selected Gram Panchayat in the Andhra Pradesh. This attempt has been made in Naryanapuram

Gram Panchayat of Warangal District in Andhra Pradesh. The main aim of the attempt is to make that Gram Panchayat as a *Model Village*. Different stakeholders involved in the process of Participatory Micro level Planning is presented in the following diagram:

Different Stakeholders in the Participatory Micro Level Planning at Village Level

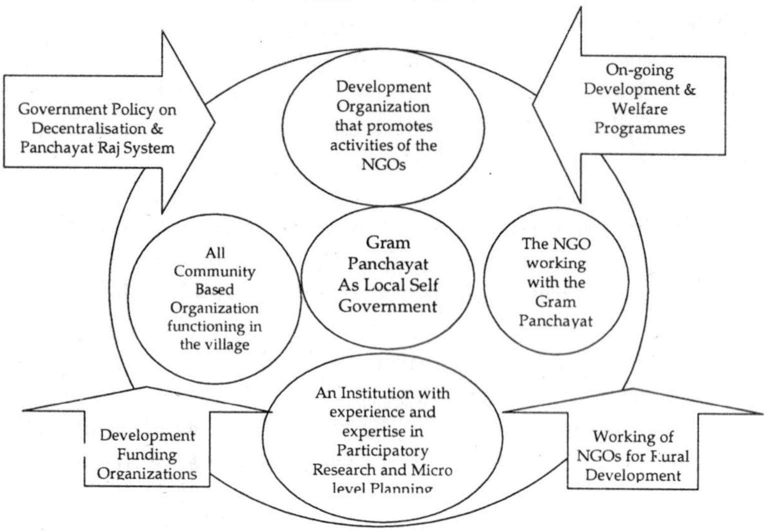

In the above figure, the larger circle indicates the village community that has various organizations ands institutions operating for the development at grassroot level such as Gram Panchayat, NGO which is working with the Gram Panchayat, Community Based Organizations (including User Groups, Clubs and People Associations) and Participatory Research Team. These stakeholders are directly involved in the process of Micro level Planning at village level.

The process of micro level planning has been done with in the existing policy environment related to the decentralization and Panchayati Raj system, functioning of different government departments that implement development and welfare programmes, existing mechanism for reaching the people with assistance of external funds. Considering these factors would at any level and also moment could have influence on the Micro level Plan of the Gram Panchayat or the NGO working with Gram Panchayat.

The Participatory Research Team from the Council for Social Development, Hyderabad, has provided professional inputs for designing the micro level plan in the Narayanapuram village. However, CWS, MARI, GP Members and Village community have participated in the process. Each one of these stakeholders have played important role during the Participatory Research carried out in the village.

The CWS has made a choice of initiating such Pilot Project with one of the Partners – namely Modern Architects for Rural India (hence forth known as MARI) based at Warangal and working for development in that district for a considerably long period of time. The MARI with its strong hold at the grassroots level has involved in the major task of Mobilization of village community, sensitization of CBOs, and Gram Panchayat for undertaking a pioneering attempt in the State to have Participatory Micro Level Plan at Gram Panchayat level.

The MARI has also played a key role in bringing together of all stakeholders involved in this process for drawing plans to make the Narayanapuram Gram Panchayat as a *Model Village*. Gram Panchayat of Narayanapuram village in the Pravathagiri Mandal of Warangal district has selected for the purpose of this pilot project. The Sarpanch and Upa-Sarpanch along with all Ward members of the Gram Panchayat are involved in the process of preparation of Micro Level Plan.

Stakeholder	*Role and Responsibility*	*Output*
Participatory Research Team of Council for Social Development, Hyderabad	Provided Research and Methodological inputs, conducted Rapid Appraisal in the village community	Analyzed the situation, Identified the thrust areas, studied the interrelationship between GP, NGO and Community. Brought out the identified areas of development issues and need for intervention

Contd....

Stakeholder	*Role and Responsibility*	*Output*
Modern Architects for Rural India (also known as MARI), Warangal	Facilitated the process, logistic management. Mobilization of community, Sensitization of Functional Committees of GP, Sensitization of CBOs in the village. Identification Social Partners/Stakeholders	Community, CBOs and GP worked together to take up various steps in preparation micro level plans
Community Based Organizations functioning in the Gram Panchayat area	Identification of Problems and their root causes, analy zing the prevailing situation in the village community, Identification of Felt-needs and prioritizing according to the needs, Identification development activities and alternatives solutions to the problems	Come out with an account of needs, issues, priorities, and possible ways and means to solve their problems and meet the demand of the community.
Village Community of Gram Panchayat area	Mapping Resources and Assets and their accessibility; provided social capital for the planning	Issues based solutions and strategies have been developed
Centre for World Solidarity, Hyderabad	Provided required funds to the planning process	GP, NGO, CBOs and Community worked together the planning process

In the process of Participatory Planning exercise, apart from Members of GP and Faculty of MARI, Members of various Community Based Organizations functioning in the village, (such as Water User Association, School Education Committee, Self-Help Groups, Mother Committees and Ryhtu Sangham) have participated and contributed. Besides these stakeholders, Villages Elders, former Sarpanch and former Members of the GP have also taken part actively and contributed for the preparation of Micro Plan for the village. The Participatory Micro level Planning has been done in truly democratic sense by involving all stakeholders in the process – starting from preliminary stage to till the approval of the Micro Level Plan Document by the Gram Panchayat.

SELECTION OF NARAYANAPURAM VILLAGE

The choice of the village has been based on the following parameters and indicators discussed and finalized by the CWS, MARI and CSD with few Panchayat leaders from the service area of the MARI in Warangal district. The parameters and indicators are – Gram Panchayat need to a small village with 1000 to 2000 population, Gram Panchayat is necessarily have all communities, Gram Panchayat headed by a SC or ST leader, Women head the Gram Panchayat, Village need to have been facing several development issue or problems. All the stakeholders have felt that a Gram Panchayat that is selected for making a Model Gram Panchayat need to be considered to undertake pilot project of this kind. As the Narayanapuram Gram Panchayat has fit-in all parameters, the same has been selected to the project.

The Micro Plan preparation has been done with Participatory Approach and techniques. The Professional of the CSD, CWS and MARI have facilitated and carried out diverse task that are already identified at field level. The planning exercise has been undertaken by using various Participatory Research and Action (PRA) methods, tools and techniques that includes -Transect Walk and Diagramming, Social and Resource Mapping, Problem and Priority Ranking with Matrix, Focus Group Discussions, Workshop for Need Identification and Pair-wise Ranking, Need Assessment, Systematic Client Consultation, Risk analysis Semi-Structured Interview with Sarpanch, Upa-sarpanch and Panchayat Secretary, In-personal Interview with key informants and community leaders and a detailed Household Survey. Combination of these tools, techniques and methods are used according to the ground reality that prevailed during time of field work, so as to bringing out the local knowledge of the community – that is Social Capital as prime input for formulating the Participatory Micro-Plan at village level.

OUTPUTS AND EXPERIENCES

The outputs of the Participatory Micro planning exercise in the Narayanapuram Gram Panchayat have been presented in this report. The report has a comprehensive Micro Level Action Plans for the socio-economic development of the people and also steps improve the basic facilities and essential services in the gram Panchayat. The report also consist of a quick assessment related to the working of Gram Panchayats in the line of its basic functions to deliver the services for betterment of the village community.

In the light of the Participatory Research and subsequent Planning process carried out in the Narayanapuram Gram Panchayat has provided some experience and lessons for all the stakeholders. It is understood that the Gram Panchayat needs to be equipped with adequate authority and resources by the State government through systematic devolution. The elected leaders are to be trained for preparation of Micro level plans.

It would be appropriate to have exclusive participatory research for major sectors – like Health and Sanitation, Education, Agriculture Development, Rural Infrastructure, Rural Livelihoods. Because, it is the same village community that is provides various inputs and responses for any kind of participatory research and planning on specific subject matter. Accordingly, it would be right to analyze various developmental issues and needs of the community. It would help to have sector-wise plans along with area plan for a Gram Panchayat.

In the whole process, it is necessary to have much more involvement of different CBOs as they are also representing mainly as organized User Groups at village level for many resources and services such as, Irrigation Water, Drinking Water, Drainage and Sanitation, Heath Services, Education, Micro-finance. When, situation analysis and planning is attempted sector wise, these User Groups or Stakeholders Associations need to be consulted extensively. It would help for maintaining the service delivery and resource management by the respective Users themselves at village level. Moreover, it needs to pave way for Asset Management by the community, as they are the owners of the Assets created in their village.

The sector-wise assessment situation with participation of different stakeholders would enable to more effectively use the tools and techniques for generation of information. It would also facilitate concurrently carry out the participatory research with more of community participation. The participatory research needs to be done on completion of the household survey for baseline data. It would help to specifically focus on the identified issue as guided by the outcome of the survey during the Participatory Rapid Appraisal in the village.

Another dimension observed is that the Gram Panchayat is closely working in partnership with the NGOs operating in the area. At the same time, relationship between Panchayat Secretary (official) and Sarpanch and Members of the Gram Panchayat (elected leaders) is found not conducive for the normal functioning of the Panchayat by way of discharging regular responsibilities for the good governance at village level. The professional capabilities of the NGO's functionaries who are working with Gram Panchayats required being periodically refreshed (otherwise continuously developed or updated) that would enable them to provide effective partnership at grassroots level to have sustainable development in the village.

ISSUES EMERGED:

The preparation of Participatory Micro Level Planning at village has come out several issues related to the aspects of present status of decentralisation and governance at village level. They are concern with various stakeholders' participation in the development of the rural areas. The emerging issues are presented are as follows:

GRAM PANCHAYAT

- As this Gram Panchayat is new formed facing so many operation al problems in running the administration.
- Though the Gram Panchayats are need to prepare Micro Level Plans, they are not adequately informed and lack in the capacity to take such process with existing resources.
- The tax and revenue collection is very poor even after having a full time Panchayat Secretary for discharging such routine functions.

- The coordination between Sarpanch and Secretary is not lacking and existing level functional coordination is not sufficient for proper management of the Gram Panchayat.
- Lack of adequate level of interaction through vertical linkages between Gram Panchayat and other upper tier PRIs.
- Inadequate coordination with various CBOs functioning in the village, particularly with Water Users Association, Self Help Groups and Rythu Sangham.
- Inadequate level of interaction between GP and Community, specifically community is not cooperating with Women Sarpanch from the ST community.
- Gram Panchayat has no much control over the existing natural resources, like land and water in the village.
- The Gram Panchayat is not having proper build to house its office and conduct the meeting.

NGO PARTNER

- Though much has been done by the NGO to build the capacity of the elected Members of the Gram Panchayat, still the institutional development has not taken place.
- Focusing only on the Mandatory functions of the Gram Panchayat in the Planning Process, instead of comprehensive planning for the area and community.
- Not according the status of local self-government to the Gram Panchayat; relationship between NGO and GP is similar to the NGO and CBOs.
- Lack of clarity between administrative and democratic decentralisation as result NGO not attempted to bring together CBOs as technical wings of the GP.

OTHER PARTNERS

Any development agency workings for the development of Model Village or Gram Panchayat need to prepare a wide-ranging participatory micro level plans covering all sectors and focusing on all sections of the village community. In such a perspective plan, role of Gram Panchayat, CBOs and NGO can be identified. It is also necessary to involve the upper tier Panchayat Raj Institutions while going in for such an exercise to ensure some amount of funds to take up the action plans prepared under the micro level planning document. It would help the Gram Panchayat to tap the people participation the planning process. Moreover, it would also help to gradually build the basic facilities in the village. Involving the people involvement through the CBOs in the process of planning is not sufficient but also required to be involved in contributing for taking up few activities with funds available with them. It is required to tap the un-used resources available with CBOs – like Water Users Association, Forest Management Committee and Self Help Groups. It is equally necessary to make the community to understand that when they are asking for certain facilities from the Gram Panchayat, they have to regularly need to pay what is due to the Panchayat from them.

NOTE

1. Authors are grateful to Council for Social Development, Hyderabad for the Institutional support in for preparing this paper. Authors have immeasurably benefited out of the discussions held with Dr. S. Vijaya Kumar, Fellow, Council for Social Development, Hyderabad on the early version of this paper, we express our sincere gratitude to him.

REFERENCES

Bibek Debroy and Kaushik. P. D. (2005) " Energizing Rural Development through Panchayats" Academic Foundation, New Delhi, Pp. 151-186.

Malik. A. S. (2005) "Local Self Government at Village Level: An Assessment" *The Indian Journal of Political Science,* Vol. LXVI (4), October-December, Pp. 773 – 792.

Participatory Micro level Planning in Narayanapuram Gram Panchayat, Warangal District, Council for Social Development, Hyderabad, 2006, A Report.

8

RURAL MARKETING AND POST-LIBERALIZED ERA: EMERGING PERSPECTIVE AND ISSUES[1]

*Awadhesh Kr. Singh**
*Satya Prakash Pandey***

The present paper purports to assess the potential of rural marketing in post-liberalized era and also to review the corporate response to the emerging changes in rural markets. Since 1991, India has been going through a process of economic reforms and liberalization. The reforms have embraced almost all aspects of the country's economy. Policies relating to industrial licensing, trade and foreign investment have undergone major changes. In addition, significant macro-economic adjustments have also taken place. Economic institutions too have undergone significant change; the banking sector and capital markets in particular, have been major targets of the change. And finally, structural adjustments covering areas like subsidies, the price environment and the public sector have also taken place. Collectively, these reforms aim at modernization of the country's industrial system, removal of unproductive controls, strengthening of private investment,

1. Paper presented at National Seminar on Agri-business Management: Opportunities & Challenges organized by Indian Institute of Rural Management, Jaipur dated 20th & 21st November, 2003.

* Faculty, MMEM Programme, Institute of Management Sciences, Lucknow University, Lucknow.

** Visiting Faculty, MA-DA Programme, Institute of Development Studies, Lucknow University, Lucknow.

including foreign investment, and integration of India's economy with the global economy. In one word, it can be said that all-round opening up of the country's economy has been the essence of the reforms (Ramaswamy & Namakumari 2002, p. 37). The programme of macro-economic adjustment and structural reforms has stabilized the economy and integrated it with world economy. The board contents of the structural reforms programme are not new. They are an elaboration and intensification of changes that began in the 1980s. These changes were aimed at increasing productive efficiency of the economy by creating a more open and competitive environment for both the public and private sector (Ahluwalia, 1993, p. 80). There seems to be a general consensus on the desirability of reforms to dismantle the bureaucratic regulatory apparatus evolved over the years that may have out-lived its utility (Kumar, 2000 p. 803).

CORPORATE RESPONSE TO THE CHANGE

The corporate sector has well responded to the new changes (Basant, 2000).

(i) The Indian corporate sector is vigorously restructuring itself to retain competitiveness. Restructuring is mainly geared towards consolidation in a few chosen areas to correct the inefficiencies created by over-diversification in the pre-reform era.

(ii) MNC's have actively participated in the mergers and acquisitions process to get market entry or to strengthen their presence.

(iii) MNC's are better placed vis-à-vis domestic firms in the acquisition game because of their deep pockets and relatively cheaper access to capital.

(iv) The reliance of the Indian corporate sector on foreign technology purchase has increased. More and more technology flows are now tied with equity.

(v) Firms are making efforts to improve manufacturing capability. This is being done through initiatives within the firm. Quality upgradation seems to be their key priority. The efforts at improving manufacturing capability may still prove to be inadequate to meet the competitive challenges.

(vi) Export based growth strategies are being adopted by some of the corporate sector firms but such strategies are not widespread; export orientation increased appreciably in the early years of reforms but has been a major collapse since 1997-98.

(vii) The performance of the Indian corporate sector in the 1990s, has shown mixed tendencies. Profitability rates, export performance as well as export to import ratios have shown varied trends across industry groups.

Tougher the competition in the business environment, increased efficiency became a must for a corporate enterprise to survive. This implied business re-engineering process to be adopted in an enterprise. This involves a fundamental change that effects multiple business functions. This required the company to look back and rethink the way it did business, and reshape and realign its strategies, business processes, technology, people and infrastructure with what the customer needed. Fundamentals of business changed, and flexibility, teamwork, customer focus, speed to market, quality management became very important for an enterprise, and the realization that being complacent with the status quo is certainly the fastest way to lose one's leadership position.

According to Khanna (1993, p. 144), following emerged to be important in the changed business environment :

(i) customer's perspective is the only perspective;

(ii) management commitment and involvement;

(iii) far reaching goals combined with continuous measurement of performance;

(iv) end-to-end view of processes, across all functional and organizational boundaries;

(v) operationist focus around customer driven business results;

(vi) the elimination on non-value added activities;

(vii) ownership at all levels of the organization and people empowered with knowledge, tools and authority;

(viii) timely dissemination of information; and
(ix) continuous improvements

RURAL MARKETING IN CHANGED SCENARIO:

The rural scene is now undergoing a sea-change, resulting from the multi-prolonged activities undertaken for the overall development of rural areas. There have been significant improvements in the rural sector in respect of agricultural production, spread of education, banking facilities, electrification, transportation, communication, etc. All these changes have led to the creation of general awareness for achieving a new and better style of living. With the increased purchasing power, access to communication and awareness about modern life-styles, the rural sector needs a better marketing thrust. The recent economic policy initiatives of the government have resulted in increased investments in the corporate sector by domestic as well as overseas investors. The growth of the corporate sector means increased production, and this, in turn, requires identification and penetration into high growth potential markets. In this context, rural markets have good prospects for most of the goods and services of this liberalized economy. It also indicates that the twenty-first century is going to see the full blossoming of the Indian rural market (Chahal and Pal, 1997, p. 223).

As change came in 1991 when Government took a series of bold initiatives to take the economy away from controls. The programme included for reaching trade, fiscal, marketing and industrial policy measures with a major thrust on improvement of competitive efficiency of Indian industries by utilizing foreign investment and technology to a much greater degree than in the past. Moreover, the new reform measures ended the regime of licensing and controls and made the industry virtually independent. Significantly, the new policy permitted the free import and export of virtually all products with some exceptions. Imports of capital goods and raw material were made more liberal. Introduction of automatic approvals of foreign technology agreements and foreign investment, restructuring of public sector. Undertakings and the thrust on export were other measures announced by the government with a view to improve the competitiveness of Indian industries and promotion of experts. In short, the force of the new policy was more on free play of market forces instead of state control in determining the country's future growth and development. For the first time, the government came out in favour of outward oriented trade and industrial policies where export marketing was given prime importance. Under the new policy, industries could expand, modernize, diversify and internationalize their operations with greater freedom (Neelmegham, 2000, p.5). This changed economic scenario gave further boost to marketing, and motivating the corporate sector to further stretch out to tap the so far largely untapped rural sector markets.

Economic reforms have enabled GDP to grow at an average annual rate of about 6.4 per cent between 1992-93 and 1999-2000. Consumption too has gone up – especially the consumption of manufactured FMCGS (Fast Moving Consumer Goods). For 1997-98, market size of a basket of 20 consumer expendable goods in the household sector is estimated at Rs. 801 billion (at current prices). Consumption of the same commodities was estimated to be Rs. 371 billion in 1992-93 showing an average annual growth of 16.7 per cent. These figures also indicate that per household consumption expenditure on the goods considered has doubled from Rs. 2387 in 1992-93 to Rs. 4736 in 1997-98. Rural India, in particular, with a share of over 55 per cent in total consumption of FMCGs has also witnessed a growth of about 14 per cent per annum during the same period. This seems to be a fairly good growth by any standard (Brahmankar and Gupta, 2000).

Indian market is undergoing a significant metamorphosis because of economic liberalization and globalisation. Many players (both national and global) are trying to capture the urban market of our country. But this market has already reached a saturation level and it is extremely difficult to tap the urban market with high profit margin. It is also not easy to penetrate profitably into the export market because of fierce competition. In export market, a firm has to face challenges from MNCs (Multinational Companies), other foreign companies and domestic firms of the concerned export market. In this cut-throat competition, everybody's market share will shrink as everyone is chasing the same market (Dey Adhikar, 1998, p. 1). This realization is forcing companies to go rural.

The 1990s have ushered in far reaching changes that influence the customer's profile and therefore the market. Literacy levels have risen (especially female literacy). The average size of the household is reducing; nuclear families are increasing. This development has particular significance for durable goods marketers; for instance, instead of a large refrigerator for a joint family, a household may now need two or three smaller refrigerators. Also, sizeable youth segment is emerging, with it's own income or pocket money, which marketers need to recognize (Godrej, 1993, p. 155). Rural India is also in the throes of change, perhaps in an even more significant manner. There has been a boon in those markets, fuelled by the penetration of media; vast improvement in infrastructural facilities like roads and shops; telecom connectivity, successive good monsoons; and high government spending. As a result, the rural component is now bigger than the urban in many product categories (Godrej, 1993). Gone are the days when a rural consumer went to a nearby city to buy "branded products and services". Time was when only a select household consumed branded goods, be it tea or jeans. There were days when big companies flocked to rural markets to establish their brands. Today, rural markets are critical for every marketer – be it for a branded shampoo or an automobile (Kannan, 2001). Lifestyles and habits of rural people are changing. Yesterday's luxuries are becoming today's necessities. There is a boom of (both domestic and foreign) brands of products.

RURAL MARKETING BOOM:

India lives in her villages. And so it would appear to India's consumers. Profitable farming and better marketing options in some states have made a large number of villagers potential consumers for consumer. Durables and FMCG (Fast Moving

Consumer Goods) companies. The size and profitability of the rural market increased with agricultural development and infrastructure facilities. The greater the agricultural development in an area, the greater the rural market. Villagers now consume everything from branded soaps to cold drinks like Pepsi to electrical appliances like high horsepower tractors. Most of the manufacturers still think that urban areas are the potential markets for their products. But the studies show that the rural share has been increasing over time. The number of items which sell less than 20 per cent in rural areas has actually declined. Now rural areas absorb more of all items. The demand pattern for consumer products has also changed. So, far the country's mega marketers, the rural reach is increasingly become the most important route to growth. Some companies like Hindustan Lever, Nirma, Parle Foods and Marico Industries are making inroads into the interland, usually displacing unbranded offerings and regional local brands. But their ingress remained restricted primarily to the 10 product categories with the highest penetration in the rural market (Chundi, 1999). According to ORG-MARG survey, these products (together with percentage penetration, and brand with highest penetration) were as follows until a few years ago : Toilet Soaps (88.26% penetration – Lifebuoy), Washing Soaps (87.4% penetration – Nirma), Edible Oils (84.67% penetration – Palmolive, Anupam, Mustard Oil), Tea (79.09% penetration– Nirma), Biscuits (59.80% penetration – Parle-G), Cocunut Oil (53.76% penetration – Parachute), Safety Razor Blades (45.34% penetration – Topaz), and Shampoos (38.28% penetration–Clinic) (Business Today– July 3, 1999).

Trends indicate that the rural markets are coming up in a big way and growing twice as fast as the urban, witnessing a rise in sales of hitherto typical urban kitchen gadgets such as refrigerators, mixer-grinders and pressure cookers. According to a National Council for Applied Economic Research (NCAER) study, there are as many 'middle income and above' households in the rural areas as there are in the urban areas. There are almost twice as many 'lower middle income' households in rural areas as in the urban areas.

As per NCAER projections, the number of middle and high income households in rural India is expected to grow from 80 million to 111 million by 2007. In urban India, the same is expected to grow from 46 million to 59 million. Thus, the absolute size of rural India is expected to be double than that of urban India. The study on ownership of goods indicates the same trend. It segments durables under three groups – (1) Necessary products – transistors, wrist-watch and bicycle; (2) Emerging products B & W TV and cassette recorder; (3) Lifestyle products – CTV and refrigerators. Marketers have depend on rural India for the first two categories for growth and size. Even in lifestyle products, rural India will be significant over next five years (Kannan, 2001).

The opportunity seems big 12 per cent of the world's population or 126 million households, lives in rural India. Purchasing power exists. Between 30 and 50 per cent of the consumption of a number of consumer goods comes from rural India. Faced with intense competition in their urban markets, where high media spends and expensive consumer promotions are the order of the day, marketers are giving up to milk the great rural opportunity (Mishra and Gupta, 1999). Rural Marketing strategies are bolstered by data indicating the latent purchasing power that consumers in rural areas have (Jacob, 2003).

CORPORATE INTEREST IN RURAL MARKETS:

Television has made inroads into rural homes. Mass-media today has enormous approach and access to rural masses, capable of influencing their habits and lifestyles, and this creating demand for the (branded) products. Corporate houses then develop new products for rural consumers and attempt their suitable positioning. For example, Hindustan Motors (HM) launched a utility vehicle, the RTV (Rural Transport Vehicle) aimed at rural markets. Watch industries found their watch brand 'Sonata' getting popular in rural areas, they formulated a new strategy tailored to the requirements of large rural markets (Rai, 2000). The recession and the knowledge that rural customers have not been tapped to their full potential has forced the companies to undertake innovative measures Hyuendai Motors India Limited (HMIL), Coca Cola India, DCM, Shriram Chemicals Limited, are all doing so (Jacob, 2003). The companies that are tapping the rural markets, are surprisingly the multinationals like Hindustan Level Ltd., who have done more to penetrate the rural market than several Indian private sector grants or even the public sector. There are three strong seasons that give multinationals this advantage of tapping rural markets. First : the companies need the resources to understand a large and diverse rural economy. The kind of exploratory study of behaviour that is needed to understand the peculiarities of each segment of the rural market will necessarily be expensive. Second : even if the companies have the resources, they need to believe the expenditure is worthwhile. This belief must co-exist with the recognition that the exercise need not always result in a profit-generating project. Third : companies must not treat the rural market as a dumping ground for lower end products designed for an urban audience. Instead, they must use their technological expertise to create specific products for the rural economy (Pani, 2000). In meeting these three conditions the multinationals have an edge over several major Indian companies. They have much deeper pockets, have an attitude for greater emphasis on research, are technologically much advanced, and are sensitive to the rural Indian markets.

At a seminar in Chennai on 'rural marketing for competitive advantage in globalised India', marketing pundits echoed that a sound network and a thorough understanding of the village psyche are a *sine quo non* for making in roads into rural market. The price-sensitivity of a consumer in a village in something the marketers should be alive to. Rural income levels are largely determined by the vagaries of monsoon and, hence, the demand there is not a easy horse to ride on. Apart from increasing the geographical width of their product distribution, the focus of corporates should be on the introduction of brands and develop strategies specific to rural consumers. Britania Industries launched 'Tiger Biscuits' especially for the rural market. It clearly paid dividend. Its share of the glucose biscuits market has increased from 7 per cent to 15 per cent (Kanan, 2001).

MARKET SIZE AND PENETRATION:

About 12 per cent of world population lives in rural areas in India. This is a huge market by world standards. According to an NCAER (1998) survey, rural consumers own only 52 per cent of available consumer durables, even though they constitute 72 per cent of total households in India. According to this survey, on an average rural households owned three consumer durables as compared to seven consumer durables owned by an average household. It also showed that purchase and use of certain durables and non-durables by consumers in rural areas is more than that of the consumers in urban areas. The durable products are : Sewing machines, radio/transistors; wrist-watches, black and white television sets, cassette recorders, bicycles, table fans and pressure cookers. However, in case of non-durables, data shows that atleast six products, rural market has a larger share than the urban.

POTENTIAL OF RURAL MARKETS:

Rural Markets have seen a big boom in terms of opportunities they provide to the corporate sector in India. Rural India had a share of over 55 per cent in total consumption of FMCG (Fast Moving Consumer Goods) and had a growth of about 14 per cent per annum during the period 1992-93 to 1997-98. This seems to be a fairly good growth by any standard (Brahmankar and Gupta, 2000). The rural market's contribution to the total national market had gone up from 28 per cent in 1985 to 40 per cent in 1990 (Chatterjee, 1992). The size of rural market in 1992 was of the order of Rs. 40,000 crores made up of Rs. 22,000 crores for non-food items and Rs. 18,000 crores for food items (Soritakki, 1992, p. 562). During the period 1992-93 to 1997-98 consumption of FMCGs had grown at a ratio of 14 per cent per annum.

According to data furnished by National Council for Applied Economic Research (NCAER) clearly showed a great rural market boob (Business World, 1999). The Chief Economist of NCAER (based on this data) clarified "that rural growth rates have already outpaced urban ones and will continue to do so through the next decade. So, a presence in the rural market, will not remain a choice, but a necessity" (Business World, 1999, p. 27). The companies will have no choice but to go rural if they must survive. Findings of the study conducted by NCAER in 1998-99 showed that, (i) Rural markets for group I durables (less than Rs. 1000 in value : items like transistors, pressure cookers, wrist-watches, bicycles, etc.) are bigger than urban markets already predicted that (ii) rural markets fro group II durables (Rs. 1001 – Rs. 6000 in value : items like B&W TVs, sewing machines, mixers, cassette recorders) will be bigger than urban markets by 2001-02; (iii) for group III durables (Rs. 6001 or more in value : like colour TVs, refrigerators, two-wheelers and washing machines) rural markets will be smaller than urban ones, even in 2006-07; and showed that (iv) rural market growth rates are faster than urban ones, even on the large bases of group I & II (Business World, 1999). The NCAER data also showed that India is now seeing a dramatic shift towards prosperity in rural households. It predicted that the lowest income class will shrink from more than 60% in 1994-95 to 20% in 2006-07. The higher income classes will be more than double. Rural economy has triggered. Ten good rains in a row from 1980-81 to have 1998-99 boosted foodgrain production. Procurement prices have also been rising. This implies growing rural prosperity and demand for goods. The NCAER data clearly showed that Rural FMCG (Fast Moving Consumer Goods) Market will bloom (Business World, 1999, p. 28-29).

Some impressive facts about rural sector:

(i) The number of rural supermarkets (haats) in India 42,000 exceeds the total number of retail chain stores in the US (35,000);
(ii) In 2001-02, LIC sold 55 per cent of its policies in rural India;
(iii) Of the two million BSNL mobile phone connections, 50 per cent are in rural;
(iv) Of the 20 million who have signed up for Rediffmail, 60 per cent are from small towns. Of the one lakh who have transacted on Rediff online shopping site, 50 per cent are from small towns;

(v) 24 million Kisan Credit Cards (KCC) issued in rural areas exceeds the 17.7 million credit plus debit-cards issued in urban India. A whopping Rs. 52,000 crore has been sanctioned under the KCC scheme;

(vi) The number of middle and higher income families (having Rs. 70,000 plus annual income) in rural (21.7 million) and urban (24.2 million) is nearly the same;

(vii) Electricity consumption by the agricultural sector has shown a sharp increase from 17.6 per cent of total consumption in 1980-81 to 29.2 per cent in 1999-00. During the same period, industry share has dropped from 58.4 per cent to 34.8 per cent (Kashyap, 2003, p. 6).

PROBLEMS & CHALLENGES OF RURAL MARKETS

Despite the vast potential in rural markets, effective taping of emerging rural markets is not an easy task for corporate houses. The problems & challenges of rural marketing include vast and scattered markets, transportation bottlenecks, seasonal and irregular demand, low standard of living and income levels of consumers, lack of desire for new lifestyle, low level of consumer's awareness, poor marketing intelligence, high inventory cost, inadequate marketing support, lack of proper planning for business operation, insufficient storage and warehousing facilities, ineffective sales force, non-suitable packaging, branding and designing of the products, penetration of low priced foreign products and high priced and large volume consumer's product etc.

CONCLUSION

Now, it is crucial for a company to redesign it's marketing-mix, because not much is left in the urban market, which is heading towards saturation. Contrary to this, the rural market has not been tapped scientifically by majority of companies. Growth prospects lie in the efficient exploitation of this market which has more than 650 million consumers. Rural India is a market with regard to which the age-old marketing story – an inland of barefoot people representing tremendous opportunity or a waste of resources for a shoemaker – is applicable. There are many reasons for companies to redesign their mix for the vast Indian market. Some of them are discussed below (Dwivedi, 1997, p. 94) :

- The changing business environment, economic liberalization, increasing competition, rising costs, lower margins, splintered market, and high consumer choice have brought the consumer to the centre stage. The silent not very demanding customer, who was ignored, has now been replaced by one who is aware and choosy.
- Rural earnings are rising rapidly and persona social familiar and cultural values are under transformation. Increasing personal disposable income will lead greater consumption of products – both durables and non-durables – making a vast potential untapped market presently not as tough as the urban, available.
- Changing buyer profile. Younger, more knowledgeable, better informed and educated sons are replacing conservative fathers in making purchase decisions or have more influential role in decision-making. The group unlike the previous generation, is more rational, less emotional and least interested in long-term association, but wants quick returns.
- It is not only the members of the elite class of urban India which now has a good percentage of upscale consumers whose purchasing power actually matches their propensity to spend. Those in rural India have discarded the ideology of simple livings of their ancestors. They wish to have all types of comforts, and for that, all types of products to boost their status.
- Media–Satellite TV and print–has played a vital role in changing the attitude of the people of India – urban and rural. Among the latter, the rate of change, and in some cases, rise in aspiration level are comparatively higher than among the former. This has rendered rural market open for reduction by marketers of most industries.

In the change scenario, the corporate houses need strategies for exploitation of potential of rural markets in India. The existing corporate strategies for taping of the rural markets need to redesign and a fresh approach. The strategies should be based on market analysis and research, location specific planning and marketing mix of products and services. The emerging role of NGO's, SHGs and other community-based organizations, so vast potential for marketing of consumer goods and services in the rural areas and with the closure interface of such organisations with corporate houses may lead to growth of rural markets as well as effective marketing of consumer goods and services in the rural areas. The traditional markets centers such as fairs and haats, may be treated as effective platforms for brand promotion, conducting marketing research, product demonstration and counseling as well as selling of the consumer products and services. Through such platforms and effective promotion of brands and new products may be ensured by the corporate houses. Importantly, the existing distribution channels are not effective, therefore, for effective physical distribution an innovative supply-chain has to be evolved and strengthened. In this regard, civil societies, internet-led services and community-based organisations may help to the greater extent to the corporate houses. The mind-set of the corporate houses should also be changed to sustain the interest and loyalty of customers through providing quality, choice and effective service rather than making profit and enhancing the market share.

REFERENCES

Ahluwalia, M.S. (1993), "Policies for the 1990s", Business India, 15th Anniversary Issue, 1993.

Basant, Rakesh (2000), "Corporate Response to Economic Reforms", Economic & Political Weekly, March 4, 2000.

Brahmankar, S.D. & Gupta, Tarun (2000), "Rural India : Market on Fast Track", The Economic Times, July 13, 2000.

Business World (1999), Issue dated 11 October, 1999.

Chahal, S.S. & Pal, Karam (1997), "Measures for Successful Rural Marketing", in Rural Marketing : Thrust and Challenges Edited by Samiuddin et. al – National Publishing House, Jaipur.

Chatterjee, A. (1992), "Gambling on the Rural Roulette", Brand Equity, The Economic Times, 8 April, 1992.

Chundi, Janaki (1999), "From Urban to Rural", Mainstream, November 27, 1999.

Dey, N.B. & Adhikari, K. (1998), "Rural Marketing : Challenges & Opportunities", Yojana Vol. 42 (5), May 1998.

Godrej, Adi (1993), "The Indian Consumer Wakes Up", Business India, 15th Anniversary Issue, 1993.

Jacob, Anil G (2003), "Picking Rural Pockets", Business Standard – The Strategist, 22 April, 2003.

Kannan, Shanthi (2001), "Rural Market – A World of Opportunity", Hindu, 11 October, 2001.

Kashyap, Pradeep (2003), "Revolution-in-Waiting", Praxis, Business Line's Journal of Management, Vol. 4 (Issue No. 2), July 2003.

Khanna, S.I.D. (1993), "Responding To Change", Business India, 15th Anniversary Issue, 1993.

Kumar, Nagesh (2000), "Economic Reforms and their Macro-Economic Impact", Economic & Political Weekly, March 4, 2000.

Mishra, Deepak & Gupta, Vinay (1999), "Rethinking the Rural Distribution Strategy", The Strategist – Special Issue on Rural Marketing, Business Standards, 27 April, 1999.

NCAER (1998), "Indian Market Demographics Report 1998", National Council Applied Economic Research, New Delhi.

Neelamegam, S. (2000), "Marketing in India : Cases and Readings", Vikas Publishing House, Delhi.

Pani, Narender (2000), "The Mirage in Rural Markets", The Economic Times, 14 July 2000.

Rai, Asha (2000), "Titan Chimes Rural Times with Sonata's", The Economic Times, August 18, 2000.

Ramaswamy, V.S. and Namakumari, S. (2002), "Marketing Management : Planning, Implementation & Control : Global Perspective Indian Context, 3rd ed. Macmillan, New Delhi.

Soritankki, C.N. (1992), Marketing Management in the Indian Background, Kalyani Publishers, Delhi. (4), October-December, Pp. 773 – 792.

Participatory Micro level Planning in Narayanapuram Gram Panchayat, Warangal District, Council for Social Development, Hyderabad, 2006, A Report.

9

PRIMACY OF PARTICIPATORY METHODS IN RURAL APPRAISAL: A MICRO STUDY

*N. Narayanasamy**
*M. P. Boraian***

INTRODUCTION

Lured by its lucrative features like simplicity, multi-disciplinary approach, visual way of data collection and analysis, people-centered participatory learning, and knowledge-based local action, a multitude of change agents have started using PRA in their sphere of profession. Practiced initially in the field of agriculture, PRA has eventually pervaded to a wide spectrum of development arenas in various parts of the world. Participatory monitoring and evaluation, using PRA methods have been found to be a viable and feasible alternative for conventional evaluation studies in the process of impact assessment. The quick spread of PRA drew sharp criticism on the efficacy of its methods which, by and large, centre around accuracy, reliability and cost-effectiveness of the data collected through PRA. The type, extent and quality of participation of people in PRA exercises have also been questioned. An attempt has also been made in this paper to ascertain the efficacy of participatory method with reference to accuracy, rapidity, cost-effectiveness and participation. The data obtained through

* Professor and Head and Reader.
** Dept. of Extension Education, Gandhigram Rural Institute (Deemed University), Gandhigram - 624 302, Dindigul Dist, Tamil Nadu.

social mapping (PRA method) has been compared with data collected through survey method in this villages. PRA took less time to gather, analyse and report the data; cost is also less under PRA method; the data collected through PRA are as accurate as collected under survey method, and participation of people in PRA is quite high and vibrant.

PARTICIPATORY RURAL APPRAISAL

Participatory Rural Appraisal (PRA) as a development methodology has primarily been evolved to appraise the rural resources, problems and requirements. In course of time, it was realized that as a development tool, it could not just stop with committing the people in analyzing their situations, conditions and problems but must go beyond this and extend to analysis, planning and action. The design of PRA therefore has to be refashioned to cover both the diagnosis and development action. PRA in the changed context has thus, been defined as a "a family of approaches and methods to enable rural people to share, analyse and enhance their knowledge of life and conditions, to plan and to act" (Chambers, 1999). Subsequently, the concept extended further to encompass not only planning but monitoring and evaluation as well. Because the design of monitoring and evaluation has to be incorporated not towards the end, but in the beginning of the project formulation process as well.

NGOs, who have been working with the people, have quickly responded to the participatory approach and started practicing "seemingly simple participatory methodologies involving disciplined observation, accurate recording and common sense analysis" (Korten, 1989). To start with, they practise the methods of PRA at the grassroots which may "provide basic information on the feasibility of beginning a project" (Rhoades, 1987). Later, realizing the efficacy of the methods experimented, they started using the methods in the area of analysis of situation, planning and implementation of projects. The results of experiments were found to be encouraging, rewarding and impressive which eventuated in the quick spread of PRA in all comers of the globe.

However, the rapid spread and application of PRA has invited sharp criticisms too. The criticisms are:

(i) they are biased, impressionistic and unreliable "(Cornwall and Jewkes, 1985). They constitute an enquiry that is 'undisciplined and sloppy'. They are said to involve subjective observations and respond fast to the selected members of the community.

(ii) terms like informal and qualitative are used to imply poor quality or second rate work.

(iii) rigour and accuracy are assumed and therefore to be in contradiction with participatory methods." (Pretty, 1995)

(iv) PRA is prone to poor and gender-sensitive.

In short, these criticisms, by and large, centre around the criteria of 'effective information supply such as timeliness (rapidity), cost effectiveness, and accuracy' (Moris and Copstake, 1983). Are these criticisms true? Does the use of participatory methods in appraising a situation result in reduction of time. Are the participatory methods cost-effective? Do they ensure accuracy of data collected? Do they lead to active participation of the people? These issues require in-depth empirical analysis because such an analysis would help position the participatory methods as a methodology of information gathering in the right perspective and it would also throw enough light on the efficacy or otherwise of the participatory methods. Hence, a study on the 'efficacy of PRA methods' was commissioned to answer these questions.

MICRO STUDY

The objective of the study is to ascertain the efficacy of participatory methods with reference to 'rapidity', 'cost-effectiveness', 'accuracy' and 'participation' in a micro rural cluster in the most backward block of Dindigul district.

The efficacy of participatory methods has been assessed by making comparative analysis of participatory method and conventional research method. We have, for the purpose of the experiments, chosen two different villages. Each village is distinctly different from the other in terms of size, caste, settlement pattern, occupation etc. For instance, a big village viz. Chellakuttiur is predominantly of nomads with joint family system as the rule. The other village viz. Karuthakkapatti is a small village. Between these two villages, a lot of differences could be seen in terms of occupation and pattern of settlement etc. The purpose of choosing two different villages for the experiment is to ensure that size and homogeneous nature of the population do not have much influence on the participation.

Our experience of organizing PRA in more than 100 villages of different size and composition have conclusively proved and that 'the size of the village in terms of number of households is a major determinant in enlisting people's participation and thereby quickly completing the appraisal' (Narayanasamy and Boraian, 1993). Similarly, a homogeneous village in terms of caste composition provides a very enabling environment to complete the appraisal as rapidly as possible. Conducting experiments on the effectiveness of PRA vis-a-vis survey in such a small, homogeneous village is likely to bring biased results. Hence, we have chosen a combination of two villages which are different in nature. We also made it a point to see that the villages are new, remote and PRA exercises were not conducted earlier. These precautions were mainly taken to affirm that the results obtained out of the exercise are bias free.

METHOD OF STUDY

'Social mapping' under PRA and conventional 'survey method' are the methods chosen to compare the data. The reason for selecting the participatory mapping from among the menu of methods is that participatory mapping has now been increasingly used as an alternative for collecting the demographic and other quantitative data (Chambers, 1998).

The type of data collected under the two methods include: religion, caste, marital status, age and literacy status of the family members, occupation, type of house, extent of land owned, and possession of livestock such as bullock, cows, buffalo, goat, sheep etc.

PRIMACY OF PRA METHODS

Having discussed the methods followed to collect and compile the data in detail, the analysis of data with reference to four criteria of efficacy viz., rapidity, cost effectiveness, accuracy and participation is presented. Details regarding the calculation of time, computation of cost and definition of concepts are given in Annexure A.

Time Consumption

The time involved to collect data under the two methods clearly shows that survey has taken 301 per cent of time than PRA for all the two villages put together. The time taken to complete a survey per household is 14.02 minutes while for the PRA, it is 4.77 minutes for all the villages put together.

Village-wise analysis of the time taken under two methods presents more or less similar trend. In big village, the survey consumed around 307 per cent of the time than PRA while it is 278 percent in a small village. However, there are variations in the time taken across the villages. For instance, the time taken to complete the survey per household for a big village is 15.50 minutes and for PRA 5.04 minutes; whereas for the small village the survey time per household it is 12.53 and 4.5 minutes respectively, (see Table 1)

The first village is a comparatively bigger village. The bigger village is likely to pose problems like building-up rapport, enlisting participation of different groups of people, finding the right key informants,bringing several kinds of leaders around, etc. All these factors have influence on duration of PRA. Hence, it is understandable that PRA, in a comparatively bigger village, takes more time.

Moreover, Chellakuttiur village has predominantly joint family system with an average family size of 7.5.

The time taken per unit (per household) under different components like rapport-building, data collection, data analysis, reporting and sharing shows that data collection takes much time both under survey and PRA followed by data analysis, rapport building and reporting. We have not shared the data collected out of survey with the respondents.

Table 1
Time taken to gather data
A comparison between Survey and PRA

Stages	*Big village* *Survey*	*PRA*	*Small village* *Survey*	*PRA*	*Total* *Survey*	*PRA*
Rapport building	290	180	94	35	384	215
	2.28	1.42	2.35	0.88	4.63	2.3
Data collection	1028	240	199	75	1228	315
	8.10	1.89	4.98	1.88	13.08	3.77
Data analysis	490	120	152	30	642	150
	3.86	0.94	3.8	0.75	7.66	1.69
Reporting	160	60	56	25	216	85
	1.26	0.47	1.4	0.63	2.66	1.1
Sharing	—	40	—	15	—	55
	—	0.31	—	0.38	—	0.69
Total % of PRA time	1969	640	501	180	2470	820
	307.65		278.33		301.25	
Time spent per unit	15.50	5.04	12.53	4.5	14.02	4.77

In the final analysis. it can be said that PRA takes much less time than the survey method whether in a big or small village. The findings of an earlier study corroborate this.1 (Rajarathinam et at. 1992). The time taken by PRA in different settings does differ. Big village takes much time to complete PRA exercise (mapping) whereas a smaller village takes less time.

While comparing the time taken to collect data under two methods, we have included only the researchers' time and not included the time spent by the participants from the community. Michael Richards et al. argue that time is one of the main factors in an analysis of cost effectiveness. If community time is not included and/or when no compensation is offered, PRA is cost-effective. They report that comparing researcher's/facilitator's and community time makes PRA absorb approximately 240 per cent more of every one's time than the survey (Richards, Davies and Cavendish. 1999). We have not considered community time for obvious reasons.

Cost-effectiveness

Robert Chambers described survey as a long and dirty method, which means data collection in a large questionnaire survey, can be costly and time consuming. The practitioners of PRA claim that it is cost-effective. The cost of collection of data under these two methods have been computed and presented in Table 2.

Table 2
Cost of data gathering
"A Comparison between Survey and PRA Methods"

	Big village		*Small village*		*Total*	
Cost details	*Survey*	*PRA*	*Survey*	*PRA*	*Survey*	*PRA*
Manpower	900	500	240	150	1140	650
Printing & stationery	375	48	65	19	440	67
Documentation	300	52	60	10	360	62
Total % of PRA cost	1575	600	365	179	1940	779
	262.5		203.9		249.0	
Unit cost	12.40	4.72	9.13	4.47	21.53	9.19

The total cost of conducting survey of 213 households works out to Rs.1940 whereas the cost of collecting the same data under PRA is Rs.779. Thus, the cost of conducting survey for a set of census data was 249 per cent more than the cost incurred on PRA for collecting the same data.

Village-wise analysis of the cost shows that the cost of conducting survey and PRA was higher in the big village than in the small village. The reason is quite obvious. The time taken to complete the survey and PRA was more in big village and therefore the highest cost. Again, village-wise comparison. of cost data (total as well as unit cost) shows that the cost of organising survey was 263 per cent more than PRA in big village and 204 per cent in small village. The results of the study have clearly shown that organising PRA for collecting census data is less costly.

Accuracy

Participatory methods have been criticized mostly on the ground that they lack rigour. The purpose of rigour is trustworthiness (pretty, 1993). Trustworthiness of data largely depends on the accuracy of data. The survey data are considered to be trustworthy, accurate and are amenable to the very powerful and rigourous techniques of modem statistical analysis" (Gill, 1993). Whereas PRA data, it is often said, are not amendable to the rigour and accuracy. This criticism to a certain extent has been answered by applying the conventional tests which involve comparison of PRA approach with others. Robert Chambers has identified four main areas where RRA and PRA have generated numerical data which can be compared with those from conventional sources. They are; farm and household surveys, wealth and wellbeing ranking; participatory mapping and village census, and rainfall (Chambers, 1998).

Table 3
Comparison of data collected through Social Mapping and Survey Method

	Big village		*Small village*		*Total*	
Household data	*Survey*	*PRA*	*Survey*	*PRA*	*Survey*	*PRA*
(1)	(2)	(3)	(4)	(5)	(6)	(7)
No. of households	127	127	-	40	40	-
Type of house						
Thatched	36	36	-	14	14	-
Tiled	72	72	-	19	19	-
Concrete	12	12	-	7	7	-
Colony	7	7	-			-
Population	954	957	3	184	184	-
Male	471	472	1	92	92	-
Female	483	485	2	92	92	-
Land Details						
Landless	71	71	-	23	23	-
< 2 acres	33	36	3	88		-
2 – 4 acres	14	13	1	4	5	1
4 – 6 acres	6	4	2	4	4	-
>6 acres	3	3	-	1	-	1

Field studies have proved that the data, especially quantitative data, collected through PRA are as accurate as the data collected through conventional methods (Chambers, 1998). Such field studies are limited. Substantial and convincing evidence need to be produced through more rigorous field studies to prove the efficacy of PRA over conventional method.

We made further attempt to test the accuracy of data collected through PRA in comparison with survey method. Enough care has been taken to see that the data collected through PRA have been triangulated. The data collected through both the methods are presented in Table 3.

Regarding the number of households and type houses, survey and PRA output provide the same results and there are absolutely no differences. There is an insignificant variation in population especially in the case of big village - the variation being three. The survey results were found to be accurate on further verification of the data by comparing PRA and survey data house by house. In the case of small village, PRA data perfectly matched with the survey data. Even such minor variations could be avoided through careful triangulation.

Data on the landless were similar in both the cases. But there are variations when the data on extent of land owned were examined. The variation is quite negligible. Here again the survey data was found to be more accurate than PRA data. This is also understandable as the data provided by participants of PRA are 'near accurate' data.

Regarding the data on cattle population, there is very slight difference between two sets of data. Here, PRA data proved to be more accurate as some of the respondents during survey have not counted 'calves' under cattle population whereas under PRA all the animals including' calves' have been considered.

Age-wise classification of the total population under the two methods also revealed a slight variation in the data. The data collected through survey was found to be more accurate.

Regarding literacy, the data collected under the two methods were accurate and exactly tallied even in the case of small village. There is slight variation between the two sets of data in big village and the survey data was found to be more accurate on further crosschecking.

It can be concluded that data collected through PRA (quantitative) could be as accurate as data collected through survey.

Participation

Participatory Rural Appraisal aims at empowerment orientation or transformational participation. This would mean active participation of people in different stages of the project viz., appraisal, analysis, planning, execution, monitoring and evaluation. Empowerment starts at the appraisal stage itself. Participants are empowered to gather data on themselves using mostly visual media. The data, thus, gathered are analysed and shared among themselves and also with the outsiders. The data analysed by them mostly help them to find out their problems and solutions and thus enable them to take decision on the further course of action. Participation of people at the appraisal state is, therefore, crucial and critical.

PRA stipulates participation of different categories of people– the old and young, men and women, literates and illiterates and so on. More specifically, outsiders should see that views/opinion/voice of the marginalized, oppressed, downtrodden, and the poor are properly and fully taken into account. But then this may not invariably happen? The reasons are many. Some are internal– related to the participants. Some are external in nature– related to outsiders We now present the involvement of people in a participatory mapping. (See Table 4).

It could be observed from the Table 4 that there were just eight participants at the start of the exercise. It slowly increased and went up to 29 at the close of 2 ¼ hours. And it came down to 18 at the close of the exercise. It may be noted that at the start of the exercise, the men were more in number whereas at the close of the exercise, women were more in number. Though we follow the rule of 'closing the group' we could not strictly adhere to such rule as participants are likely to join the middle of the exercise and some are likely to leave. We cannot force them to remain throughout the exercise. Further, the village being comparatively bigger with a high population, it took much time for us to collect the data. As the time passed, the interest of some participants waned and hence they left. However, it should be noted that a majority of the participants stayed back till the exercise was over.

Table 4
Participation in Social Mapping at Chellakuttiur

No. of participants	*Participants at the beginning*			*Participants who joined*			*Participants who left*			*Participants at the end*		
Duration (minutes)	*Male*	*Female*	*Total*	*Male*	*Female*	*Total*	*Male*	*Female*	*Total*	*Male*	*Female*	*Total*
0 - 45	5	3	8	3	3	6	-	-	-	8	6	14
45 - 90	8	6	14	3	4	7	-	-	-	11	10	21
90 - 135	14	10	21	6	3	9	3	1	4	17	12	29
135 - 180	17	12	29	1	2	3	4	1	5	14	13	27
180 - 225	14	13	27	-	-	-	2	1	3	12	12	24
225 - 270	12	12	24	-	-	-	-	-	-	12	12	24
270 - 315	12	12	24	-	-	-	4	2	6	8	10	18
315 - 360	8	10	18	-	-	-	-	-	-	8	10	18

Total time taken = 360 minutes*

* Time spent on rapport - building is not added here

** Time spent is related to activities like drawing of the map, data collection, data analysis, reporting and sharing of data

The other village is comparatively smaller. It took less time to complete the exercise. The team could sustain the interests of the participants. Only very few participants left in the middle of the exercises. There were 13 at the beginning and it rose to 20 at the close of the exercise. Barring a only man and a woman who left in the middle of the exercise, all the other members stayed throughout the exercise. Among them, an equal number of men and women were present throughout the exercise. (See Table 5).

The analysis shows: (i) presence of women and men nearly of equal number; (ii) a sustained physical presence of participants throughout the exercise; and (iii) the influence of time over their participation. As the time for completing the exercise increased, the participants were likely to leave.

Active Participation

We have so far analysed the physical presence of participants in the exercise. Now, we will examine the 'active participation of the participants in the exercise. In an exercise like mapping, every one cannot actively participate at a time. Some may participate 'by gathering material for the exercise'; some may participate by actually 'drawing the map on the ground'; and some may participate by 'giving information' and so on.

This would mean that all could not actively participate throughout the exercise. Yet, if a participant contributes in one form or the other in successful completion of the exercise, he/she may be termed as an active participant. Table 6 gives the extent of active participation in different stages of the exercises. It may be noted that of the 49 participants from the two villages put together, around 7 per cent of the participants were active. Village– wise analysis shows that the percentage of active participants was found to be more in the case of smaller village. For instance, the percentage of active participants was 85 in Karuthakkapatti, whereas in Chellakuttiur, it was 65.

It could also be noted that women were found to be more active in general. For instance, of the total of 12 women

Table 5
Participation in Social Mapping at Karuthakkapatti

No. of participants Duration (minutes)	*Participants at the beginning*			*Participants who joined*			*Participants who left*			*Participants at the end*		
	Male	*Female*	*Total*	*Male*	*Female*	*Total*	*Male*	*Female*	*Total*	*Male*	*Female*	*Total*
0 - 45	6	7	13	2	2	4	-	-	-	8	-	17
45 - 90	8	9	17	1	1	2	-	-	-	9	10	19
90 - 135	9	10	19	2	1	3	1	1	2	10	10	20

Total time taken 135 minutes

Table 6
Extent of active participation in Social Mapping

Stages	*Chellakuttiur*			*Karuthakkapatti*			*Total*		
	Male	*Female*	*Total*	*Male*	*Female*	*Total*	*Male*	*Female*	*Total*
Gathering the participants for mapping	3	4	7	1	4	5	4	8	12
Gathering the materials for mapping	1	3	4	2	4	6	3	7	10
Mapping	3	2	5	2	2	1	5	4	9
Giving information	4	3	7	3	3	6	7	6	13
Analysis of information	1	2	3	2	1	3	3	3	6
Reporting	1	1	2	1	1	2	2	2	4
Number of active participants	10	9	19	8	9	17	18	18	36
Passive participants	7	3	10	2	1	3	9	4	13
Total no. of Participants	17	12	29	10	10	20	27	22	49

participants in Chellakuttiur, 75 per cent were active; whereas the percentage of active men participants was 59. Similar trend where 90% of women were active, as against 80% for men could be seen in other village too. Participation in different stages of PRA exercise indicates the involvement of women in all stages. However, they are found to have played a predominant role in gathering the participants and the material for mapping. In activities like 'mapping, giving information and analysis of information, their participation was found to be nearly equivalent to men.

CONCLUSION

The empirical analysis of comparison of the data collected under 'participatory mapping' and 'survey method' has conclusively proved that a PRA method like participatory mapping help in gathering, analyzing and reporting the data in a shorter period of time than the survey method. The time taken to complete a PRA, if we consider the 'community time', is most likely to exceed the time taken under survey methods. But then the community time need not be considered as the multiple benefits that the community members derive because it is likely to outweigh the cost in terms of the time they spent. PRA method is found to be 'cost-effective' as the cost of conducting survey to collect census data is more than double the cost of organising PRA method. Regarding accuracy, there is very negligible variation in the data collected under the two methods. In some cases, the data collected through PRA are found to be more accurate whereas in some other cases the survey data is / found to be accurate. The overall analysis shows that PRA data can be as accurate as survey data.

Participation in PRA is quite high and active. Contrary to some of the findings of the earlier studies, the women participated very actively. Their participation, if properly facilitated, would be better than the participation of men. The participatory methods, therefore, proved to be effective. However, it must be noted that we have experimented with participatory mapping only for collection of quantitative data.

But then, PRA's strength lies in the collection of qualitative data too. PRA's efficacy in gathering, analyzing and reporting of qualitative data is therefore a potential and promising area for systematic research by social scientists.

ACKNOWLEDGMENT

This is part of a major research project on 'Efficacy of Participatory Methods: An Enquiry into NGOs Experiences' funded by ICSSR, New Delhi. The authors are grateful to ICSSR for its financial support.

We thank Sri. B. Baskar, Research Assistant in the ICSSR project who provided support in data collection, compilation of information, and computerization of data, enabling the preparation of this paper.

NOTES

1. Gubert observes that as per his results, the formal survey required 5 to 7 times more working days as the informal survey and the time needed to publish the results was three times longer for the formal survey. See Gubert, Jean Pierre, "Comparing two methods for implementing farming systems surveys in the Imbo Region of Burundi, 11th FSRIE Symposium, October 1991, Michigan State University, Michigan. Rajarathinam *et al.*, have estimated that survey of 412 households have taken 776 person hours as against 76 person hours in PRA.
2. The PRA team of GRI facilitated modeling exercise in a Pillaiarnatham village. The water distribution system was depicted in the model. It was found that the Harijan colony with 40 households did not have even a single water tap, whereas each non-harijan street with 25 to 30 houses has two or three taps. This immediately created an awareness among the harijans and started demanding water taps in their colony. This immediately led to an action plan which we subsequently implemented.

REFERENCE

Chambers Robert, (1994), Participatory Rural Appraisal: Analysis of Experience, World Development, 22 (9), p. 1253.

Chambers Robert, 1998, Whose Reality Counts? Putting the First Last, London, Intermediate Technology Publications, p. 122.

Cornwall Andrea and Jewkes Rachal, (1995), What is Participatory Research, Social Sciences &Medicine, 41 (12), p. 1667.

Gill, Gerry, O.K., (1993), The Data's Lousy, But its all we've got (Being a Critique of Conventional Methods), Gate Keeper Series, No.38, London, International Institute of Environment and Development, p. 13.

Korten C. David, (1989), Social Science in the Service of Social Transformation, in Cynthia Veneracion (Ed.), A Decade of Process Documentation and Research. Reflections and Synthesis. (5 - 20) Manila: Ateneo de Manila University, p. 6.

Moris John and Copstake James, (1983), Qualitative Enquiry for Rural Development: A Review. London. International Technology Publications, p.34.

Mukhe~ee Neela, (1997), Participatory Rural Appraisal and Questionnaire Survey, New Delhi, Concept Publishing Company, p.108.

Narayanasamy. N., and Boraian M.P., (1993), Community Participation in Big and Small Villages, RRA Notes, (18) pp. 44 - 46.

Narayanasamy N., (1994), PRA Exercise in an Indian Village: A Retrospective Evaluation or the First Exposure to the Process, PRA Notes. (19), pp.19- 23.

Pretty N, Jules, (1995), Regenerating Agriculture: Policies and Practices for Sustainability and Self-reliance, New Delhi, Vikas Publishing House Pvt. Ltd., p.178.

Pretty N, Jules, (1993), Participatory Inquiry and Agricultural Research, London: Intemational Institute of Environment and Development.

Rajarathinam *et al.*, 1992, Validating Wealth Ranking of PRA and Formal Survey in Identifying the Rural Poor, Vellore,RUSHA.

Rhoades E. Robert, (1987), Basic Field Techniques for Rapid Rural Appraisal, in Proceedings of the 1985. International Conference on Rapid Rural Appraisal, p. 114.

Richards Micheal, Davies Jonathan and Cavendish William, (1999), Can PRA Methods be Used to Collect Economic Data? A Non-timber Forest Producer Case Study from Zimbabwe, PLA Notes, (36), pp. 38-39.

ANNEXURE 'A'

CALCULATION OF TIME AND COST

Calculation of Time: A team of two investigators, after proper orientation, has been deployed in the field to gather data under survey method. They have been asked to note the time taken to collect the data from each household. The same team was given the responsibility of analyzing the data and reporting the analysis. They noted the time taken to complete the data analysis and reporting. Thus, the total time taken to complete the task under survey was arrived at. While organizing PRA, a team of three members trained in PRA was deployed in the field. They were entrusted with the responsibility of gathering information using participatory mapping. The data as collected through survey method was gathered through mapping too. The team was asked to note the time taken to complete the process of data gathering, analysis, reporting and sharing. The time taken under these two methods have been compared and analysed.

Computation of Cost: How do we arrive at cost? It is not easy to arrive at the relative cost of two methods through simple comparison, as there are many factors, which influence both actual cost and imputed cost of undertaking conventional surveyor PRA type of studies. Such factors are:

- Planning and design for data collection
- Training in PRA or conventional survey
- Size of the area to be covered
- Mode of transport
- Materials used in data collection
- Number of investigators -facilitators
- Duration of enquiry, methods, analysis and results
- System for dissemination of results.

For calculating the cost: we have considered three broad components, viz., manpower charges, printing and stationery and documentations. Calculation of time for different stages of data collection, analysis and compilation largely helps in computing the manpower charges involved in the process. The cost of the other two components can be easily worked out.

Efficacy: Efficacy with reference to accuracy was tested by cross-checking and comparing the data collected under two methods.

Participation of people: The team, identified the key informants to start with, and invited them to take part in participatory mapping. A member of the team was given the task of observing the time at which the exercise was started and the time at which the exercise was closed. He was also asked to note down the number of participants sex-wise, (at different time intervals) in terms of how many persons were present in the beginning, how many joined at different time intervals and how many left.

Rapidity or Time involved: The factors to be considered for the time taken to complete the process of data collection, analysis and reporting are: (Mukherjee, 1997).

- Training time
- Time taken for conducting PRA / Survey
- Time required for the type and volume of data to be collected
- Time taken for cross checking of data
- Time required for data management
- Time taken for dissemination of data

The steps involved in conducting PRA method which influence time and duration are:

- type of data required;
- rapport building;
- techniques whether 'visual' or 'verbal' or 'a combination';
- probing on various issues;
- copying of 'visual' output on paper;
- taking of notes; and
- cross checking of data (Mukherjee, 1997).

The training time has not been considered since only the personnel already trained were deployed for conducting PRA and also for survey. All the other factors have been carefully considered and incorporated for analyzing the time to collect a set of quantitative data under PRA and survey.

10

SUSTAINABLE RURAL DEVELOPMENT THROUGH PEOPLE'S PARTICIPATION

M. Perumal*

INTRODUCTION

The catalytic role of popular participation socio-economic development has gained a special significance in promoting a self-reliant development process in all societies-developed or developing, tribal or non-tribal. It has been discussed and commended in numerous conferences, seminars and publications during the last decades. The *United Nations Economic and Social Council* has recommended that the Government should adopt participation as a basic policy measure in national development strategy. They should encourage the widest possible active participation of all individuals and national non-governmental organizations in development process in setting goals, formulating policies and implementing plans.

It is well accepted that "Participation of the people in institutions and systems which govern their lives is essential for realignment of political power in favour of disadvantaged groups and for social and economic development." It has rightly been defined as the "involvement of members of society in the decision-making process of the system." It has also been defined as an "organised effort to increase control over resources and

* Lecturer in Economics, Urumu Dhanalakshmi College, Tiruchirappalli.

regulative institutions in a given social situation on the part of groups and movements of those hitherto excluded from such control. In *the terminology suggested by David Easton,* individual's political acts constitute inputs into the process of decision-making for territorial community. In can, therefore, be seen a civic duty, as a sign of political health, as the best methods of ensuring that one's private interests are not neglected and as a *sine qua non* of democracy.

Participation, thus has a very wide meaning. But we take a very limited view of it. To us it means the involvement of a significant number of people in situations or actions which enhance their well-being, *e.g.*, their income, security of self-esteem. *To administrators,* participation is relevant to the implementation of policies and programmes. They regard participation as that element of the external environment which exercise corrective or at least moderating influence on certain pathological features of public bureaucracy. It also works as a force to keep bureaucracy oriented toward programmatic goals.

PARTICIPATION IN DECISION-MAKING

It begins with the identification of local and the ways to approach it through a particular project. For most of the rural development project, this initial state is crucial stage. At this stage the involvement of the people provides necessary information about the local needs. It also prevents misunderstandings as to the nature of the problem and the strategies proposed for its resolution, as where it should be located, the ways it would be financed and staffed, the path by which people will participate in the project, and the contributions they are expected to make are some of the initial decisions in which local people can be involved. Participation in operational decisions may be conceived as relating to specific local organisations which have been established by the project or linked to the project to involved people in the delivery aspects.

PARTICIPATION IN IMPLEMENTATION

It may occur, in three ways, First: by contribution in regard to resources as provision of labour, cash, material goods and information. Local people lend their labour to the digging of wells, giving of land and labour for schools, contribution of timber for the construction of schools and health centers, construction of village roads with the governmental assistance, supporting positively to the Grain Goals and by giving information with regards to crop yields, tenure arrangements, pest problems, sources of nutrition and so on.

Another way of involving rural people in the implementation process is the participation through project administration and coordination activities. Local people, in this process, can participate in two ways either as an employee or as a member of various projects and administrative units, advisory boards, implementation committees or decision making bodies. They can also be members of voluntary associations who are playing their role in the welfare of the local people and also act as an effective pressure group. Many development workers have gained new insights by discussing development problems with the local people. The local people are able to put forth rational suggestions which could produce quick results.

Finally, enlistment in programme is perhaps the most common form of participation. In the tribal areas, the tribal families are enlisted in the project programme. However, it seems essential to distinguish between enlistment and participation in benefits. Enlistment does not necessarily ensure benefits where the latter is concerned essentially with benefits.

PARTICIPATION IN BENEFITS

While we agree that participation in benefits is one of the more passive kinds of participation. It is so important in the field of socio-economic development that it cannot be overlooked. The people may participate as material, social and personal beneficiaries of administration. Material benefit has been regarded as increase in consumption, income or assets. It is well known that consumption increased assets can be seen in the question of land, livestock, implements, improved farm dwelling savings and so on.

In the fold of social benefits come the public goods. It may be characterized as services or amenities, such as, health clinics, water system, improved housing facilities, improved seeds, use of fertilizers and better roads. As the rural development projects are designed to be more 'integrated' and as efforts are being made to improve the quality of life for the people, there is a great need of participation in social benefits.

The concept of sustainable development is basically an improvement on the concept of development. It is a concept of eco-friendly development, based on the will and aspirations of the people and executed with the active participation of the local people in the formulation and execution of projects and in the enjoyment of its benefits. In fact, it has refined the concept of "growth".

Sustainability strongly reinforce permeation of quality in development efforts. If exposes pronounced concern for accountability, ethics, morality, cultural moorings, and ethos as well as environment. It concern transcends passing considerations – both national and international – with a vigilant eye on needs of distant future and future generation. The sustainability angle assumed the most fundamental priority after grim realities of environmental degradation, caused by hedonistic pursuit of consumerist and wasteful model of industrial development world over, got clearly linked with the survival of human species and the natural habitat.

The World Commission on Environment defined sustainable development as 'development that meets the needs of the present without compromising the ability of future generation to their own needs, Naturally, Community participation is essential it refers to an active process where by beneficiaries influence the direction and execution of development project benefits. So definition of sustainable development stress that development must be participatory and must involve local people in decision-making. Again, the community participation in sustainable development schemes means their participation in planning, implementation and monitoring of such activities. The approach is that we, the present generation, have inherited a certain amount of ecology and environment surrounding in terms of land, water and air, where we leave it to the next generation, we should leave it at least in the same condition. So, our institution, rules and regulations, and their enforcement should be such as to play positive role to stop environment degradation. For all these we should encourage community participation.

Mr. Albert Gore Propose a Marshall Plan designed to stop environment destruction. His premise is that human civilization is out of balance with nature. Currently humans pose a strategic threat to the Earth, and in turn, the environmental poses a strategic threat to civilization by way of global warming and ozone depletion. He also describe out consumer mentality as dysfunctional. Keeping environmental as central organising principle the first strategy suggested by him under the Global Marshal Plan is to stabilize population. This would be accomplished by the international funding of functional literacy programmes – programmes designed to reduce infant mortality and, finally, to have birth control possible. The rest, such as, sharing of appropriate technologies agreement exploiting environment economically only to a limit, global education on information etc. will follow.

Now coming to literacy and its impact on sustainable rural development we must know that Bihar belongs to the category of *BIMARU* States as called by *Ashish Bose*, an eminent demographer about Bihar, Madhya Pradesh, Rajasthan and Uttar Pradesh so far as female literacy is concerned. The regional concentration of female literacy is highlighted by the fact that 155 of the 247 districts whose female literacy rates are lower than the national average are concentrated in these four States.

The picture is very grim in Bihar. In 1991 the literacy rate of Bihar was 38.54 per cent. The literacy rate of women indicates the ironical situation here. It is only 22.9 per cent in Bihar, is at the bottom in the literacy attainment, especially that of women. There are about 16 districts in Bihar where literacy rate is less than 20 per cent among female. In Kishanganj and Araria it is as low as 11 per cent and 14 per cent respectively.

The other 14 districts are Madhepura, West Champaran Madhubani, Saharsa, Palamu, Sitamarhi, Sahibganj, Katihar, Purnea, East Champaran, Gopalganj, Khagaria and Godda. So districts with lowest female literacy rate are mainly found in North Bihar. Out of the 17 districts with low literacy rate 10 are from North and the rest from Santhal Pargana and Chhotanagpur plateau.

It is good news that under the aegis of the National Literacy Mission, the Total Literacy Programme (TLC) has been introduced in 13 districts of Bihar, namely Madhubani, Madhepura, Saharsa, Begusarai, Khagaria, Supoul, Siwan, Bhojpur, Aurangabad, Munger, Jamui, Dumka and Chanbad.

It is heartening to note that Madhwapur block to attain total literacy. While Dumka Achieve the distinction to be declared as the first literate district of Bihar begging the first "Mahila Samridhi Award 1994" by the Honourable P.M.

The Zila Saksharta Samiti Khagaria formed on 31st March 1994 with a mission to achieve total literacy in the district with 2.6 lakh learners in the first phase with a total budget of Rs. 1,69,000/- with an estimate of Rs. 65 as cost per learner. A total of 71,302 people was made literate during last one year out of 170,000 admitted at different centers in 127 Panchayats completing primer I by the Improved pace constant learner method and put under the category of neo-literates. Under the plan altogether 2.6 lakh persons in the age group of 9-35 years with an approved budget of Rs. 1.69 crore, 35 key Resource persons, 175 Resource persons, 500 Master trainers for primer II and 30000 volunteers, are to be made literate. But the working has been hampered due to assembly and parliamentary poll and now, due to the high food.

However, even if the Mission, may get its target fulfilled in total it will leave behind a vast army of illiterate numbering 5,63,328 people. After the perusal of above date it seems certain that total literacy in this district is a distant dream to be achieved easily.

The declaration of the Honourable Prime Minister to raise investment in the education sector to six per cent of the G.D.P. in the 9th plan from the present 3.27 per cent augurs well certainly, a step in the right direction. Also, the union Minister for Human Resource Development announced that education would get a fillip with allocation being enhanced from present Rs. 18000 crore to Rs. 9000 crore.

The total campaign must be backed with a full fledged scheme of compulsory primary education as adult education and elementary education is complementary to each other. The District Primary Education Programme (DPEP) launched by the experience to Bihar Education Project, UP Basic Education Project and AP Primary Education Project.

The scheme of Charwaha Vidyalaya first established in 1993-94 is a concept so astoundingly unique in its dimension and philosophy that it has been globally recognized as a experiment which deserve unreserved laurels.

'Earn while learn' and education at doorstep is the mission. The Planning Commission gave special grant for the scheme. During 1993-94 the state government set up 131 of these Vidayalays with a plan to add 100 more.

The World Conference on Education for all held in Jomtien *(Thailand) in 2000* evolved a strong consensus that education is the single most important element combating poverty, empowering women, protecting children hazardous and exploitative labour practices and sexual exploitation, promoting human rights and democracy protecting the environment and influencing population growth. It is why the World Bank has identified illiteracy as the major stumbling factor in poverty alleviation in India and prescribed for enhanced investment on education. Even Prof. Amartya Sen, the noble laurite economist has stressed the point that India should do better do better on the from of elementary education and nutrition by investing more as well managing them efficiently. So there exists a clear cut co-relation between literacy and rural development particularly sustainable rural development.

REFERENCES

R.P. Mishra, "Group Action and Popular Participation", in R.P. Mishra, Local Level Planning and Development, P. 213.

Among the latest of these meetings is the International Seminar on Popular Participation Organised by DTCD, United Nations at Ljublihjana, Yugoslavia, 17-25 May 1982.

See, John M. Cohen, *et. al* Participation at the Local Level: A Working Bibliography.

U.N. Document No, E/CN 5/526, Para-4, Quoted in S.N. Mishra, and other, Participation and Development, P. 24.

FAO World Conference on Agrarian Reform and Rural Development, 12-20 July, 1979. Quoted in R.P. Mishra, Local Level Planning and Development, op. cit., p. 232.

G.A. Almond and G.B. Peweil, Comparative Politics: A Development Approach, p. 53.

Andrew Pears and Matias Stiefel, Debater's Comments on Inquiry in Participation: A research Approach, UNRISD, Paper, October 1980, p. 2.

I.M. Cohen and others, participation at the Local Level : A working Bibliography Quoted in S., N. Mishra, participation and Development, op. cit., p. 25.

C.P. Singh, Tribal Development Administration, Mittal Publication, New Delhi, 1994, p. 174.

Scchhidananda, "Strategies of Rural Development in India," in L.P. Vidyarthi (Ed.) Rural Development in South Asia, p. 74.

S.N. Mishra, Local Level Planning and Development, pp. 36-37.

11

LOCAL KNOWLEDGE AND SUSTAINABLE DEVELOPMENT: A CASE OF KONDA REDDI TRIBE

*K. Anil Kumar**

INTRODUCTION

Local/indigenous knowledge encompasses the body of knowledge, which indigenous people have accumulated over generations concerning their environment. It includes knowledge on identification, utilization and management of resources built through observation, experimentation and innovation. Although it is passed on from generation to generation it is not static. It is this knowledge that has guided men through ages in living within their environment.

Many indigenous communities, they are wholly or partly dependent on the forest to eke out their livelihood. Their belief systems, social, economic and ritual activities are intricately interwoven around the forest and hills. Indigenous people and forests are ecologically and economically inseparable. They have co-existed since times immemorial and will continue to co-exist in a mutually reinforcing relationship. The indigenous people hold this symbiotic relationship in great esteem and they regard various species of forest as their kith and kin.

This complex of knowledge, beliefs and practices is generally known as indigenous or local knowledge. It is the

* Research Scholar, Dept. of Anthropology, University of Hyderabad, Hyderabad.

only major resource of the people who have limited access to basic and essential material resources. In developing countries communities' use of indigenous knowledge also represents the richness of the poor.

The importance of local knowledge in resource use can be perceived by looking at simple facts: 85 % to 90% of the basic livelihood needs of the worlds poor (more than half of the worlds population, including indigenous and local communities) are based on direct use of biological resources (and related local knowledge) for food, medicine, shelter, transport, etc., In the 1950's and 1960's theorist of development saw indigenous/local knowledge as inefficient, inferior and an obstacle for development. The value of local knowledge in facilitating development is gradually being recognized by national and international development agencies. Nevertheless, these systems are not yet recognized as the product of holistic perceptions to many professionals working in forest, agriculture and rural development departments.

In recent years, alarmingly high rate of deforestation in many developing countries has been a matter of concern for the people living there and for the development administration. The process of deforestation certainly affects the economy of the state concerned, but more than that it affects the forest dependent communities, as it is closely linked with their subsistence. There are many forest communities, who still depend upon forest exclusively for their food.

Today there is consensus on the need to see development in terms of long-term sustainability. This has led many people to argue that in order to ensure a more socially and ecologically sound approach to development, it is necessary to understand, respect and utilize the local knowledge systems (Berkes and Folke, 1994; Hecht and Posey, 1998). Although the value of local knowledge systems in facilitating development is gradually being recognized by national and international development agencies, these systems are not yet familiar to many professionals working in agricultural and rural development (Warren and Rajasekaran, 1991).

In the last two decades research and development experts have promoted indigenous knowledge as a key to sustainable development (Brokensha *et al.* 1980; Chambers *et al.* 1989; Warren *et. al.* 1989). Since then a wealth of information on indigenous knowledge pertaining to soils, plants and animals has been complied (*e. g.* Bizimana 1994; Walker et al. 1999).

In this backdrop, the paper attempts to view local knowledge and use of forest plant products with the help of a case study of *Konda Reddis* (PTG) in East Godavari District of Andhra Pradesh, Southern India. The paper focuses on the ethno-ecological knowledge and management of local resources. The study shows both local practices and native perspective, is capable of forming a basis for sustainable development. The paper ends with a discussion of the need to protect and promote local knowledge gradually, being lost, due to pressures from globalization and modernization.

PROFILE OF THE KONDA REDDIS AND FOREST ECOSYSTEM

The *Konda Reddis* are one of the Primitive Tribal Groups inhabiting the southern state of Andhra Pradesh. *Konda Reddi* tribes' are mostly concentrated inhabited in the hilly tracts and cleared forest areas in the districts of East Godavari, Khammam, and West Godavari and are found scattered in the districts of Warangal and Vishakhapatnam of Andhra Pradesh. The major tribes inhabiting in the East Godavari district are *Konda Reddi, Koya, Konda Dora, Valmiki, and Konda Kammara* etc. *Reddis* speak a corrupt form of Telugu Language and they known with varied names *Pandava Reddis, Raja Reddis,* hill *Reddis* etc.

Reddis dwell in the interior areas have a greater level of dependence on the local natural resources. Their adaptation to the physical environment is seen in the material culture and in particular technology. Forest plant species ensure Reddis subsistence, his shelter, inspires, his love, his marriage, his recreation and his happiness. Trees caution his action and motivate his behaviour. Therefore Reddis evolved an elaborate system of rituals that bind them with the trees. Their intimacy with the trees is expressed in their folksongs, which they sing for themselves and passed on to the future generations. This deep bond is one of continuity between man and trees, rather than an opposition between them, as has been the characteristics of the western disjunctive thought.

They live by shifting and settled cultivation. Supplementary subsistence support is derived from the bounty of nature in the form of seasonal edible fruits, roots, tubers, green leaves, mushrooms, insects, honey, gum, *Caryota urens* and *Borassus palm* sap etc. their village social organizations revolves around many exogamous steps or *intiperulu*. So far as the subsistence is concerned, steps are not hierarchical, as the resources under the jurisdiction of the political boundary of the village are communally owned, and the concept of private property is extremely limited, although it is not altogether absent. Patriarchy and patriliny are the basic rules of family organization among them and hence the status of women is relatively lower, despite their higher contribution to the family economy.

Though *Reddis* are agriculturalist, either shifting or settled agriculture, is the main source of livelihood. They depend on the forest produce to eke out their subsistence. Forest provides various edible fruits; tubers, roots and leaves etc., throughout the year besides numerous items of Non-timber forest produce to cater to their consumption as well as commercial needs. Forests also provide varieties of medicinal plants herbs etc., to cure their health care.

Other traditional taboos are scrupulously followed by the Reddis and this negative life sustaining restrictions facilitate production, protection, and welfare of the community. They do not touch any crop or fruit either cultivated or available in the forest unless it is offered to their deities on the auspicious occasion. These celebrations are generally organized in such a way that all these crops, fruits etc. attain maturity and full growth.

The social organization of the *Reddis* is based on certain totemic clans. The community is divided into different clans and the members of each clan claim mythical affinity with animate and inanimate objects and species available in the forest. They claim their decent from animals, plants etc. but they did not remember.

Beef eating is a taboo; while pork eating is common among them. They worship village God, Goddess and the spirit of hills *Rajulbabu/Adavirajulu, Bairudu, Parentalu* etc., Belief in magic, sorcery and witchcraft is very common, and call wizards at the time of illness. *Reddis* are animists in religion, although they worship some of the Hindu pantheon. *Gangalamma* is the chief protector deity of the *Konda Reddis*. Most of their rituals are connected with the harvesting vest of different crops-cultivated and wild. Ancestral spirits are remembered and worshipped because of their benevolence.

Konda Reddis acquaintance with the forest flora and fauna is spontaneous and natural. When a child is about three years old, he/she starts accompanying the parents to the fields and forests. This is a process of early socialization of identifying the species of plants and animals and getting to know their uses. Further this knowledge gets consolidated. When the child moves into the deep forest with the peers and gets the opportunity to examine the reliability of the knowledge passed on to him with mutual discussion and experimentation with other age mates. When the child grows up to adulthood, there is further acquisition of innovative and elaborate floral and faunal knowledge for the survival of self and other members of the family.

In 1940s, Furer-Haimendrof studied them, eventually throwing some light on their beliefs concerning human sacrifice, and publishing a monograph, The *Reddis* of the Bison Hills: A Study in Acculturation (1945). It is only the major study carried out by him among the *Reddis*. He is of the firm opinion that they are very primitive autochthones ethic stock of the region, despite their names being associated with the clean Hindu landed aristocratic caste of *Reddi* of Andhra Pradesh.

The research among the *Konda Reddis* of the village *Utalapalem* in the East Godavari district indicates that the adult members of the tribe are able to easily recognize about 400-500 species of plants, their availability, growing conditions and possible uses. That includes trees (*chettlu*), climbers (*teegalu*), creepers (*nela teegalu*), tubers (*dumpalu*), green leaves (*akukuralu*), roots (*verlu*), mushrooms (*kokulu*), herbs (*mokkalu*), grasses (*gaddi*), bushes (*tuppalu*), bamboos (*veduru*), parasites (*antulu*) etc.

In this article examine the *Reddis* local knowledge in a number of forest plant species used in large quantities within the village ecosystem. From forest they usually collect various edible tubers, roots, leaves and seeds, mushrooms and flowers etc. *Reddis* possess local knowledge about the utility of numerous plant and animal species available in the forest. Their knowledge about flora and fauna of the area in which they are inhabiting is extra ordinary and they have devised several techniques for their utilization in sustainable way. The *Reddis* know exactly which type of products to collect, as well as the proper season and time of day. The tools and implements devised by them are very simple. The various food getting devices like bows, varieties of arrows, traps, snares etc. indicate that primitive tribes are not wanting in ingenuity and skill. They never overexploit the forest resources, and are very precise about the time that a particular plant or shrub should be picked, dug or cut. They never cut trees entire that have religious or economic value.

KONDA REDDIS PERCEPTION ABOUT THE ENVIRONMENT

Reddis carry both kinds of feelings, of reverence and fear towards the forest. They perceive forest as their father, (A*daviraju/*) mother (Adavithalli/Prentalu) and god or mountain God (*Konda Devudu/ Birudu*), Goddess (Kondathalli/ Nilaramma) are the terms refer for forest, which means forest is everything for them. Because, forest provides everything for them for their survival and paradoxically it also is symbolized as evil at times, it is foreboding, uncontrollable and dangerous. *Reddis* think that forest is the habitat of evil spirit and ghosts who attack on people when they are in forest. *Konda Reddis* attach a type of mixed emotions of fear, respect and wonder towards the forest and other natural components. The hills and mountains, which are considered to be the symbols of the power and the domain of nature, are considered to be majestic and mysterious, uncontrollable and threatening. They do have belief that the hills and mountains, which surround the village, protect the people and village from natural calamities. Forest plays an important role in the religious life of the people. They are viewed as the abodes of gods and Goddess and places of infinite beauty, yet they also have an element of wilderness, desolation and terror. They have negative, undesirable places as well as positive feeding objects, which are part of the forest.

Water bodies like streams (*Uta*) and river (*Caluva*) are revered as they the source of life. Streams are considered to be village deity *Gangalamm*. Land too is perceived as mother Goddess (*Bhudevi*), who ceaselessly blesses them and provide them with agricultural produces. During the time pollution caused due to the various life cycle occasions such as birth, puberty and death, they cleanse themselves in the stream water, which is believed to make them pure. During the period of menstruating women is prohibited to enter into the farms and other religious places/occasions, as it is considered to be a sin for polluting it. *Reddis* perform *Gangalamma* festival to propitiate the goddess of water to have sufficient rains for them to cultivate. In sense this festival can be noted as the annual harvest festival where all the harvested grains are ablated to the *Gangalamma*. This is an annual festival, the celebration of the festival is held for three days in the month of (March-April), which is celebrated elaborately since the whole village has by this time complete their agricultural activities. The deity seated under an old *Burugu* tree located in the grove. A stone is placed under the tree to symbolize the deity. Country chicken and goats are offered every year so as to gain good will. They believe in supernatural powers, deities and benevolent and malevolent spirits, which are responsible for ecological happenings. All the religious belief, practices and ceremonies are associated with the physical environment. They appease or worship God and Goddess by celebrating rituals/festivals in order to get a good harvest and to be free from disease and other misfortunes. They worship the ancestral spirits on every important life cycle ceremonies and village festivals. Reddis believe that their lives are ordained by certain spirits and deities and are thus engaged in occasional offerings towards the supernatural powers.

Thus, *Reddis* perform worship their natural components whether it is land for agriculture practiced, forest, hill, streams etc. The whole agriculture activities like preparation of agriculture fields, manuring of the fields, sowing seeds, ripening of the crops, harvesting and eating of the first produce are associated with rituals and festivals celebration by the *Reddis.* Community *Gangalamma* festival also indicates the precautions that they take to over come natural calamities and scarcity of products. The community celebrates its rejoicing and its sense of renewed social solidarity with feasting, drinking and dancing. It can be summed up that their belief systems, social, economic and ritual activities are intricately interwoven around the forest and hills.

Like other indigenous societies in India, *Konda Reddis* also depend to a large extent on forest resources to eke out their subsistence. People gather many forest products for food, drink, fodder, medicine, and house construction material as well as for agricultural or other domestic purposes. There is a seasonal variation in the availability of different products through out the year for household consumption. Forest products also contribute to the individual household income. In some households products not consumed domestically are sold and the money used to buy food. In others, the money earned from forest products is the major source of income.

KONDA REDDIS LOCAL KNOWLEDGE AND USE OF FOREST PLANT PRODUCTS

Reddis collect several green leaves from the forest as their food items some of them are presented in Akukura/Kura is the local term used for green vegetable leaves by the *Reddis*. They identify the greens leaves by seeing the leaf shape and size of the plant. *Reddis* are familiar with locations of green leaves plant spread in the forest area and often knowledgeable about the availability season of a wide variety of these plants. Depending up on the season and weather condition, *Reddis* mostly in groups of four to five persons set out early in the morning or during daytime go to collect leaves from the forest. They look for tender leaves in a plant to obtain good taste and mature leaves left for the next season. They gather few leaves from the each plant without uprooting or harming the whole plant.

Reddis are familiar with locations of tuberous plant spread in the forest area and often knowledgeable about the availability of a wide variety of these plants. The emic view of forest and its resources are so rich among *Reddis* that they can easily select a place for digging in search of tuber after observing the herbs and creeper or leaves grown on the earth. They make use of these resources to an extent. The availability of tubers wild and semi-wild, which are collected from the forest used for consumption.

Dumpa/kanda/gadda are the terms used for tubers (*Dioscorea spp.*) by the *Reddis*. *Reddis* identify the tubers by the location of plant or creepers. They also identify variety of tubers by seeing the leaves of the plants, size of the tuber plant, size and maturity of the leaves of the plants. Depending up on the season and weather condition, Reddis mostly in groups of four to five persons set out early in the morning or during daytime. They look for drying plants with ripe yellow leaves to obtain good and mature tubers. They gather the tubers from the soil without uprooting or harming the roots of associated plants and also left a small portion of the tuber back in the pit and cover it with loose soil.

According to Reddis fully matured, big, repined and tastier tubers are available between December to May and in rest of the periods, the tubers are not tasty or fully mature. Before consumption of tubers, a long process is involved to remove the high content of toxic components. Sliced tubers of *Nalla Gadda, Nara dumpa, Vayamu dumpa, Velichanda Gadda* are kept in running water for a day, after through wash, and boiled with leaves of tamarind. The water is decanted, then cooked and consumed by the *Reddis*. Among tuberous plants, some tubers also used as medicine by the *Reddis*.

Depending on the season Reddis engaged in food gathering activity. Forest provides numerous edible fruits throughout the year to cater to their consumption. They eat several edible fruits from the forest while they are working in the forest and fields.

Reddis houses are constructed with the materials available in the local forest. In their vicinity, Borassus palm (*Thatichettu*), trees grow abundantly. They use it leaves for thatching their houses. They use particular trees as central pillar, side poles, beams, and etc. they used types of fibre for tying, bamboo is used for making walls, roof, fencing etc. in this way, they utilize the locally available forest products in the house construction. Plants used for construction of house, making furniture, used for agriculture and hunting implements and fibre for ropes etc.

A traditional building method of house, which make use of locally available natural material, have for centuries provided shelter for the *Reddis* and have become part of the knowledge base of this society. Construction wood is used in the form of poles, beams and roof for houses, huts, fences and shelter. *Konda Reddis* make use of trees found in the forest for the construction of their houses. Different trees are used for particular parts of the house. Building methods and organizational structures are determined by traditional beliefs, norms, and values and by availability of materials.

Traditionally, the men are responsible for constructing the wall and roof frame, thatching the roof, and making the sun dried mud. Women assist the men by collecting leaves for thatching, plastering the walls, and preparing the mud and dung surface of the floor.

The woods of all these trees are resistant to the insects and will last long. *Gesari* wood is used to make small wooden stools known as *peeta, which* enables them to sit and work conveniently. They make spoons with the wood of trees like *theddu pala, cheedi*. They manufacture furniture like table, stools, chairs etc. from the trees wood of *ganneru, adaviteku, errodimanu* (rose wood), v*epa*, etc.

Most common implements seen with the Reddis are *nagali* (plough), *kathi* (knife), *kodavali* (sickle), *goddali* (axe), *golli, vaaluva, gonapam,* bows and arrows (*inti badha*) digging stick etc. All these implements are manufactured by them and approach the blacksmiths for iron parts. Every individual prepare his own plough with the help of blacksmith. They use different kinds of woods for manufacturing different implements.

Konda Reddis use bamboos for making bows and arrows. The bow is made up of bamboo while the string of the bow is made up of *jeelugu marra,* which is very strong. The edges are tied with *jeelugu naara,* which is a thin peel of the *jeelugu* tree. The arrow is made by a thin bamboo, which is fixed with an arrowhead made up of iron. The handle of the sickle is prepared by bamboo (*veduru).*

PLANTS USED FOR DRINK

Toddy is extracted from mature trees of thati chettu, jeelugu chettu, etha chettu throughout the year. It takes nearly maximum 20 years for a plant to reach maturity. In summer season *Reddis* collect *Ippa* flower (*Madhuca latifolia*) which are either used for making drinks or sold in the local periodic market. Plants used for tapping toddy extract liquor and used for other purpose.

Forests also provide varieties of cosmetics plants to cater to their hygiene. The *Reddis* identify and collect cosmetics to their use as well as for commercial needs. They used Sikum (*Acacta sinuate*), Kunkudu (*Sapindus emarginatus*) and *Yelakkaya* for head bath. *Yelakkaya* tree fruit used for dandruff alleviate. After collecting fruits they allow to dry for few days. Dry fruits crush properly and than mix in water for sometime and than they apply on the head while talking bathing. In the village many people use this as a shampoo and said that it is better than shampoo. According to *Reddis* taking bath with their cosmetics hair will become strong and black.

Various types of livestock play a vital role in the agriculture-based economy of *Konda Reddis*. Goats, chickens, cows, oxen, buffaloes and dogs are found among them. Fodder that is given to these animals. Fodder is another plant product collected in the forest by *Reddis* for their livestock. Depending on the season types of fodder is available. The knowledge of fodder in the forest is so rich among these people that they can easily select which herbs, creepers and plant leaves are good as a fodder. Leaves and twigs of plants mentioned in the table are especially collected (cut and carried) for their domestic animals.

Konda Reddis depend totally on the forests for the fuel wood for cooking as well as for lighting bonfires to fight with cold during winters. Manta *pullalu/karralu* are the terms refer to firewood. They do not cut any trees for the firewood unless they are scarcity. They only collect dry fallen tree branches (*pullalu*) and dry fallen wood of the trees. In case if they come across any dry and dead trees in the forest, they cut them and use them as firewood.

On certain days of the season (winter and summer), the *Reddis* women walk in groups to the forest and collect firewood for household consumption. They store the firewood close to the settlement and use it according to their requirements. In this way they make the best possible use of the available time and resources.

The majority of all forest plants collected by the *Reddis* are used for medicinal purposes. Other parts of plants are often used in other ways. In the present investigation it was found that plant species are used as medicine among the *Reddis*. These are presented in table 9; the table also lists the parts used, the purpose for which they are used, and how they are prepared. The plants medicines are prepared in various ways. For medicinal purposes, leaves, bark, fruits, seeds, root is often used; this is either drunk or rubbed on the body to treat one or more diseases or conditions. Most of the plant parts are used, by simply crushing a particular part of the species with a crushing stone and wood. But some are made by boiling plant part with water after decanting and cooling; the liquid is drunk or applied.

In the village *Reddis* go to a medicine men and women (*Vydudu/Vejju*) mainly to have their problem diagnosed, even though they know something about medicinal plants themselves. The effectiveness of the herb depends on knowledge of the exact nature of the disease. The response to a particular dosage may from person to person, while the same person may also react differently at different times. Thus the patient himself will often experiment with a particular remedy and work out a suitable dose.

Medicine men also believe that certain plant parts should be harvested during a particular stage in their growth. Since few people have detailed knowledge of the best stage or time to collect these herbs, they are almost totally dependent on medicine men and women. The rules governing the time of collection, the part of the plant to use, storage, and preparation are known only to local faith healers, and for this reason they command considerable respect in Reddis society.

Reddis are the most dependent and believe on herbal treatment, and they also have a greater understanding of herbal plants. Not only the medicine men, but also every elder in the village has a good knowledge of the medicinal value of some herbs, usually those plants used to treat common diseases like cold, cough, fever, stomach ache, swelling cuts, and wounds. While the youth of the community have little knowledge of herbs, they do have faith in the efficacy of these medicines. In general, members of these tribal groups tens to keep the more detailed information about medicine plants to themselves, and sometimes medicine men do not even pass on their knowledge to members of their own family.

It is clear from the above description, that traditional knowledge system of medicine to cure various diseases among *Reddis* depends upon their forest environment. *Reddis* are still practicing ethno-medicine even though modern medicare is available to them.

PLANTS USED IN RELIGION

Konda Reddis believe that their Gods and Goddesses dwelling in forests and they consider forests and hill as their sacred places. They celebrate annual rituals and ceremonies in honour of these forest concerned deities. They believe that if they do not propitiate the forest gods and Goddesses properly, they and their domestic animals will not be protected from wild animals and attack evil spirits while moving in the forests. Cutting of these God and Goddess abode trees and even using the wood of these trees other than religious purpose from the particular place are considered to be taboo.

Religious beliefs and ritual practices are complete with the tree worship because many of the tree species are mythically connected with various Gods and Goddesses to secure a formal religious status for them. Besides number of plants parts are of economic, societal and medicinal values for the *Reddis*. Certain plant species and its parts play a significant role in the ritual and the life of the village people. *Reddis* consider number of plant species as sacred trees. The sacred groves i.e. *Gangalamma* is the space allocated for the village deity and all the activities related to them are carried out as a collective phenomena.

They use plant parts in the ritual celebrations are *Pala chettu* (*Mimusops hexandra*) is a tree, which found to be present in each grove as this is the dominant tree species growing in this region. The sacred site in the grove is mainly located under one such *Pala* tree. Different parts of this tree are used in the ritual of *Gangalamma* festival. The branches are used for decorating the place of ritual. Leaves are used for making plates and cups used in offering made to the deities and later on for distribution of sanctified food. If it is not available they use the leaves of *Adda chettu*. The branch of *Somi* tree is used for making idol of *Gangalamma. Rella (Cassia fistula)* and *Nallamaddi, Yegesi* trees are used in celebration of *Gangalamma* festival. The tree wood is used for making cradle (*Vuyala*) to *Gangalamma*. The flowers of *Pala chettu* and *Rella chettu* are used for worshiping *Gangalamma*. Similarly the fruit seeds of *Amodam* tree are considered to be sacred. They extract oil from the seeds for light at *Gangalamma* deity.

The tree Neredu (*Syzygium cuminii*) considered to be sacred and different part of this tree is used in celebration of marriage ritual. At the time of marriage or before construction of house, two days before they first dig the pillar of *Neredu* at North side. The twig of this tree is used in warding away of evil eye. The pillar of *Neredu* is tied with the leaves of *neredu, mamidi* and *raavi* along turmeric rice and 1-2 rupees, which signs as *Murthum rata* (Inaugural pillar) on the eve of auspicious occasion. The leaves of the tree are considered to be auspicious and symbolize prosperity, fertility and productivity. The tree log is used for making elevated platform (*Peetalu*) to sit bride and bridegroom at the time of marriage. To seek good life for married couple it is necessary to plant a *Neredu* branch at the corner of the house or marriage *pandalam*.

The *Reddis* celebrate many festivals and rituals with the leaves of mango (*Mangifera indica*), which stands for purity, sanctity and prosperity. The leaves of mango are used to decorate the entrance of the huts doors. The bark of mango and raw turmeric are made into paste, mixed with water and sprinkled on the bride and bridegroom at the time of marriage, to get rid of all misfortunes and evil eyes. *Pacha pasapu (Curcuma longa)* and *Kunkuma* (Vermilion) has high religious value for the *Reddis*. At the time of every ritual and festival without turmeric and vermilion they don't perform any ritual and festival. They grind turmeric and applied to bride and the bridegroom to give marriage bath and it is considered as purity. In the marriage ritual at the time of tying *mangalasutram* elder people sprinkled *talambralu* (Rice and turmeric mixed powder) as a kind of blessing to get rid of misfortune. They also apply to God and Goddess at the time of ritual. After applying the turmeric they put vermilion dot.

Pedda tungagaddi (*Cyperus rotundus*) the root of the grass is used in *gandam* and the paste is applied on the body of bridegroom at the time of marriage as good perfumer. The leaves of *Pala*, *Neredu* and mango tree wood quash by mixing turmeric in pot full of water use to sprinkle a mixture of water at the place of death and at the burial place to make them free from pollution. They offer grains on the leaves of *Pala* and *neredu* trees in honour of the departed soul. If the pregnant women die they stroke *Udike manu* tree wood nails to the hands and legs and also apply *chedi* to the eyes and burn to the body to free from pollution.

ECONOMIC RELATIONSHIP WITH FOREST

Since the forests surround the *Reddis* dwelling, they are wholly or partly depended on the forest for consumption as well as commercial needs. There is seasonal variation in the availability of different forest products. Including men, women and children are engaged in activities related to the gathering of minor forest produce to supplement their meagre income.

SOCIAL ORGANIZATION FOR PRESERVATION OR CONSERVATION OF NATURAL RESOURCES

Other traditional taboos are scrupulously followed by the *Reddis* and this negative life sustaining restrictions facilitate production, protection, and welfare of the community. They do not touch any crop or fruit either cultivated or available in the forest unless it is offered to their deities on the auspicious occasion. These celebrations are generally organized in such a way that all these crops, fruits etc attain maturity and full growth.

As for preservation or conservation of the habitat and surrounding natural resources, the *Reddis* strictly observe certain social norms. These norms regulate and guide natives in the process of exploitation of natural ecosystem and aim at conservation of natural ecosystem. This shows the natives awareness to the conservation and maintenance of natural ecosystem. The social norms emphasize the following view in the process of conservation of the natural resources. In the village every household is restricted not to over exploit the natural resources such as excess cutting of wood, edible leaves, fruits, tubers etc. According to them causing wastage, which may lead to scarcity of forest items. The villagers cut the timber only for their domestic purposes. They cut down forest wood to make agriculture implements such as plough, handle for certain other tools and for house construction. A part from the uses, the *Reddis* do not specifically cut the wood for firewood rather, they collect the already slashed and half burnt wood from *podu* fields. They only cut dry and fallen branches and bark of trees and utilize as firewood in their homestead. *Konda Reddis* believe that unnecessary and excess felling of trees and greenery lead to the destruction of natural resources, which ultimately may affect their livelihood. Another reason for not cutting wood for domestic purpose is that of the abundant availability of dry and fallen trees in the forest. Though the

Reddis cut the trees and forest growth on the hill slopes for *podu* cultivation, they observe three years of fallen period for regeneration of forest growth. The *Reddis* conserve the forest resources in order to practice *podu* cultivation again in the same patch after three years. It is to not that they conserve forest growth in the *podu* to reoccupy and continue *podu* cultivation in the same patch. . *Reddis* possess indigenous knowledge about the utility of numerous plant species available in the forest. In addition to the conservation of forest growth in the forest and *podu* fields, the *Reddis* conserve most of the tubers and roots by leaving a small piece of tuber or root in the earth for further germination. So that to collect the same in the forthcoming season While collecting the broomsticks they select the only fully-grown and matured plants and while cutting any tree they take care to see that ripened seeds fall on the ground for regeneration. At the time of bamboo cutting they cut one foot above or fully matured species and not tender ones. Similarly while picking the beedi leaves *Reddis* leave all the tender leaves to facilitate for growth of the plant into a big tree after as this tree yield them fruits. A part from household level of conservation of natural resources especially land, forest growth and edible forest products, the *Reddis* show concern about the conservation of fruit bearing trees and water resources at community level. In the study village the community owns certain number of jackfruit, tamarind, mango, cashew nut and caryota trees. The community as a whole takes the responsibility to safeguard them and take measures to replace it with the same plant species in the case of damaged trees. Like this the *Reddis* as a whole attempts to conserve the natural resources.

RESEARCH METHODOLOGY

The present study is basically a qualitative micro-level study aimed at understanding the *"Local Knowledge and Use Forest Plants* among the *Konda Reddis*. The fieldwork was undertaken in the village, *Utlapalem,* under Addateegala Mandal in East Godavari district of Andhra Pradesh. In order to fulfill the aim of the study, qualitative and quantitative anthropological tools and techniques has been used. Local or traditional knowledge is generally passed by word of mouth through generations and is not often recorded in writing. Gathering information of this nature therefore requires techniques such as observation, participant observation, schedule, interviews, focus group discussion, guided field walk, case study, schedules, using detailed checklist and key informants.

The observations presented here are based upon a participatory study carried out over a period of one year. Fields visits were undertaken together with the locals, in order to identify forest plant species as medical, economic value and household importance. Detailed checklist data are supported by field observations during which some of the species referred to by local name could be identified and the scientific name provided. Plant species used for any purpose, together with the local name, the part used and the mode of utilization were recorded and a comprehensive list drawn up. This was done with the help of local medical practitioners known as *vydudu*, Magician (*vejju*), as well as village headmen, women, elders, curers, and knowledgeable persons in the village.

CONCLUSION

Recapping of the above description on the local knowledge use of forest plant products among the *Konda Reddis* of Andhra Pradesh clearly explored that local knowledge is closely bound up with their way of life. These have faced a series of challenge in the recent past. The rules and regulations that have traditionally governed they are breaking down, and the homogeneity of the individual society is giving way to heterogeneity of settlement. The traditional beliefs and indigenous knowledge of the people are now being questioned by the younger generation, whose task it is to keep that culture alive. The causes factors of these problems are many, and have to do with economic, social and political. The traditional role of neighbours acting as each other's 'keepers' during misfortune or happiness is diminishing.

Another factor responsible for change is the migration of youths from tribal areas to the plains and semi-urban and urban centres, in order to take up employment there. In the course of time these youths begin to relinquish their traditional and adopt modern culture. Yet another problem in maintaining traditional culture and indigenous knowledge results from the loss of the natural forests. Forest depletion caused by various factors has led to the loss of natural pockets of indigenous flora and fauna. With the degradation of forest, they are not getting any kind of fruits in good quantity. The need for documentation is doubly acute in view of the rapid socio-economic and cultural changes taking place in these tribal communities.

It will be unethical for the academicians or researchers who are associated with local knowledge studies in tribal areas to undermine their indigenous knowledge system in the wake of global market force. Hence, it is important for us to explore its importance, which can be aligned with the socio economic development of the society or community. Subsequently, it is important to record this knowledge, not just to store it, but also to keep it alive and make it available for future use. This implies maintaining the ecosystems or natural habitat, as well as the socio-cultural organizations of the local people (cf. Maikhuri *et al.* 1996, 1998). However, this would conflict with the autonomy of the people involved. It seems that the only alternative is to carefully record the knowledge and insights of the people living within these societies.

The recognition and reinforcement of indigenous knowledge systems can form the basis for an alternative development model. The capacity of these systems to integrate multiple disciplines, and the resultant synergism are beginning to demonstrate higher levels of efficiency, effectiveness, adaptability and sustainability than many of the conventional technology systems (Mathias-Mundy, 1993).

Innovation in indigenous knowledge systems must be encouraged, so that individuals can find new opportunities to mitigate the effects of the scarcity of natural resources, migration from rural to urban areas, drought, wars and unfavourable market conditions. If indigenous knowledge systems are to continue to contribute to the quest for sustainable development, their capacity to focus on diversity and locality as well as to innovate on the basis of gendered-knowledge-generating processes must be recognized and respected. In view of the indigenous wisdom available among the indigenous groups, there is an urgent need to document properly the indigenous knowledge systems of the various indigenous groups in the country and also promote such life sustaining aspects of culture of various indigenous communities in India. So that the development consider from grass root level.

Therefore, it would be wise to protect and promote indigenous knowledge and wisdom widely in order to reduce poverty among indigenous people. Thus, the above information is highly valuable as it has development among the indigenous communities over generations. So, it is time for academicians, scientists, planners, NGOs, to take care to practice and to intimate proper documentation of indigenous knowledge systems in a more scientific way.

NOTE

1. The present paper is a part of the U.G.C. funded major research project, "Indigenous Knowledge, Natural Resource Management and Development in a forest-based Community of Andhra Pradesh." The earlier version of the paper was presented in National Seminar on Strategies for Poverty Reduction in Tribal Areas 20-22 March 2006, organized by National Institute of Rural Development (NIRD) Rajendranagar, Hyderabad-30. The author thanks the U.G.C. for the financial assistance provided for the project. I am greatly indebted to my research supervisor Prof. K.K. Misra for his valuable guidance. I Specially thank my wife Parvathi, who has been a constant source of support for me.

REFERENCES

Chambers, R., A. Pacey and L.A. Thrupp (eds) (1989), Farmer First:Farmer innovation and agricultural research. London: Intermediate Technology Publications.

Furer-Haimendrof, C von & Elizabeth Furer-Haimendrof (1945), The Reddis of Bison Hills: A Study in Acculturation, London: Macmillan & Co. Ltd.

Hill, C. (1993), 'Healthy communities, healthy animals: Reconceptualizing health and wellness', pp 4-32 in indigenous and local community knowledge in animal health and production systems: Gender Perspectives. Ottawa: The World Women's Veterinary Asscociation.

Howes, M. and R. Chambers (1979), 'indigenous technical knowledge: analysis, implications and issues', IDS Bulletin 10(2):5-11.

Maikhuri, R.K., S. Nautiyal, K.S. Rao, and K.G. Saxena (1996) Ecology and Socio-economy of Transhumanse Communities of Garhwal Himalaya. Final progress report. DST, New Delhi.

Maikhuri, R.K., S. Nautiyal, K.S. Rao, and K.G. Saxena (1998), 'Role of medicinal plants in traditional health care system: a case study from Nanda Devi Biosphere Reserve,' Current Science 75(2):152-157.

Murdoch, J. and J. Clark (1994), 'Sustainable Knowledge'. Geoforum 25(2):115-132.

Norgaard, R. (1992), 'Coevolution of economy, society and environment', pp.76-88 in P. Ekins and M. Max-Neef (eds) Real-life economics: Understanding wealth creation. London: Routeledge.

12

REFLECTION OF TRIBAL DEVELOPMENT PROGRAMMES: A CASE OF MANIPUR

*M. Romesh Singh**

The Government of India has been taking special care concerning the welfare of the tribal people ever since independence. During pre British period, the tribal communities in India remained fully or partially isolated from others in the country, and they remained backward. The British policy of isolation increased the misery of the tribal communities (Vidyarthi LP: 1986; Sahay BN: 1997). The founder of Indian constitutions seriously considered about the miserable conditions of the tribals who were segregated from the national mainstream and provided special measures to improve their socio-economic condition.

Over five decades of independence witnessed the arrival of various committee reports dealing with socio-economic situation of the tribal population, and evaluation of functioning of development agencies and their policies. Based on this reports new strategies, initiatives and approaches came into existence for the development of tribals. Consequently, efforts were made in successive five year plans to uplift the poor tribal living in our country (Rao PV: 2001). Inspite of all these efforts, desired results have not been achieved. Tribal studies carried out by various scholars' throws light on

* Associate Fellow, Council for Social Development, Southern Regional Centre, Rajendranagar, Hyderabad-30, E-Mail: m_romesh@yahoo.co.in

different problems of tribal development and offer valuable suggestions for the betterment of tribal communities. Tribal development involves development of groups, which are at different stages of socio-economic development. Hence no plan strategy can work unless we pragmatically honour some of the compulsions of the tribal situation and imbalance in development not only requires comprehensive planning, but also a different type of administrative edifice. It cannot be administered from above; it has to organize from below (Sharma B D: 1978,1984; Ratha SN: 1982; Roy Burman: 1989). However, some other studies suggested that the plans must be regional with a slant on ethnicity. The plans should ensure that socio-economic barriers and carriers would be so focused as to have a desirable change within a limited period (Pande: 1977;Sharma BD: 1970, Basu A R: 1985; Ansari SA: 1986; Sudarshan V and Xavier R: 1996).

Continuous efforts have been made to ameliorate the living condition of the poor tribals. However, it has been percolated to few elite groups and deprived the deserving people. As result, it leads to disparity of development progress in tribal society. It is mainly due to improper implementation of the programmes, lack of awareness etc. It is an urgent need to reexamine the situation as to avoid further negative consequence. Otherwise, issue of disparity among tribal group will become serious threat to future prosperity of the country. Considering this fact, the present paper attempts to explore imbalance of development progress in tribal areas of Manipur through micro level study. Moreover, paper highlights reason for disparity among tribes and its possible remedies to fill the gap in planning and policy.

METHODOLOGY

The data highlighted in this paper is based on the extensive field work conducted in two tribal villages in Manipur. Social research tools/techniques and methods are used for data collection.

The villages that were taken up for the present study come under the jurisdiction of Machi block of Chandel district in Manipur, situated near Kakching town of Thoubal district of

Manipur. One of them is Khangshim village, which is located at a distance of 2 k.m. on the N.H. 39 linking between Kakching to Moreh and Chandel district. The other one is called – Minou village, which is 15 kms away from Kakching town and comes in the right side of the N.H.39 running between Kakching and Imphal. Minou village is a hundred years old hill village whereas Khangshim village is thrity years old plain village.

HISTORY OF DEVELOPMENT PROGRESS IN TWO VILLAGES

The Minou village is situated on hilly terrain. It came to public view in 1940s. It is located in a forest region with the people living a nomadic but a self-sufficient life. However, with the beginning of community development programme, the village was linked to mainstream through many ways. To begin with, the Chief Commissioner of Manipur laid a footpath, which linked Machi block to Pallel. This enabled the tribes of Machi block to come in contact with others down the valley. This contact resulted in ideas of education coming to the minds of Minou villagers. These ideas lead them to construct a school, which was administered by the village authority. After five years of its inception, the government of Manipur adopted the school during the tenure of Naga MLA.

The PWD added to the development process by expanding the footpath to semi pucca road in 1980. Jeeps started plying from then on. Later, the roads were widened after which trucks and lorries started plying on this road.

In 1973, a post office was established at Minou village but without proper building. However, the setting up of post office not only strengthened the communications but also brought awareness among the villagers about the written mode of communication.

Later on, Minou village received few basic requirements like establishment of Anganwadi Centre at the village, and availability of two hand pumps for drinking water, access to electricity facilities etc. However, Minou villagers still require more infrastructures to meet their daily needs and to improve their style of living.

Whereas Khangshim village is situated within the vicinity of the Kakching town NH 39, which is connected to Moreh, passes by the side of this village. This geographical nearness gives Khangshim an advantage over Minou in terms of development and social outlook. High literacy rate, contact with bureaucrats, and awareness of development process were at the higher level among Khangshim villagers when compared to that of Minou villagers.

Although Khangshim village had a late start when compared to Minou, the welfare programmes it received in the last 30 years are wide and rich as compared with other villages in Manipur in general. To begin with, the Bazaar shed was established in 1970s quite adjacent to the Khangshim village. This enabled the villagers to sell their products outside. It was established to provide marketing facilities among the tribals living in this block. But major beneficiaries are the Khangshim villagers since it is near to the village. Some of the villagers managed to do regular types of small business in this bazaar to sustain their livelihood.

The community development programmes enriched with the setting up of various infrastructure facilities in Khangshim village i.e., school building, culverts, public latrine, Bore well, two ring wells. The establishment or construction of a Church building and digging of community pond are examples of villagers involvement in community work. The nineteen eighties (1980) witnessed the arrival of electricity supply to the village. Telephone facilities are also available in Khangshim village, which is also not there in many tribal villages like Minou village.

DEVELOPMENT PROGRAMMES IN THE STUDY VILLAGES

Developmental schemes are carried out for the benefit of tribals basically aim at narrowing down the gap between the tribal and non-tribal areas by increasing the productivity and income level of beneficiaries. For that, the two major sources of finances are the special central assistance fund and state plan outlays. The programmes under the special central assistance are under agriculture, horticulture, small-scale industries, fishery, and animal husbandry, which are mainly aimed at the economic development of the tribals. The infrastructure development programmes included water supply scheme, construction of suspension and wooden bridges, inter village road, construction of school, community hall etc. Besides this, welfare schemes comprising of the programmes dealing with the financial assistance for medical treatment, imparting training to tribal youth, and housing schemes were carried out. Development schemes implemented in the studied villages are discussed in the following heads.

AGRICULTURE

In Minou and Khangshim village, agriculture represents a peculiar mix of tradition and modernity. Agriculture of this area is subsistence agriculture. To provide better water facility for the farmers, a check dam was constructed at Khangshim village in 1995. However, check dam failed to provide water due to poor quality of the materials used in the construction of dam, unskilled work and dam directly facing to the speedy flow of water during rainy season. After 1 ½ year of its construction, the check dam was washed away by the heavy flow of the stream. Hence, agricultural practices in these areas are totally dependent on rainfall.

In addition to this, high yielding variety of paddy was supplied to increase the rice production of farmers. And four persons from Khangshim village received HYV seed provided by the agriculture department, Chandel district. But it could not yield good quantity especially in jhum land. Reasons for not getting high yield among the farmers are due to jhum cultivation. Moreover, after sowing of HYV paddy, it required follow up steps like timely application of chemical fertilizer and pesticide for better yield. These HYV varieties are only suitable for wet cultivation. Generally villagers don't go for fertilizers especially in jhum cultivation, and most of the people cannot afford to buy. Moreover, HYV sowing should be done at appropriate time and fertilizer should be used at suitable period. Water supply is quite necessary in time. Since people are dependent upon the rainfall, it is unthinkable to get water in time. However, HYV benefited the villagers who are economically sound and practiced plain cultivation in the villages where fertilizers and pesticides are used extensively. But, these HYV varieties gave benefit only to some villagers who possess land in plain area, and can afford to use chemical fertilizer. Majority of the tribals are practicing jhum cultivation that is their way of life, and are not benefited by introduction of HYV. Generally, majority of the tribals are practicing jhum cultivation and sustaining their life. And HYV is introduced to improve the production level of the poor farmers and it failed to provide benefits to the poor tribals who are engaged in jhum cultivation. These varieties of seeds were introduced by the government agencies without taking into consideration of jhum land condition and its suitability. Government agencies are not taking much initiative to improve the productivity level of jhum farmers, which constitute major population of Manipur tribals. It is necessary to take up jhum control measures suitable to the tirbals. Another problem is the absence of individual ownership of land in the hill areas as the land in the hill areas belong to the community or village chiefs. Suitable land tenure system has to be evolved for introducing land ownership for permanent improvement of the land by the individuals.

Besides, tribals are cultivating cash crops like vegetables, ginger, maize, potatoes,banana, sugar cane, maize, etc., in jhum area, and leaving half of the area for paddy cultivation, for the consumption of family. Cultivation of these cash crops help to supplement their income.

The inception of Manipur Tribal Development Corporation (MTDC) and Directorate for Development of Tribal and Backward Classes(DDTBC) implemented cash crops schemes to the tribal farmers. In the Minou and Khangshim villages, seven persons got benefit from these agencies, and benefits given to them are for cultivation of sugarcane, potato, ginger and maize. Similarly, this schemes also failed to provide benefit due to improper implementation and lack of proper management of the schemes. Moreover, these schemes had been distributed to the undeserving clients, at the same time deprived the deserving clients who were capable of doing such cultivation.

These programmes mostly benefited the tribal elites who are practicing settled agriculture in both the villages. Moreover, poor tribals are totally neglected from getting such schemes. The schemes implemented for the upliftment of the poor tribals are giving more benefits to the economically better off families, instead of serving poor tribal families. It can be highlighted that planning and strategies for tribal development in Manipur lack proper initiatives and understanding of the tribals living conditions. Because, agriculture related schemes launched in Manipur are generally in tune with the plain lifestyle and not conducive for hill areas. To develop tribals in Manipur, it is necessary to initiate agriculture scheme related to jhum cultivation.

ANIMAL HUSBANDRY

Animal husbandry is one of most important bases for development of tribal economy as the hilly terrain and nature of soil is not very conducive for agriculture. The tribals by nature are non-vegetarians and they prefer rearing animals.

Government paid attention to animal husbandry among the development programmes undertaken in these areas, For increasing their breeds, pigs, bullocks and buffaloes etc., were distributed. Both bullocks and buffaloes are very important animals for agriculture. For poor tribal farmers, it is difficult to purchase bullocks or buffaloes on their own. Only seven households were able to get benefit from this scheme. The study revealed that distribution of buffaloes/bullocks should be given more attention rather than spending money on other schemes, because beneficiaries could earn something out of this scheme, either by selling them to the butchers for meat or to be used in agricultural work. Moreover illness or sickness is rare to the bullocks/buffaloes and villagers also consumed meat or beef extensively during Christmas or marriage ceremonies. It can be used both the way i.e., consumption or agriculture work.

Subsequently, Piggery scheme is also implementing through different agencies during different plan periods and five villagers were given piggery scheme in the form of six piglets each. Out of the five beneficiaries, only one household in Minou village got assistance. Unfortunately, this scheme has not really benefited the beneficiaries as the pigs died in an early age. The piglets that were distributed in these villages could not survive due to improper feeding, lack of awareness about diseases etc. Beneficiaries suggested that instead of this piglets, agencies should give middle aged pigs which don't require much attention like piglets. Generally, villagers are not able to take special care of animals since they are engaged in various kinds of agricultural works and wage labour throughout the year.

Over all, the animal husbandry schemes show positive results as compared with agricultural related schemes. Infact, these schemes have more scope for getting successful results in these areas since tribals are using them for multiple purposes. However, it is again benefited by the people who are skilled in bribing officials and influence the officials. They are most eligible applicants for any type of scheme implemented by government agencies in Manipur.

EMPLOYMENT AND TRAINING PROGRAMMES

Subsidiary occupations for the majority of the tribal people are small and village industries. Under this sector of development, tribal families are provided with training in knitting, tailoring, and carpentry. Besides, under the self employment schemes, a grocery shop, tea stall, and small scale business were also provided by various government agencies.

Carpentry training had been introduced to the tribal people in district headquarters and forty people from different tribal villages were trained under TRYSEM. Trainees have been provided Rs.200 as stipend during their training period. Duration of the training was only for two months.

Under this scheme, carpentry instruments were issued to those who have received training under TRYSEM. Carpentry instruments were provided to 4 persons in Khangshim village and one person in Minou village. This scheme was aimed at providing good income to the carpenter since there is a lot of demand for wooden furniture, construction of houses in hills and plains area. But TRYSEM beneficiaries are failed to derive income from carpentry work because they cannot compete with the plain people due to lack of skill and improper training provided in a very short period.

WEAVING

Since the tribal women in Manipur are well known experts in weaving activities. Weaving and knitting schemes are distributed in cash and kind. Out of the ten beneficiaries, only two are from Minou village. Study reported that majority of the beneficiaries did not utilize the scheme for actual purpose since the beneficiaries were provided in the form of cash. Tribal families are always in need of money and they utilized the money for their family purpose in various ways, i.e., treatment, running tea stall, house construction etc. Once the scheme got sanctioned, none of the officials came to the village for inspection or inquiry about beneficiaries' work. There are two beneficiaries in Khangshim village who do weaving and supplement their family economy from their earnings.

It is always felt that providing weaving machine to the beneficiaries instead of giving money is always better in long run. Similar schemes are being implemented by various agencies, leading to overlapping of programmes. It leads to the maximum benefit to some particular group or villages who have more access to the officials in various departments. That's why, Minou villagers got very less benefit in any schemes when compared to that of Khangshim villagers.

It is very necessary to specify particular department, to look after the specific scheme, which will be provided to beneficiaries as to avoid the overlapping of programmes from departments like DRDA, MTDC, DDTBC etc.

PRIME MINISTERS' ROJGAR YOJANA

The scheme started in Manipur in the year 1994. So far more than 7900 educated unemployed youth have been assisted through the scheme (DDTBC:1999). In Khangshim village, there are two persons who received PMRY scheme.

In general PMRY scheme spent lots of money for unemployed youth, but success rate of this scheme is very low. As mentioned by two beneficiaries, as per the guidelines all the selected candidates under PMRY have to undergo training. The concerned officials have to provide the training to the candidates by making the necessary arrangement. But in practice, there was no such training given to selected candidates. Once the scheme is sanctioned, there is no further communication or interaction between beneficiaries and concern officials. No more enquiries about the progress of the candidates. This leads to unsuccessful results. None of the youth from Minou village got PMRY due to their ignorance and not having influential persons in the village. This scheme rather disappoints the youth than serving its purpose.

SMALL SCALE BUSSINESS

Under self employment schemes, two persons in Minou and three persons in Khangshim were provided assistance through IRDP for starting small scale business. Each beneficiary started running pan shops and tea stall respectively. Beneficiaries who are running pan shop and tea stall at Khangshim village are doing good business but its quite opposite in Minou village as two beneficiaries in this village are not able to get income out of this business due to less customers. It leads to close down of the shop and started engaging themselves in wage labour. Hence, it is important to assess the suitability and feasibility of programmes before implementing in tribal village. These schemes are more suitable for Khangshim village since it is situated near NH 39 where lot many people gather in this area. Beneficiaries are successful in sustaining their livelihood.

HOUSING SCHEME

Housing scheme has been implemented through various development agencies. Poor people who cannot afford to construct houses were provided in the form of zinc sheet (35 pieces) for covering the roof of the house. Majority of the beneficiaries revealed that it is not sufficient to cover the whole roof of the house. They required extra pieces of zinc sheet to cover the whole roof. The beneficiaries who couldn't afford to buy extra zinc sheets covered their house roof by mixing zinc sheet and thatch. It looks very ugly especially on a newly constructed house. People do not prefer to mix these two types. Thus, zinc sheet provided to the poor tribal families for housing scheme were sold to other villagers, because they are neither sufficient to construct a new house nor villagers could afford to buy additional requirements. Villagers expressed that it could have been better if government provides money instead of zinc sheet, with proper inspection and guidance, so that a poor person also can construct a thatch house with a low budget.

PEOPLE'S PARTICIPATION:

For the success of any development programme, people's participation is most important. The programmes and schemes on village level development activities are successfully executed whereas the family oriented schemes or individual schemes are less successful. The success of the village development programmes are because of the involvement of village authority who are capable of organizing social activities in the village. Even the funding from the development agencies is inadequate. Village autnority can mobilize money from the villagers to make a scheme successful. The money released from government is sufficient, if not misused. It is quite clear that sanctioned amounts of the scheme are misused in different ways like bribing the officials, paying for extortions by insurgents etc. As a result, villagers get very less financial assistance from officials. However, for the community development programmes like labour work for construction of culvert, market shed, digging ring well, construction of school building, inner village road, leveling of play ground etc., are done by the villagers under the supervision of village authority. In fact the involvement of the villagers of Khangshim and Minou in village development programmes is quite impressive.

PROBLEMS FACED BY THE VILLAGERS

The problems faced by villagers of Khangshim and Minou villages; tribal people have a number of problems which need the attention of administration, voluntary agencies, social reformers etc.

The villagers of Minou are facing shortage of water. There are only two under ground bore water hand pumps available to supply water to the villagers for their daily consumption. And also these water sources are located at outer areas of the village. Therefore, villagers residing in the inner area of the village have to go a long distance to fetch water for drinking and other purposes. Number of attempts have been made to install more under ground bore water hand pumps, but the attempts failed due to lack of financial support from government side. Moreover, it is costly to install under ground bore water hand pumps especially in hill areas.

Another important problem is the absence of health centre in these two villages especially in the Minou village. Whenever emergency health problems come among the villagers, it gives a lot of trouble to the patient because of non-availability of first aid medical facilities. However, Khangshim villagers are better in this situation since they are very near to Kakching town, where a hospital and more clinics are available. At the time of emergency health problems, number of villagers have died in Minou village due to the non availability of first aid as reported by the villagers. Besides, transport facilities are also not easily available whenever somebody wants to take a patient to town area. These are major problems which have to be taken under consideration very seriously.

Delay in budget provision proved to be a major obstacle in the development work. In case of Khangshim village, community hall has been under construction since last three years and not yet completed. Due to delay in funding, some part of the hall, which had already been constructed, is also slowly getting damaged day by day. Village Authority has been trying hard to complete the construction by collecting funds from various sources. But It is difficult task for them to complete without the financial support from government agencies.

In Minou village transport facilities are available only once in a day for going to the town and coming back to the village.

Because of poor transportation facilities, due to poor quality of road construction (muddy road), they are totally cut off from town during rainy season. Sometimes, it affects their family economy especially for the people who have to go out of their village for selling their products. Whereas Khangshim village is far better in terms of transport and market facilities, since they are close to Kakching town and being roadside of National high way 39 connecting nearby town. The villagers are thus able to avail more facilities in terms of selling and buying. They don't have the kind of problem that is faced by Minou villagers during rainy season.

SUMMARY AND CONCLUSION

The study villages have been provided with various development schemes like agriculture and allied activities, animal husbandry, self-employment and training programmes by the state government development agencies, for their socio economic development. Unfortunately, most of the development schemes have failed to serve the real purpose due to many constraints. Development scheme's benefits differ from one village to another and from individual to individual depending upon the availability of influencial and educated persons living in particular villages. As such, majority of the benefits are gained by Khangshim villagers and even more by elite groups within the village. The Minou villagers suffered due to lack of basic infrastructure in their village. The existence of imbalance in development among tribals in these areas is clearly seen from this study.

However, the financial packages from Center are meant for development of all the villages. But, the development activities carried out in these two villages show an imbalance in some way or other. For instance, the villagers of Khangshim are obtaining more facilities like public latrine, anganwadi center building, community hall, wells etc provided by the government whereas it is not so in Minou Village which is located in a remote hilly area.

In Manipur, villages are located both in the hilly terrain and in the plain as well. As we have seen in the case of Minou and Khangshim, the villages belonging to hilly terrain don't enjoy as much wealth and progress like that of the villages in the plain area. It is clearly understood that settlement of Minou village is much older than Khangshim village. As they are easily accessible to the plain area, having more educated people, it is noticed that development agencies are also taking interest to the Khangshim village. Whereas, Minou village is not easily accessible to the plain area due to poor transport facilities and moreover, development personnel are also not interested to take up development initiatives due to the "unrest problems" existing in the hill areas. The "unrest problems" in the sense that various groups of insurgents moving in the hill areas and Naga and Kuki conflict in hill areas, make the officials reluctant to reach hill villages. As a whole, hill areas like Minou village are not favourable for development activities. The difference between the socio-economic growth of Minou and Khangshim is a classical example of such differences in the growth of Manipur's tribal areas.

Besides, there are other parameters that aid the development process. They include literacy level, their contact with government officials and presence of wealthy, educated people in the village. These factors are more crucial than allocation of finances itself. If the village has higher literacy rate and has a wealthy educated class living in it, the village will attract more development activities. The Minou village doesn't have a powerful people to procure the development process as that of Khangshim village. The difference of socio-economic growth between Minou and Khangshim villages is essentially created because of these differences, i.e., hilly terrain, poor literacy, poor transport and communication, unrest problems etc.

Apart from this, the planning and development strategy for the tribal development in Manipur is common for both the hill and plain areas. There is no separate planning and development strategies for tribals who are living in the hill areas. Majority of the tribals are living in the hill areas whereas very few populations live in the plain areas. They have different kinds of lifestyles, which cannot be treated as common with regard to their development activities. Moreover, tribals living in plain areas are more advanced and well educated, which do not require much attention like hill people. Even though, the plain people were more benefited from many development programmes carried out by the government agencies that were basically meant for the poor tribals. Hence, the common planning and development strategies also led to the deprivation of majority of the tribals living in hill areas.

REFERENCES

Ansari, S.A. (1986), *Socio-Economic Development in Tribal Areas of Manipur*, Delhi, B.R.Publishing Corporation.

Basu, A.R. (1985), *Tribal Development Programmes and Administration in India*, New Delhi, National Book Organization.

Benota, M. (1991), *Tribal Development in Manipur During Plan Period (1951-1991): An Assessment.* Imphal, Centre for Tribal Studies, Manipur University.

Pande, M.K. (1977), *Social Life in Rural India.* Calcutta, India Book Exchange.

Rao, P.V. (2001), *Tribal Development: Policy and Practice.* New Delhi, Sarup and Sons.

Ratha, S.N. (1982), *Planning for Tribal Development*, New Delhi, Inter India Publications.

Roy, Burman (1989), *Problems and Prospects of Tribal Development in North-East India. Economic and Political Weekly. April, Vol.24(13).*

Sahay, B.N. (1997), *Approach to Tribal Welfare, New Delhi, Yojana, January, Vol.41.*

Sharma, B.D. (1978), *Tribal Development: The Concept and the Frame.* New Delhi, Prachi Prakash.

Sharma, B.D. (1984), *Planning for Tribal Development.* New Delhi, Prachi Prakashan.

Sudarsan,V and Xavier, R (1996), *'Tribal Scenario and developmental Planning in Tamil Nadu'* in Mann, R.S (ed) 1996 Tribes of India: Ongoing Challenges. New Delhi; M.D. Publications, Pvt. Ltd.

Vidyarthi, L.P. (1986), *Applied Anthropology in India.* Allahabad, Kitab Mahal.

Government of Manipur (1999), *District Socio-Economic Review of Chandel District 1997-98*, *Imphal, Directorate of Economic & Statistics.*

Government of Manipur (2000), *Revised Replies to Questionnaire regarding Implementation of Safeguards & Development Programmes for Scheduled Castes & Scheduled Tribes, Imphal, Department for Development of Tribals and Scheduled Castes.*

SECTION III

WOMEN DEVELOPMENT

13

INTER-STATE INTER-REGIONAL VARIATIONS IN PERFORMANCE OF BANKING INSTITUTIONS IN FINANCING WOMEN SELF-HELP GROUPS

*I. Sundar**

INTRODUCTION

Banking institutions play a significant role in the implementation of anti-poverty programmes in India. Their role has been realized since the rural sector in past has by and large remained a neglected sector and banking facilities were not available to the rural sector. Further, whatever little credit facilities were available to the rural sector went mostly to big farmers. Hence, there was need to expand banking facilities in rural areas. In consequence of these rural branches of Commercial Banks expanded sharply since 1969, due to nationalization of banks. Despite this situation, there exists a problem of inadequate banking institutions to cater to the financial requirement of the rural population. To solve this problem, in 1972 the banking commission recommended the establishment of a chain of rural banks in addition to rural branches of Commercial Banks with the objective of converting of primary cooperative societies into institutions offering full banking facilities.

Regional Rural Banks have been established after realization of the inadequate services of the cooperative credit sector and

* Lecturer in Economics, Directorate of Distance Education, Annamalai University, India.

the expansion of branches of Commercial Banks in the rural areas would not go for enough. Before the establishment of Regional Rural Banks, there existed cooperative credit. The concept of cooperative credit has come into existence mainly to weed out the evils associated with credit provided by the moneylenders in rural areas. Cooperative credit converts the static rural credit system into a dynamic one. Now there are three major banking institutions, viz., Commercial Banks, Regional Rural Banks and Cooperative Banks that are entrusted with the responsibility of implementing anti-poverty programmes in general and women empowerment programmes in terms of financing women self-help groups in particular. This paper attempts to examine the performance of these banking institutions in financing women development programmes in terms of self-help groups in different parts of the country.

METHODOLOGY

This paper analyses the performance of Commercial Banks, Regional Rural Banks and Cooperatives Banks in financing women self-help groups in India. This study is undertaken in two dimensions. The first dimension relates to individual regional analysis, covering the states and union territories in each region. India has six regions, viz., Northern region, North-eastern region, Eastern region, Central region, Western region and Southern region. All the regions are specifically analyzed in the study. The second dimension of the study relates to inter-regional variations in the performance of banking institutions in the implementation of financial assistance programme to the women SHGs. The indicators relate to the number of SHGs in each state and region, extent of bank credit given in each state and region and per group bank credit in each state and region. The analysis covers both aggregate total performance of banking institutions in financing women development programmes and also bank-wise performance analysis. The result of this study is interpreted with the help of simple statistical tools of percentage and average analysis.

RESULTS AND DISCUSSION

Data presented in table 1 indicate the performance of banking institutions in financing women self-help groups in India. It could be noted that in the Northern region, 19321 women self-help groups are covered by three groups of banks, viz., Commercial Banks, Regional Rural Banks and Cooperative Banks. As on March 2002, these banks have sanctioned credit amount of Rs. 373.1 millions to the Self-help Groups (SHGs). The per group bank credit is worked out to Rs. 19311.1 during the same period of analysis. Among the banks in the Northern region, Commercial Banks occupy the first position (44.83%) in coverage of women self-help groups in their bank credit scheme, Regional Rural Banks the second (37.28%) and Cooperative Banks the last (17.89%). A similar situation has been observed with respect to sanctioned bank credit amount. The Northern region has 5 states and one union territory. Among them the banking institutions of Rajasthan state have covered more than a half of the self-help groups (65.03%) of the Northern region and also sanctioned credit amount. The bank-wise performance analysis reveals that the role of Commercial Banks is quite encouraging in their coverage of women self-help groups and also sanction of credit amount, Regional Rural Banks the second and Cooperative Banks the last.

The banking institutions in Himachal Pradesh state come second in the Northern region with respect to coverage of women self-help groups (26.24%) and also in sanctioned credit amount. In this state the performance of Cooperative Banks is quite encouraging in terms of coverage of SHGs and sanctioned credit amount Haryana state banking institutions occupy the third position in the Northern region in their coverage of women self-help groups (5.02%) and also sanctioned credit amount (9.99%). It is significant to note that Cooperative Banks have not involved themselves in assisting women SHGs. However, Regional Rural Banks in Haryana state have covered 72.47 per cent of the women self-help groups and sanctioned Rs. 17.31 millions of bank credit to the women SHGs.

Table 1
Performance of Banking Institutions in Financing Women Self-help Groups in the Northern Region

State	Commercial Banks		Per capita loan per SHG (in Rs)	Regional Rural Banks		Per capita loan per SHG (in Rs.)	Cooperative Banks		Per capita loan per SHG (in Rs.)	Total		Per capita loan per SHG (in Rs.)
	No. of SHGs	Bank Loan		No. of SHGs	Bank Loan		No. of SHGs	Bank Loan		No. of SHGs	Bank Loan	
Haryana	267 (3.08)*	19.88 (13.26)*	74831.4**	703 (9.76)*	17.31 (11.84)*	24623.0**	–	–	–	970 (5.02)*	37.29 (9.99)*	38443.22**
Himachal Pradesh	2078 (23.99)*	20.07 (13.32)*	9658.3**	678 (9.41)*	12.19 (8.33)*	17979.3**	2313 (66.93)*	48.24 (63.30)*	20856.0**	5069 (26.24)*	80.5 (21.58)*	15880.8**
Punjab	181 (2.09)*	7.68 (5.10)*	42430.9**	71 (0.99)*	5.83 (3.99)*	82112.6**	155 (4.48)*	5.54 (7.27)*	35741.9**	407 (2.11)*	19.05 (5.11)*	46805.8**
Jammu & Kashmir	145 (1.67)*	2.58 (1.71)*	17793.1**	134 (1.86)*	1.00 (0.68)*	7462.6**	21 (0.61)*	0.14 (0.18)*	6666.6**	300 (1.55)*	3.72 (1.00)*	12400.0**
Rajasthan	5979 (69.04)*	99.77 (66.23)*	16686.7**	5618 (77.98)*	109.92 (75.16)*	19565.6**	967 (27.98)*	22.29 (29.25)*	23050.5**	2564 (65.03)*	231.98 (62.17)*	18463.8**
New Delhi	11 (0.13)*	0.57 (0.38)*	51818.1**	–	–	–	–	–	–	11 (0.05)*	0.57 (0.15)*	51818.1**
Total	8661 (100.00)*	150.65 (100.00)*	17394.0**	7204 (100.00)*	146.25 (100.00)*	20301.2**	3456 (100.00)*	76.21 (100.00)*	22051.5**	19321 (100.00)*	373.11 (100.00)*	19311.1**

Source: NABARD's Online Data upto March 2002
* Figures in parentheses denote column percentage
** Figures in parentheses denote row percentage.

Punjab State's banking institutions occupy the fourth position in their coverage of women self-help groups (2.11%) and also sanctioned banks credit (5.11%) in the Northern region. In this state, the performance of Cooperative Banks is quite low as they have covered less than 10 per cent of the SHGs and also sanctioned bank credit, indicating the low role of cooperative institutions in poverty alleviation in the state. The banking institutions of Jammu and Kashmir state occupy the fifth position in their coverage of women self-help groups (1.55%) and also sanctioned bank credit. The reason for poor performance of banking institutions in the state may be due to terrorists' distributive activities and such activities hinder the normal economic activities. In this state also the performance of Cooperative Banks is quite discouraging in their coverage of SHGs and also sanctioned bank credit. Only Commercial Banks in the union territory of Delhi have covered 11 women self-help groups and sanctioned 0.57 million rupees. Among the banks in the Northern region, the per group bank credit is quite large in New Delhi, Punjab and Haryana states and it is the lowest in Jammu and Kashmir.

A study of data in table 2 indicates the performance of banking institutions in financing women self-help groups in the North-eastern region. This region has seven states viz., Assam, Manipur, Meghalaya, Sikkim, Tripura, Nagaland and Arunachal Pradesh. The Commercial Banks in the North-eastern region have covered 1990 women self-help groups in their credit schemes and sanctioned a credit amount of Rs. 25.40 millions upto March 2002. More than a half of the self-help groups have been covered by Regional Rural Banks in the state. The Cooperative Banks have played the least role in catering to the financial needs of women self-help groups. Among the states in the North-eastern region, the majorities of the self-help groups are benefited by the banking institutions of Assam (68.72%) and also availed themselves of the benefit of bank credit. In this state, most of the self-help groups are covered by Regional Rural Banks (81.93%) and also in the sanctioned bank credit. The Cooperative Banks role is very low. Meghalaya state's banking institutions take the second position in their

Table 2
Performance of Banking Institutions in Financing Women Self-help Groups in the North-Eastern Region

State	Commercial Banks		Per capita loan per SHG (in Rs)	Regional Rural Bank		Per capita loan per SHG (in Rs.)	Cooperative Banks		Per capita loan per SHG (in Rs.)	Total		Per capita loan per SHG (in Rs.)
	No. of SHGs	Bank Loan		No. of SHGs	Bank Loan		No. of SHGs	Bank Loan		No. of SHGs	Bank Loan	
Assam	179 (17.48)*	1.84 (13.48)*	10279.3**	839 (81.93)*	11.66 (85.42)*	13897.4**	6 (0.59)*	0.15 (1.10)*	25000.0**	1024 (68.72)*	13.65 (53.74)*	13330.0**
Manipur	134 (100.00)*	2.61 (100.00)*	19477.6**	–	–	–	–	–	–	134 (8.99)*	2.61 (10.28)*	19477.6**
Meghalaya	62 (34.64)*	5.48 (94.65)*	88387.0**	117 (65.36)*	0.31 (5.35)*	2649.5**	–	–	–	179 (12.01)*	5.79 (22.80)*	32346.3**
Sikkim	23 (100.00)*	0.44 (100.00)*	19130.4**	–	–	–	–	–	–	23 (1.54)*	0.44 (1.73)*	19130.4**
Tripura	2 (28.57)*	0.16 (48.48)*	80000.0**	3 (42.86)*	0.15 (45.46)*	50000.0**	2 (28.57)*	0.02 (6.06)*	10000.0**	7 (0.48)*	0.33 (1.30)*	47142.8**
Nagaland	–	–	–	15 (100.00)*	0.58 (100.00)*	38666.6**	–	–	–	15 (1.01)*	0.58 (2.28)*	38666.6**
Arunachal Pradesh	108 (100.00)*	2.00 (100.00)*	18518.5**	–	–	–	–	–	–	108 (7.25)*	2.00 (7.87)*	18518.5**
Total	508 (34.09)*	12.53 (49.33)*	2465.3**	974 (65.37)*	12.70 (50.00)*	13039.0**	8 (0.54)*	0.17 (0.67)*	21250.0	1490 (100.00)*	25.40 (100.00)*	17046.9**

Source: NABARD's Online Data upto March 2002

* Figures in parentheses denote column percentage

** Figures in parentheses denote row percentage.

coverage of women SHGs (12.01%) and also sanctioned bank credit (22.80%) as on March 2002. In this state, Regional Rural Banks have shared a major role in financing women self-help groups, whereas, the Cooperative Banks have not played any role in assisting women self-help groups. The banking institutions in Manipur state occupy the third position (8.99%) in their coverage of women self-help group and also in sanctioned bank credit (10.28%) during the period of analysis. In Manipur state, only Commercial Banks have covered women SHGs and also financed those groups under anti-poverty alleviation programmes.

Arunachal Pradesh state's banking institutions rank fourth in order in catering to the financial needs of women self-help groups (7.25%). It is heartening to note that the role of Regional Rural Banks and Cooperative Banks is not reported in the state and only the Commercial Banks have done the job. The banking institutions in Sikkim state occupy the fifth position with respect to coverage of women self-help groups (1.54%) and also sanctioned bank credit. Here also Commercial Banks alone have financed women SHGs.

The banking institutions in Nagaland state take the sixth position (1.01%) in their coverage of women self-help groups which are done only by Regional Rural Banks. Tripura state's banking institutions are put at last in order in the North-eastern region in their coverage of women SHG. Among the states in the North-eastern region, per group loan amount is found to be the highest in Tripura state and lowest in Assam. The per group loan sanctioned level declines as the number of groups increases and the vice versa.

A keen observation of data in table-3 indicates the performance of banking institutions in financing women development programmes in the Eastern region. This region has 4 states and one union territory viz., Bihar, Jharkhand, Orissa, West Bengal and the Andaman and Nicobar Islands. Eastern region's banking institutions have covered 45892 women self-helps and sanctioned a credit amount of Rs. 467.51 millions as on March 2002. The per group bank credit is worked out to Rs. 10187.1. Among the states in the Eastern region,

Table 3
Performance of Banking Institutions in Financing Women Self-help Groups in the Eastern Region

State	*Commercial Banks*		*Per capita loan per SHG (in Rs)*	*Regional Rural Banks*		*Per capita loan per SHG (in Rs.)*	*Cooperative Banks*		*Per capita loan per SHG (in Rs.)*	*Total*		*Per capita loan per SHG (in Rs.)*
	No. of SHGs	*Bank Loan*		*No. of SHGs*	*Bank Loan*		*No. of SHGs*	*Bank Loan*		*No. of SHGs*	*Bank Loan*	
Bihar	1942	9.31	4794.0**	1956	25.60	13087.9**	59	3.24	54915.2**	3957	38.15	9641.1**
	(49.08)*	(24.41)*		(49.43)*	(67.10)*		(1.49)*	(8.49)*		(8.62)*	(8.16)*	
Jharkhand	1894	55.50	29303.0**	2304	38.65	16775.1**	–	–	–	4198	94.15	22427.3**
	(45.12)*	(58.95)*		(54.88)*	(41.05)*					(9.15)*	(20.11)*	
Orissa	5994	45.67	7619.2**	12432	134.77	10840.5**	2127	26.28	12355.4**	20553	206.72	10057.8**
	(29.16)*	(22.09)*		(60.49)*	(65.19)*		(10.35)*	(12.72)*		(44.79)*	(44.23)*	
West Bengal	4806	28.07	5840.6**	3226	25.49	7901.4**	9111	73.63	8081.4**	17143	127.19	7419.3**
	(28.03)*	(22.07)*		(18.82)*	(20.04)*		(53.15)*	(57.89)*		(37.35*)	(27.22)*	
A & N Islands (UT)	–	–	–	–	–	–	41	1.30	31707.3**	41	1.30	31707.3**
							(100.00)*	(100.00)*		(0.09)*	(0.28)*	
Total	14636	138.55	9466.3**	19918	224.51	11271.7**	11338	104.45	9212.3**	45892	467.51	10187.1**
	(31.89)*	(29.64)*		(43.40)*	(48.02)*		(24.71)	(22.34)*		(100.00)*	(100.00)*	

Source: NABARD's Online Data upto March 2002

* Figures in parentheses denote column percentage

** Figures in parentheses denote row percentage.

Orissa, state's banking institutions occupy the first position (44.79%) in their coverage of women SHGs and also sanctioned credit amount. In this state, Regional Rural Banks have covered more than a half of the SHGs and also provided the same level of bank credit.

The performance of Cooperative Banks is quite discouraging in their credit coverage to the women self-help groups. West Bengal state's banking institutions take the second position in their coverage of women self-help groups (37.35%) in the provision of credit under various anti-poverty programme of the government. It is significant to observe that the Cooperative Banks have covered more than a half of the women SHGs under their credit scheme. In the Eastern region, Jharkhand state's banking institutions take the third position (9.15%) in their coverage of women self-help groups in provision of credit. In this state, Regional Rural Banks have covered more than a half of the SHGs (54.88%) in their credit scheme. However, Commercial Banks have sanctioned more than a half of the (58.95%) credit in the state.

Bihar state's Commercial Banks occupy the fourth place (8.62%) in their coverage of women SHGs and also Sanctioned credit in the Eastern region. In this state, Cooperative Banks have played the least role in catering to the financing needs of the women SHGs. In the Andaman Nicobar Islands only the Cooperative Banks have covered 41 SHGs under their credit scheme. Among the states in the Eastern region, the per group credit is the highest in the Andaman and Nicobar islands and the lowest in Bihar.

A study of data in table-4 indicates the performance banking, institutions in financing women SHGs in the central region. This region has four states viz., Madhya Pradesh, Chhattisgarh, Uttar Pradesh and Uttaranchal. Central region's banking institutions have covered 48181 women SHGs in their credit scheme with a sanctioned amount of Rs. 569.11 million. Their per group credit amount is worked out to be Rs. 11811.9. Among the states in the central region, the banking institutions of Uttar Pradesh state occupy the first position (68.73%) in their

Table 4
Performance of Banking Institutions in Financing Women Self-help Groups in the Central Region

State	*Commercial Banks*		*Per capita loan per SHG (in Rs)*	*Regional Rural Banks*		*Per capita loan per SHG (in Rs.)*	*Cooperative Banks*		*Per capita loan per SHG (in Rs.)*	*Total*		*Per capita loan per SHG (in Rs.)*
	No. of SHGs	*Bank Loan*		*No. of SHGs*	*Bank Loan*		*No. of SHGs*	*Bank Loan*		*No. of SHGs*	*Bank Loan*	
Madhya Pradesh	2456 (30.77)*	51.66 (33.13)*	21034.2**	4850 (60.77)*	74.08 (47.51)*	15274.2**	675 (8.46)*	30.18 (19.36)*	44711.1**	7981 (16.56)*	155.92 (27.40)*	19536.3**
Chhattisgarh	314 (8.34)*	1.20 (4.71)*	3821.6**	2312 (61.44)*	19.09 (74.86)*	8256.9**	1137 (30.22)*	5.21 (20.43)*	4582.2**	3763 (7.81)*	25.50 (4.44)*	6776.5*
Uttar Pradesh	10575 (31.94)*	57.96 (22.69)*	5480.8**	22388 (67.61)*	196.85 (77.06)*	8792.6**	151 (0.45)*	0.63 (0.25)*	4582.2**	33114 (68.73)*	255.44 (44.88)*	77006.70*
Uttaranchal	2940 (88.48)*	121.41 (91.80)*	41295.9**	362 (10.89)*	10.41 (7.89)*	28756.9**	21 (0.63)*	0.43 (0.33)*	20476.1**	3323 (6.90)*	132.25 (23.24)*	39798.3**
Total	16285 (33.80)*	232.23 (40.81)*	14260.3**	29912 (62.08)*	300.43 (52.79)*	10043.7**	1984 (4.12)*	36.45 (6.40)*	18371.9**	48181 (100.00)*	569.11 (100.00)*	11811.9**

Source: NABARD's Online Data upto March 2002

* Figures in parentheses denote column percentage

** Figures in parentheses denote row percentage.

coverage of women self-help groups and also sanctioned credit amount.

Madhya Pradesh state's banking institutions come next in their coverage of women SHGs and in the sanction of credit (16.56%). However, they have covered 27.40 per cent of the sanctioned bank credit of the central region. Among the banking institutions in Madhya Pradesh state, Regional Rural Banks have covered the majority of the SHGs and also in sanctioned loan amount Chhattisgarh state's banking institutions occupy the third position (7.81%) in their coverage of women SHGs in their credit scheme. However, they lag behind Uttaranchal state's banking institutions with respect to sanctioned credit amount and also per group credit amount.

A keen observation of data in table-5 indicates the performance of banking institutions in financing women development programme in the Western region. This region has 3 states, viz., Goa, Gujarat and Maharashtra. The Western region's banking institutions have covered 29,318 women self-help groups in their credit scheme and they have sanctioned a credit amount of Rs.515.12 millions. Their per group credit provision amount is worked out to Rs.17,570. The banking institutions of Maharashtra state have covered about two-thirds of the women SHGs in the Western region in their credit scheme. In this state, Commercial Banks have covered the majority of the SHGs followed by Regional Rural Banks and Cooperative Banks.

Gujarat state's banking institutions come next in position (32.39%) in their coverage of women SHGs in their provision of credit in the Western region. The performance of Cooperative Banks is the least in the state with respect to coverage of SHGs in the provision of credit. Goa state's banking institutions are placed at the last in order (0.69%) with respect to coverage of women SHGs in provision of credit under various anti-poverty programmes. Regional Rural Banks have not involved themselves in financing women SHGs in Goa state and most of the groups and credits are covered by the Commercial Banks in Goa state.

Table 5
Performance of Banking Institutions in Financing Women Self-help Groups in the Western Region

State	Commercial Banks		Per capita loan per SHG (in Rs)	Regional Rural Banks		Per capita loan per SHG (in Rs.)	Cooperative Banks		Per capita loan per SHG (in Rs.)	Total		Per capita loan per SHG (in Rs.)
	No. of SHGs	Bank Loan		No. of SHGs	Bank Loan		No. of SHGs	Bank Loan		No. of SHGs	Bank Loan	
Goa	179	5.91	33016.7**	–	–	–	24	1.28	53333.3**	203	7.19	35418.7**
	(88.18)*	(82.20)*					(11.82)*	(17.80)*		(0.69)*	(1.40)*	
Gujarat	6760	45.29	6699.7**	2403	34.51	14361.2**	333	5.11	15345.3**	9496	84.91	8941.6**
	(71.19)*	(53.34)*		(25.31)*	(40.64)*		(3.50)*	(6.02)*		(32.39)*	(16.48)*	
Maharashtra	11438	278.66	24362.6**	6315	116.74	18486.1**	1866	27.62	14801.7**	19619	423.02	21561.7**
	(58.30)*	(65.87)*		(32.19)*	(27.60)*		(9.51)*	(6.53)*		(66.92)*	(82.12)*	
Total	18377	329.86	1794.6**	8718	151.25	17349.1**	2223	34.01	15299.1**	29318	515.12	17570.0**
	(62.68)*	(64.04)*		(29.74)*	(29.36)*		(7.58.)*	(6.60)*		(100.00)*	(100.00)*	

Source: NABARD's Online Data upto March 2002

* Figures in parentheses denote column percentage

** Figures in parentheses denote row percentage.

Data presented in table 6 indicate the performance of banking institutions in financing women development programmes in the Southern region. The Southern region has four states and one union territory viz., Andhra Pradesh, Karnataka, Kerala, Tamil Nadu and Pondicherry. The Southern region's banking institutions have covered 358689 women self-help groups in their credit scheme and sanctioned a credit amount of Rs. 8313.14 millions upto March 2002. Their per group credit provision level is worked out to Rs. 23,176.6. Among the banks in the Southern region, Commercial Banks have covered more than a half of the SHGs in their credit provision (60.16%) followed by Regional Rural Banks (34.02%) and Cooperative Banks (5.82%). Among the states in the Southern region, the banking institutions of Andhra Pradesh occupy the first position (67.95%) in their coverage of women SHGs in their credit scheme and also sanctioned credit amount (62.7%). In this state, the role of Cooperative Banks is the least in coverage of women SHGs and also sanctioned credit amount. The banking institutions of Tamil Nadu state and Pondicherry come next in position (17.62%) in their coverage of women SHGs in their provision of credit under various anti-poverty programmes. Here also Cooperative Banks play the least role. Karnataka state's banking institutions have covered 10.32 per cent of the SHGs of the Southern region and provided of credit and it occupies the third position in the Southern region. In this state, though the Regional Rural Banks lag behind Commercial Banks in their coverage of women SHGs, they have sanctioned more bank credit and also per group credit than others.

The banking institutions of Kerala state are placed last in their coverage of women SHGs (4.1%) and in provision of credit in the Southern region. The majority of the SHGs and sanctioned credit amount are covered by Commercial Banks in Kerala state. Among the states in the Southern region more amount of the group credit is given in Tamil Nadu state than in others.

Data presented in table 7 indicate the region-wise performance of banking institutions in financing women development programmes. The Northern region's banking institutions have covered 3.84 per cent of the women SHGs in

Table 6
Performance of Banking Institutions in Financing Women Self-help Groups in the Southern Region

State	*Commercial Banks*		*Per capita loan per SHG (in Rs)*	*Regional Rural Banks*		*Per capita loan per SHG (in Rs.)*	*Cooperative Banks*		*Per capita loan per SHG (in Rs.)*	*Total*		*Per capita loan per SHG (in Rs.)*
	No. of SHGs	*Bank Loan*		*No. of SHGs*	*Bank Loan*		*No. of SHGs*	*Bank Loan*		*No. of SHGs*	*Bank Loan*	
Andhra Pradesh	149279 (61.25)*	3353.90 (64.34)*	22467.3**	89042 (36.54)*	1778.62 (34.12)*	19975.0**	5393 (2.21)*	80.05 (1.54)*	14843.3**	243714 (67.95)*	5212.57 (67.71)*	21388.0**
Karnataka	17118 (46.22)*	217.85 (30.46)*	12726.3**	11735 (31.69)*	302.17 (42.25)*	25749.4**	8179 (22.09)*	195.17 (27.29)*	23862.3**	37032 (10.32)*	715.19 (8.60)*	19312.7**
Kerala	10011 (67.83)*	199.52 (58.68)*	19930.0**	3478 (23.57)*	63.80 (18.76)*	18343.8**	1270 (8.60)*	76.70 (22.56)*	60393.7**	14759 (4.11)*	340.02 (4.09)*	23038.1**
Tamil Nadu & UT of Pondicherry	39372 (62.31)*	1373.98 (67.18)*	34897.3**	17757 (28.10)*	479.71 (23.45)*	27015.2**	6055 (9.59)*	191.67 (9.37)*	31654.8**	63184 (17.62)*	2045.36 (24.60)*	32371.4*
Total	215780 (60.16)*	5145.25 (61.89)*	23844.8**	122012 (34.02)*	2624.30 (31.57)*	21508.5**	20897 (5.82)*	543.59 (6.54)*	26012.8**	358689 (100.00)*	8313.14 (100.00)*	23176.4**

Source: NABARD's Online Data upto March 2002

* Figures in parentheses denote column percentage

** Figures in parentheses denote row percentage.

their credit scheme and they have covered 3.64 per cent of the total bank Credit provided in the country. In this region Commercial Banks occupy the first position in financing women development programmes, Regional Rural Banks the second and Cooperative Banks the last.

The banking institutions in the North-eastern region have covered 0.29 per cent of SHGs and 0.24 per cent of the total bank credit given to the women SHGs in the country. The majority of SHGs and bank credit have been covered by the Regional Rural Banks in the North-eastern region. The role of Cooperative Banks is found to be the least.

Eastern region's banking institutions have covered 9.12 per cent of SHGs in the country, but they have covered 4.58 per cent of the total bank credit given to the SHGs in the country. In this region also Regional Rural Banks occupy the predominant position in catering to the financing needs of the women SHGs.

The banking institutions of the Central region have covered 9.58 per cent of the women SHGs in the country and 5.56 per cent of the disbursed bank credit. The performance of Cooperative Banks is the least in this region. The Western region's banking institutions have covered 5.87 per cent of the women SHGs in their credit scheme and they have taken 5.02 per cent of the total credit disbursed in the country. In this region, the Commercial Banks have played a major role in their coverage of women SHGs and also provision of loan amount.

It is significant to note that the banking institutions in the Southern region have covered 71.34 per cent of women SHGs in their credit plan in India and they have also covered 80.99 per cent of the bank credit provided to the SHGs in the country. In this region also, Commercial Banks have played a major role in their coverage of women SHGs and also in sanctioned loan.

At the All India level the banking institutions have covered 502891 women SHG in their credit plan and sanctioned a credit amount of Rs. 10263.37 millions as on March 2002. At the All India level, Commercial Banks occupy the first position in

Table 7
Region-Wise Performance of Banking Institutions in Financing Women Self-help Groups

Region/State	Commercial Banks No. of SHGs	Commercial Banks Bank Loan	Regional Rural Banks No. of SHGs	Regional Rural Banks Bank Loan	Cooperative Banks No. of SHGs	Cooperative Banks Bank Loan	Total No. of SHGs	Total Bank Loan
Northern Region	8661 (44.83)*	150.65 (40.38)*	7204 (37.28)*	146.25 (39.19)*	3456 (17.89)*	543.59 (6.54*)	19321 (3.84)**	373.11 (-3.64)**
Northern Eastern Region	508 (34.09)*	12.53 (49.33)*	974 (65.37)*	12.70 (50.00)*	8 (0.54)*	36.45 (6.40)*	1490 (0.29)**	25.40 (0.24)**
Eastern Region	14636 (31.89)*	138.55 (29.64)*	19918 (43.40)*	224.51 (48.02)*	11338 (24.71)*	104.45 (22.34)*	45892 (9.12)**	467.51 (-4.55)**
Central Region	16285 (33.80)*	232.23 (40.81)*	29912 (62.08)*	300.43 (52.79)*	1984 (4.12)*	34.01 (6.60)*	48181 (9.58)**	569.11 (-5.5)**
Western Region	18377 (62.68)*	329.86 (64.04)*	8718 (29.74)*	151.25 (29.36)*	2223 (7.58)*	76.21 (20.43)*	29318 (5.83)**	515.12 (-5.02)**
Southern Region	215780 (60.16)*	5145.25 (61.89)*	122012 (34.02)*	2624.30 (31.57)*	20897 (5.82)*	0.17 (0.67)*	358689 (71.34)**	8313.14 (-80.99)**
Grand Total	274247 (54.53)**	6009.07 (58.54)*	188738 (30.53)*	3459.44 (33.70)*	39906 (14.94)*	794.88 (7.76)*	502891**	10263.37 (100.00)**

Source: NABARD's Online Data upto March 2002

* Figures in parentheses denote column percentage

** Figures in parentheses denote row percentage.

financing women development programme, Regional Rural Banks the second and Cooperative Banks the last.

It could be seen clearly from the above discussion that the banking institutions in the Southern region have covered more than two-thirds of the women SHGs in their credit plan and they have also covered most of the given bank credit to the SHGs in the country. The reason is women SHGs programmes have been vigorously implemented in the Southern states, notably Andhra Pradesh and Tamil Nadu. The banking institutions of the central region occupy the second position in their performance on financing women SHGs and Regional Rural Banks have played a major role in their coverage of women SHGs in financing them to sustain their economic empowerment. In the central region, the banking institutions of Uttar Pradesh alone have played a significant role in their coverage of SHGs. The performance of SHGs coverage is quite low in Chhattisgarh state and Uttaranchal states since they are newly formed states. The Eastern region's banking institutions are put third in order in their coverage of women SHGs in their credit plan along with disbursed bank credit to the SHGs in the country. In this region, Regional Rural Banks have played a major role in their credit coverage of women SHGs. Though Bihar is the second largest state in India, it has covered a low proportion of women SHGs under its bank credit programmes. The banking institutions in Orissa and West Bengal states in the Eastern region have got considerable level of coverage of women SHGs in their credit plan.

The banking institutions of the Western region are the fourth in order in their credit coverage of women SHGs in the country. This region has got a major benefit from the Commercial Banks. The banking institutions of Maharashtra state are noteworthy in their coverage of SHGs and also sanctioned bank credit. The Northern region's banking institutions occupy the fifth position in their credit coverage of women SHGs and the North eastern region's banking institutions are placed last category in this regard. The performance of banking institutions in financing women development has some short-comings. In order to overcome those short-comings, the following suggestions may be considered:

1. Though Bihar state has more poor households, the coverage of women SHGs is quite low. Hence, the government of Bihar should form more women SHGs and they should take proper steps in making availability of bank credit to the members of SHGs.
2. In some states, the Cooperative Banks do not involve themselves in financing women development programmes, as in Haryana, Manipur, Meghalaya, Sikkim, Nagaland, Arunachal Pradesh and Jharkhand. Hence, efforts should be made to involve Cooperative Banks in financing women development programmes. Further, women SHGs are to be motivated to get membership in Cooperative Banks.
3. There is a need to form more SHGs in the newly bifurcated states like Chhattisgarh and Uttaranchal and they should be made accessible to bank credit.
4. The North Eastern region is a most backward state in the country, where the performance of banking institutions in credit coverage of women SHGs is quite discouraging. Hence, the governments of Manipur, Meghalaya, Sikkim, Tripura, Nagaland and Assam states should take appropriate steps to encourage poor women to form self-help groups and thereby make accessible to bank credit.
5. Regional Rural Banks do not involve themselves in financing women development programmes in some states like Manipur, Sikkim, Arunachal Pradesh and the Anadaman and Nicobar Islands. Hence efforts are to be made to start more number of Regional Rural Banks in these regions.
6. The proportion of bank credit in relation to number of SHGs is quite low in some States/ UTs in terms of per group credit. Hence, there is a need to increase the per group credit with a view to make the utmost benefit of bank credit to all the members of a self-help groups.

7. The government should allocate more funds for rural development particularly banks credit for the benefit of poor women in the backward and isolated areas.

REFERENCES

Abudl, M., and D. Dakshinamurthy, (1983), Rich Farmers Garb all Benefits, Leave Poor Farmers in the Lurch, Yojana, Vol. 27, No. 13, July p. 23.

B.S. Mathur, (1968), "Increasing Agricultural Productivity, Role of Institutional Credit, "Journal of Productivity, Vol. 9 No. 2, p. 98.

Bhabatosh Dutta, (1979), Regional Rural Banks, Report of the Review Committee, RBI, Bombay.

First Five Year Plan, Planning Commission, Government of India, p. 163.

Harpal Singh, (1974), Regional Rural Banks, Yojana, Vol. 23, December 16, p. 13.

Recommendation of the Dantwala Committee, (1979), Compiled by AN. Popat, Faculty Member SPBT College, Bombay, April p. 3.

GOI (1972), Report of the Banking Commission, Government of India, p. 490.

14

DEPRIVATION OF WOMEN IN EDUCATION AND EMPLOYMENT IN INDIA: AN HISTORICAL PERSPECTIVE

D. Pulla Rao

INTRODUCTION

Equal opportunities in education and employment will constitute the basic strategy for management of gender diversity. Till very late, women are biased against in both these fields and hence they are left far behind their male counterparts in all fields of modern life. Women did not have their due share in the major fields of human activity, *i.e.*, social, economic and political. Lack of equal access to education deprived their due share in science and technological fields as well. Thus, the single factor i.e., lack of equal access in education deprived equal opportunities to women in all most all modern fields of human life.

Though women constitute about 50 per cent in the total population of the country, most of them are engaged as illiterate, untrained daily wage workers in the primary sectors like agriculture and its allied activities, construction, mining, petty trade etc. In the total labour force, the women labuor constitute about 45.6 per cent in the rural sector and 20.9 per cent in the urban sector for the year 1999-2000. The share of women labour in the organized sector, which requires education, is miserably low at 14.94 per cent in the public sector and 24.16 per cent in the private sector in the year 2001. It is estimated that there are less than 30 female employees for every one-lakh females in the public sector. The rate of female absorption though appears slightly higher in the organized private sector still, it was less than 50 females for every one lakh females in the country as on 31st march, 2002.

Even the rate of growth of women employment over the last 6 years *i.e.*, 1993-94 to 1999-2000 is not encouraging at all. At the over all level, it is less than one per cent (0.8 per cent in rural India and 1.5 per cent in urban India).

The deprivation of women in the economic sector has its reflection in the political sector as well. There are only 44 women M.Ps in the present Lok Sabha who constitute only 8.16 per cent in the total strength of 539.

Thus, it is understood that the women in India are not provided equal opportunities for a better living. The root cause for this one sided management of human affairs could be pinned to lack of equal access in education and employment. It appears that there is a historical deprivation for women in education. The ills of today have their roots in the educational history of India, over the centuries.

In this paper we wish to examine the historical deprivation of women both as the school/college going children as well as teachers at the school education level.

OBJECTIVES

The specific objectives of this paper are:

1. To estimate disparity index between male and female literacy rates for the last 100 years *i.e.*, from 1901-2001.
2. To estimate the growth of enrollment of girls in primary, upper primary, secondary/higher secondary and higher education in India for the last 50 years i.e. from 1950-51 to 1999-2000, and
3. To examine the increase in the number of women teachers employed in primary schools, upper primary schools and high/higher secondary schools for the last 50 years *i.e.* from 1950-51 to 1999-2000.

THE DATA

The secondary data relating to the literacy rates of male and female enrollment of students by sex in primary, upper primary and secondary/higher secondary level and the number of teachers by sex working in primary, upper primary and high/higher secondary schools for the period 1950-51 to 1999-2000 in India are obtained from the Census reports, Selected Educational Statistics, Ministry of HRD, Government of India and Ministry of HRD, Government of India, Annual reports.

SPECIAL SCHEMES AND PROGRAMMES FOR PROMOTING EDUCATION OF GIRLS

Several strategies were adopted to promote education of girls in independent India. Theoretically, all formal and non-formal education and training programmes are open to women also alongwith their male counterparts. However, separate provisions are made for opening of separate institutions or separate wings for women / girls exclusively. Education is free for girls up to the higher secondary stage and several states have made education free for girls right up to the university level as well. Besides, there are other incentives like free noon meals, free books, free uniforms, scholarships for good attendance, bicycles, etc.

In the first three Five Year Plans, girls' education was covered under special component plans with additional allocations. In the Eighth Five Year Plan, a central scheme was introduced to provide funds to the state governments to hire a woman teacher for all single teacher primary schools and also towards cash awards and prizes for villages, blocks and districts with good performance in female education / literacy. Girls belonging to scheduled castes and scheduled tribes received additional benefits for showing better school attendance. In some states girls/women receive a little high amount of scholarship particularly at the post matric and technical educational level as a special incentive for promotion of women education. As a result of the protective discrimination policies under constitutional provisions, the enrollment of the SC and ST girl children has considerably improved.

FEMALE LITERACY

Female literacy is considered to be a more sensitive index of social development compared to overall literacy rates. Female literacy is negatively related with fertility rates, population growth rates, infant and child mortality rates, and shows a positive association with female age at marriage, life expectancy, and participation in modern sectors of the economy. Inspite of the entire above special constitutional provisions and governmental efforts, in the field of education, the disparities between male and female are still large. The gap between the literacy rates of males and females has been persisting since 1901 when the female literacy rate was only 0.60 per cent as against 9.83 per cent among males. The disparity index (ratio of male literacy rate to female literacy rate) in 1901 was 16.38. On the eve of the initiation of planned economic development in 1951 the literacy rate of women was 7.93 per cent. And women education received a phenomenal jerk from 1961. One can notice a double-digit growth rate in that year and it continued to grow at an increasing rate thereafter and even surpassed the cutoff level of 50:50 by the year 2001 (for details please see Table 1).

Table 1
Sex Differences in Literacy Rates in India (1901 to 2001)

Year	*Male literacy rates*	*Female literacy rates*	*Disparity index*
1901	9.83	0.60	16.4
1911	10.56	1.05	10.1
1921	12.21	1.81	7.6
1931	15.59	2.93	5.3
1941	24.90	7.30	3.4
1951	24.95	7.93	3.1
1961	34.44	12.95	2.6
1971	39.45	18.69	2.1
1981	56.50	29.85	1.9
1991	64.13	39.29	1.6
2001	75.85	54.16	1.4

Source: Census Report, 2001

PERCENTAGE SHARE OF FEMALE ENROLLMENT TO TOTAL

Let us now examine the progress of girls' enrollment in primary, upper primary, secondary/higher secondary and higher education stages. As shown in Table-2 in 1950-51, the enrollment of girls was 28.1 per cent at primary school stage, 16.1 per cent at the upper primary stage, 13.3 per cent at secondary/higher secondary level and 10.0 per cent in higher education level compared with the corresponding percentage of 71.9, 83.9, 86.7 and 90.0 per cent among boys. By 1999-2000, the situation has considerably improved at all levels, in favour of females to 43.6 per cent at primary level, 40.4 per cent at upper primary level, 38.9 per cent at secondary/higher secondary level and 39.9 per cent in higher education as against 56.4 per cent in primary stage, 59.6 per cent in upper primary stage, 61.1 per cent in secondary/higher secondary level and 60.1 per cent in higher education stage among boys.

Table 2
Percentage of girls enrollment to total enrollment by stages 1950-51 to 1999-2000

Year	*Primary Stage (I-V)*	*Upper Primary Stage (VI-VIII)*	*Secondary/Higher Secondary(IX-XII)*	*Higher education*
1950-51	28.1	16.1	13.3	10.0
1960-61	32.6	23.9	20.5	20.4
1970-71	37.4	29.3	25.0	20.0
1980-81	38.6	32.9	29.6	26.7
1990-91	41.5	36.7	32.9	32.3
1999-2000	43.6	40.4	38.9	39.9

Sources: 1. Selected Educational Statistics, Ministry of HRD, Govt. of India.
2. Ministry of HRD, Govt. of India, Annual Report, 2000.

It is evident from the growth rates shown in Table–3, the enrollment of girls has increased at a faster rate than that of boys at primary, upper primary, secondary/higher secondary and higher education level. During our study period (1950-51 to 1999-2000) the Annual Compound Growth Rate of enrollment of girls was 4.53 per cent as against 3.12 per cent of boys in primary stage. The corresponding figures were 7.31 and 4.31 in upper primary stage, 8.34 and 5.30 in secondary/higher secondary stage and 10.66 and 6.87 in higher education respectively. The foregoing analysis shows that during the whole period of 50 years after implementation of our constitution, the growth rate of enrollment of girls has been higher than that of boys.

Table 3
Annual Compound growth rate of enrollment by stages 1950-2000

Stage	*Annual compound growth rate during 1950-51 to 1999-2000*	
	Boys (%)	*Girls (%)*
Primary	3.12	4.53
Upper Primary	4.31	7.31
Secondary/higher secondary	5.30	8.34
Higher education	6.87	10.66

Note: Computed on the basis of enrollment of boys and girls in different stages

ENROLLMENT OF FEMALES IN HIGHER, PROFESSIONAL AND TECHNICAL EDUCATION

By 1999-2000 there are 7494 colleges for general education, 540 engineering colleges, 755 medical colleges, 818 Colleges of Teacher Training, and 308 universities including institutions of national importance and research institutions serving more than six million students and scholars in India. There are 1066 Polytechnics, TTIs 4171 and 1319 Teacher Training Schools in 1999-2000.

Though, the share of girls in various faculties has increased very substantially during the last four decades, they continued to be way behind in Arts with 44.7 per cent, Science with 35.6 per cent, Commerce with 31.6 per cent, Education with 47.0 per cent, Engineering and Technology with 19.5 per cent, and Medicine with 38.0 per cent to reach the ideal 50:50 ratio (Please see Table 4)

Table 4
Enrollment of femal·s as percentage to total enrollment in higher education by faculty

Year	*Arts*	*Science*	*Commerce*	*Education*	*Engg./ Tech.*	*Medicine*
1960-61	18.6	0.0	1.1	32.5	0.8	20.4
1970-71	33.5	18.8	2.8	37.3	1.0	21.3
1980-81	37.5	27.9	15.2	46.7	4.6	23.8
1990-91	39.8	36.8	24.0	44.4	10.9	34.3
1999-2000	44.7	35.6	31.6	47.0	19.5	38.0

Source: Dept. of Education Human Resource Development Govt. of India

PROGRESS OF FEMALE TEACHERS

The number of total teachers at the school stage increased phenomenally. During 1950-51 to 1999-2000, at the primary stage their numbers has increased from 538 thousand to 1.9 million and at the upper primary (middle) stage their number has increased from 86 thousand to 1.3 million. As regards high/ higher secondary stage their number has increased from 127 thousand to 1.8 million. With regard to women teachers, the increase is from 15 per cent to 35 per cent at the primary stage; 36 per cent at the upper primary stage; and from 16 per cent to 33 per cent at the secondary/higher secondary level. It is a healthy trend that the number of women teachers is on the raise because of two reasons (1) that it contributes to gender equality, and (2) the women teachers exhibit care and patience, their general traits, in teaching children.

ANNUAL COMPOUND GROWTH RATE FOR WOMEN TEACHERS

We had computed the annual growth rate for the female and male teachers separately for the period 1950-51 to 1999-2000. The results are presented in Table 6

During the period of our study (1950-51 to 1999-2000) the Annual Compound Growth Rate of female teachers was 4.34 per cent as against 2.01 per cent of male teachers in primary schools. The corresponding figures were 7.43 per cent and 4.98 per cent in upper primary schools and 6.96 and 4.85 in high/higher secondary schools respectively. These data indicate that the participation of women has been increasing and increasing at a faster rate than that of male teachers.

Table 5
Percentage of female teachers to total teachers by type of schools (In thousands)

	Primary			*Upper primary*			*High/Hr. Secondary*		
Year	*Male*	*Female*	*Total*	*Male*	*Female*	*Total*	*Male*	*Female*	*Total*
1950-51	456	82(15)	538	73	13(15)	86	107	20(16)	127
1960-61	615	127(17)	742	262	83(24)	345	234	62(21)	296
1970-71	835	225(21)	1080	463	175(27)	638	474	155(25)	629
1980-81	1021	342(25)	1363	598	253(30)	851	669	257(28)	926
1990-91	1143	473(29)	1616	717	356(33)	1073	917	417(31)	1334
1999-2000	1246	658(35)	1904	814	464(36)	1278	1169	579(33)	1748

Sources: (i) Selected Educational statistics, Ministry of HRD, Govt. of India, 1996-97, 1999-2000

(ii) Ministry of HRD, Govt. of India, Annual Report, 1996-97, 2000-01

Note: Figures in parenthesis indicate percentage share of female teachers to total teachers at each stage.

Table 6
Annual Compound growth rate of teachers by type of schools 1950-2000

	Annual compound growth rate during 1950-51 to 1999-2000	
Stage	*Male teachers (%)*	*Female teachers (%)*
Primary	2.01	4.34
Upper Primary	4.98	7.43
High/Higher secondary	4.85	6.96

Note: Computed on the basis of male and female teachers appointed in different stages of schools.

To repeat, the number of women teachers reached an all time high at primary, upper primary and high/higher secondary stage in 1999-2000. The number of both male and female teachers in primary, upper primary and high/higher secondary stage shows as increasing trend over the period of our study. It is particularly noteworthy that the index of female teachers recorded a much higher increase than that of the male teachers. This may be due to implementation of reservation policy in some states in the country in favor of women teachers.

CONCLUSIONS AND RECOMMENDATIONS

From the above analysis it may be concluded that India started at a very low note in respect of female education in the beginning of the century. Education appeared to be almost the male affair and hence they had grabbed all the employment opportunities, all through the ages.

The situation started changing with achieving political independence for the country. The female literacy received a boost particularly from 1961 onwards and along with it, the lady teachers employment had also received a boost.

With the launching of several literacy missions like National Adult Education Programme (NAEP-1978), National Literacy Mission (NLM-1988), Total Literacy Campaigns (TLCs-1989) and Jan Shikshan Nilayams (JSNs-1993), the momentum picked up in both these fields, i.e. education and employment.

However, as noted in our introductory part, the women lag far behind their male counter parts in all major fields i.e. social, economic and political. Unless some new strategies are evolved out for management of gender diversity the progress of women in India will be retarded for some more decades to come.

REFERENCES

Chalam, K.S. (1988), *Education and weaker sections*, Inter-India Publications, New Delhi.

Chauhan, C.P.S., (1990), *Higher Education in India: Achievements, Failures and strategies*, Ashish Publishing House, New Delhi.

Government of India, Dept. of Education, *Annual Report*, Ministry of Human Resource Development, New Delhi, 1998-99.

Mira Seth (2001), *Women and development – The Indian experience*, Sage Publications, New Delhi.

Naik, J.P. (1975), *Elementary education in India – a promise to keep*, Allied Publishers, Bombay.

Nayar, Usha and Janak Duggal (1995), *Women's Equality through curriculum*: Hand Book for Primary Teachers, NCERT.

Nayar, Usha: *Study on Universalization of primary education of rural girls in India,* 1991, Published by the NCERT, 1993 UNESCO.

Rajput, J.S. (1993), *A problem of dropouts, The Hindustan Times, July 10,* New Delhi.

Sakuntala Narasimhan (1999), *Empowering women– an alternative strategy from rural India,* Sage Publications, New Delhi.

Sangeetha Purushothaman (1998), *The empowerment of women in India– grassroots women's networks and the state,* Sage Publications, New Delhi.

15

"A STUDY OF VALUE ADDITION BY THE HOUSEWIVES TO THE FAMILY INCOME THROUGH EXTENDED - SNA ACTIVITIES"

Lakshmi Kulashetra and Sunita Gupta

DISCRIMINATION OF WOMEN IN STATISTICAL DATA

During the decade of 1980, due to feminist movement, issues involving women have received a lot of academic attention but these do not reflect the full extent of Indian women's involvement in productive activities both within household and outside in the wider economy. Human development report 1995 reveals that women work longer hours than men nearly in every country. Of the total burden of work, women carry on an average 53% in developing countries and 51% in industrial countries. Of men's total work time in industrial countries, roughly 2/3rd is spent in paid SNA activities and 1/3rd unpaid Non– SNA activities. For women these shares are reversed. In developing countries more than 3/4th of men's work is in SNA activities. So, men receive the lion's share of income and recognition for their economic contribution, while most of women's work remains unpaid, unrecognized and undervalued. (EPW Oct. 96; Gupta 1998:73).

Within traditional GDP and GNP categories, the whole spectrum of social productivity from the reproduction of human beings in the household to the maintenance of relationships that promote the cohesion of community are ignored. Country's economic performance is historically evaluated from its labour force statistics and national income accounts. Both these have been defined by relating them to the market, or to the performance of some work 'for pay or profit'. "A man or woman who is doing only household duties or making something only for domestic consumption (and not for sale) is not doing any work in Census terminology" (Census of India, 1961, para 84). The devaluation of this work runs parallel to the subordinate status of women who do most of this 'caring and sustaining'. To link productivity only with paid employment continues to render invisible the enormous amount of unpaid work that women do that under girds and subsidizes all other kinds of work. (Juan Somavia, 1993, Summation of exchange of views of the first session of the preparatory committee for the world summit for social development 1993).

This implies that unremunerated work is not to be included in national income, and a person performing it not be counted as a member of the labour force. Thus, such work is considered to be economically insignificant. This results in a lowering of national income and work participation estimates. These loopholes have been to some extent filled up by 1991 Census in India by directing census takers to ask more "probing questions" about women's economic role in the household and to treat as economic activity any service or work which is productive, "even if it does not have a monetary value". This was a positive step to improve the visibility of women's work. (Rao & Pathak; 1996 ; 32).

PRODUCTION BOUNDARY OF 1993 SNA

SNA 1993 describes the SNA conceptual system which is applicable to economies around the world. The production boundary of the United Nations National Accounting system defines the range of economic activities falling within the production boundary as:

1. The production of all individuals or collected goods that are supplied to the market.
2. Own account production that is retained by producers for final consumption or gross capital formation.
3. Own account production of housing services such as services by ownership of dwellings, and/or

4. Domestic or personal services produced by employing paid domestic servants.

PRODUCTION BOUNDARY WITHIN HOUSEHOLDS

Production boundary within household includes:

1. Production of agricultural products, subsequent storage,
2. Gathering of uncultivated crops,
3. Forestry, woodcutting and collection of firewoods, hunting and fishing; mining; supply of water etc.
4. Processing of agricultural products such as threshing and milling grains, making ghee, butter cheese, slaughtering of livestock, producing poultry, utensils, baskets; weaving of clothes etc.

At present goods produced and consumed by households are in general not covered in National Accounting System except the agricultural production by households whether used for self-consumption or sold. The reason for including this agricultural production is that the approach for this sector is the production approach where total output is estimated as producing area and per hectare production norm. It is important to note that even for agricultural production sector, the backyard production of households is not covered, as this area is not a part of area under production of crops in the revenue records. (Indian Economic Journal Vol. 45, 1997).

The 1993 SNA excludes production of all personal and domestic services for own final consumption within households such as children and elder care, cooking, cleaning etc.; except for paid domestic services and owner occupied housing on the grounds that:

1. These activities are self-contained; with limited repercussion on the rest of the economy; decision to produce a household service entails a simultaneous decision to consume that service. This is not true for goods.
2. As the vast majority of households domestic and personal services is not produced for market, there are

typically no prices that can be satisfactorily used to value such services.

3. If personal and domestic services by members of households for own final consumption are included, all persons engaged in such activities would become self-employed making unemployment virtually impossible by definition. (Indian Economic Journal Vol. 45, 1997).

It has been widely accepted and expressed via many studies on women's work that these accounts under-estimate women's work and exclude large number of economic activities undertaken by women, especially in developing countries, where the work is either unpaid or invisible. Since government policy makers do not view women as productive workers, they are not brought into the mainstream of planning process and the economy. The exclusion of unpaid work from national income accounts and labour force participation depresses the estimates. The worldwide facts and statistics about the status of women show that nearly 11 trillion dollars (Jha 1998) is missing from the global economy each year because of unpaid housework, child care, agriculture and labour performed by women. According to official Indian statistics (NSS, 1981) women continue to lag behind men in all spheres of life – social, political and especially economic. During the decade of 1980 due to the feminist movement issues involving women have received a lot of academic attention.

UNPAID WORK IN DEVELOPING COUNTRIES

In poor rural areas of developing regions, a considerable amount of unpaid work is required to maintain in the well being of family members. Only a few studies are available on subsistence work and housework, however, covering three countries in southern Asia, women and girls in these countries spend from 3 to 5 more hours per week in unpaid subsistence work than men – carrying water and wood, growing and processing primary agricultural products for their families, for example – and an additional 20-30 hours more per week in unpaid housework, women spend 31 to 42 hours per week in unpaid housework, according to these studies, while men spend between 5 and 15. Women's total work time ranges from 53 hours per week in Bangladesh to 69 in India and 77 in Nepal, while men's ranges from 46 in Bangladesh to 56-57 hours per week in India and Nepal. Women do the largest share of subsistence work – generally including carrying water, fetching wood and food processing – whereas men's time for paid work is as much as twice that of women. Table 1 explains that men work longer hours in paid economic activities, while women spend more time in household work. Some experts hold that if women's unpaid work were factored into national accounting system, GDP would increase by 30 to 40 percent.

Table 1
Time use in Three South Asian Countries 1989-1992

Country	*Hours/week of Economic Activity (paid & subsistence)*	*Hours/week of House work*	*Total work Hours/week*
Bangladesh (15+)			
Male	41	05	46
Female	22	31	53
Nepal (15+)			
Male	41	15	56
Female	35	42	77
India (18+)			
Male	47	10	57
Female	35	34	69

Source: Compiled by Statistical Division of the United Nations Secretariat

UNDER-ESTIMATION OF WOMEN'S ACTIVITIES IN DOMESTIC FIELD

Until recently, this type of work was not considered as a substitute for market oriented goods and services and was excluded from the definition of economic activity, and hence, was not included in national income accounts. Obviously, this led to depressed estimates of national income and women's contribution to labour force. This practice of exclusion of domestic work from national accounts was questioned (Boserup E, 1970). This can be avoided by including the value of domestic work in national accounts. Though this task was considered to be farfetched and unacceptable around 1970's due to absence of statistical information, it has now become an important issue and constructive work. Household tasks are of two types:- (1) Housework (2) Care giving.

Table 2

SNA Activities	*Extended SNA Activities*	*NON-SNA Activities*
(A) Primary Production activities Crop farming,	(A) Care for children, the sick, elderly, and disabled for won household	* Learning
• Kitchen gardening etc.	(B) Kitchen Management	* Social and cultural activities, mass media, etc.
• Animal husbandry	(C) Household maintenance,	* Personal care and self-maintenance
• Fishing, Forestry,	(D) Community services and help to other households	
• Horticulture, Gardening		
• Collection of fruits, water, plants etc., storing and hunting		
• Processing and storage		
• Mining, quarrying, digging, cutting etc.		
(B) Secondary Activities		
• Construction Activities		
• Manufacturing Activities		
(C) Trade, Business, and Services		
• Trade and Business Services		

Report of the time use Survey Conducted by the CSO during 1998-99, in the Six Selected States Women & Men in India 2000, CSO, Ministry of Statistics & Programme Implementation, GOI.

Housework

Housework involves a range of activities the purpose of which is to maintain household members preparing and cooking meals provides food which enables household members to replenish their energy levels. Satisfactory nourishment is essential if men, women and children are to be able to continue with their daily productive activities. The endless battle against dirt' and to grime battle to guard against disease and to help to protect the general health of the population, cleaning rooms', washing clothes and dishes are other examples of household services which facilitate the continuance of productive activities. Advances in technology have however changed this trend as capital assets have been substituted for labour force. The introduction of automatic washing machine, microwave oven, vacuum cleaner etc. all reduced the number of hours which the average household needs to spend upon domestic tasks; but these appliances still require some labour input. This labour input is still overwhelming by a women's input. (Sue Hatt; 1997: 38).

Nair (1988) observed that women's work does not figure any where in national accounting and she is ironically addressed as non-working women. The major problems faced by enumerators is that most of the labour takes place in what is called as the fifth world – the kitchen. (cited in Saroj Kashyap – 2000, Perspective on Indian Women p 235). Economists do not assign monetary value to this labour but use a category *not economically active home makers* to cover women having this type of occupation. (Boulding : 1977, pp 17-18).

Care giving– Childcare and elderly care

Childcare however is rather different since it does involve the full-time attention of an adult during pre-school years. The provision of care requires the presence of a caregiver. The extent of this commitment reduces as children grow older and become more self-reliant. The duration of the commitment is limited but once again it is seen as the mother's role to provide the care.

The presence of young children in a household increases the amount of work to be done, but studies often find that this extra work is almost all undertaken by the woman. Men usually confine their domestic activities to repairing household equipment, mowing the lawn and keeping the car in running order. Their contribution to household tasks seems to remain constant regardless of the size of the household whilst a woman's workload is significantly affected by the presence and the number of children in the household (Warde and Hetherington 1993).

Whilst the time spent on childcare is falling, the elderly are growing as a proportion of the total population. Nearly 18 per cent of the population in India were over the age of 65 in 1997 (CSO 2000). The elderly are more likely to require care from other family members in future decades and the provision of this care too falls predominantly to women. Unlike childcare, eldercare is hard to anticipate and can be an open-ended commitment. Although housework and childcare requires the exercise of a considerable number of skills – such as time management, negotiation, interpersonal communication and forward planning – skills gained within the household is rarely recognized in the labour market.

Full time homemakers sacrifice years of seniority and experience in employment in order to provide household services and become heavily dependent upon their partner for their material well-being thus reducing their economic independence. Moreover monetary rewards are not the only determinant of the standard of living. We also need to consider the quality of life within the household. Children represent the future generation and their care within the home will affect their economic, social and emotional well-being later in life. Their ability to take their place in the world of the twenty-first century will depend in part on the quality of their experiences in their early years. The skills which workers bring to the labour force, are not acquired in formal education alone; the domestic environment plays an important part in producing the citizens of the future. The care of children is an important economic activity and the future generation might well benefit from experiencing both men and women in the parenting role. (Sue Hatt : 1997 : 48).

Many household tasks are unrelenting. Meals must be prepared three times a day. Child care cannot be delayed until there is free time. On Saturday, women work almost two more hours than men and on Sunday, an hour and a three quarters more – a difference that widens if the family has young children. (data from survey from 18 industrial countries. Mukta Gupta p. 75).

Housework and care giving are areas of economic activities, which economists and statisticians have largely ignored. Housework and childcare are not through there are difficulties in proper classification, and valuation of domestic services, these are not impossible to deal with. This requires frequent sources of data collection, elaboration of statistical information, removal of male bias from studies, and a wider awareness regarding women's contribution to work and economic acitvity.

In the Report of the time use survey conducted by the CSO during 1998-99, in the six selected states, the activity classification was so developed that all the activities can be grouped into 3 categories. The activities under these 3 categories are shown in the table.

According to time use survey conducted by CSO, in the six states of Haryana, Madhya Pradesh, Gujarat, Orissa. Tamil Nadu and Meghayala, on the average, male spent about 42 hours in SNA activities as compared to only about 19 hours by females. However, situation completely changes when we consider Extended-SNA activities. In these household and care related activities, male spent only about 3.6 hours as compared to 34.6 hours by females. Therefore female spend about ten times more time in extended activities, as compared to male. In NON-SNA activities, which pertains to learning, leisure and personal care, male spent about 8 hours more as compared to female. On the average 71% of the time spent in NON-SNA activities. The SNA and Extended-SNA contribute for 18% and 11% respectively. (Table 3) (CSO 2000).

SIGNIFICANCE OF THE STUDY

Chapter 4 of HDR 95, 'Valuing Women's work' is sensitive, well informed and raises the issues that feminists – both academicians and activists – have been grappling with for many decades–coming into international advocacy from Mexico 1975, (the first UN conference on women) through Nairobi 1985, (the third UN conference on women), and Beijing 1995 (the fourth UN conference on women) to the present time. There is a strong case for monetization of non-market activities on the grounds that–

Table 3
State-wise Weekly Average Time (in hrs.) Spent on SNA, Extended-SNA and NON-SNA by Sex and Place of Residence

Combined States	*Rural*			*Urban*			*Total*		
	Male	*Female*	*Total*	*Male*	*Female*	*Total*	*Male*	*Female*	*Total*
SNA	42.31	22.53	32.72	41.06	9.16	25.77	41.96	18.72	30.75
Extended-SNA	3.74	33.95	18.40	3.44	36.44	19.26	3.65	34.63	18.69
NON-SNA	121.98	111.50	116.89	123.47	122.44	123.03	122.42	114.58	118.62
Total	168.03	168.98	168.01	167.97	168.04	168.06	168.06	167.93	168.06

Report of the time use Survey conducted by the CSO during 1998-99, in the Six Selected States Women and Men in India 2000, CSO, Ministry of Statistics & Programme Implementation, IGO.

(1) Not giving an economic valuation to these activities risks seriously under-estimating the contribution of women and reduces women to virtual non-entities in most economic transactions – such as property ownership or offering collateral for bank loans.

(2) Because, status in contemporary society is so often equated with income earning power, women suffer a major under valuation of their economic status.

(3) Men's paid work in the market-place is often the result of 'joint production', much of which might not be possible if women did not stay at home looking after the children and the household.

(4) Now, however, as increasing numbers of women move into the paid labour force, the opportunity cost of such production is becoming dearer, and economists are more interested in assigning a valuation.

There exists a fundamental belief that people, who are economically productive, do the real work and housework is not real work at all. Any academic study of household labour therefore must challenge at least this assumption that household work can have no monetary value. Women concerned must be incorporated in development plans. With this background in mind, the present study was undertaken to study the problem.

OBJECTIVES

Major objectives of the study are 1. To review the National Accounting System and it's in built problems for dealing with work situations that are common to all developing countries; to develop a model for the quantification of the services of the housewives in monetary terms and to estimate the housewives' time allocation on various household activities to estimate the value addition to the family income by the housewives.

RESEARCH METHODOLOGY

To capture the activity of production of goods and services within the households, there is only one comprehensive technique – the systematic time use surveys, where one gets on idea of the amount of time spent by households, in particular by females. Taking wage rates as proxies from other sources, value of these goods and services can be imputed.

The Present Study has been conducted into Two Stages:

(A) Estimating the volume of labour inputs put into household domestic activities by housewives, usually expressed in labour time. This is measured in hours and minutes per day, and averaging it over the week and month.

(B) Assigning this input a market value of housewife's service in her various capacities.

ASSUMPTIONS

(a) The question of value is simplified by assuming that one hour of market and one hour non-market work have the same value.

(b) Productivity differences between market and non-market work and quality of work have not been considered.

(c) No division has been made on the basis of skilled and unskilled labour. All the activities have been assessed on the wage rate for unskilled work.

(d) A working day for women was considered of 14 hours, from 6 a.m. to 8 p.m.

(e) Personal or non-economic activities (NON-SNA) have not been included in the study. The distinction between economic and personal or non-economic activities have been made by applying the third person principal.

(f) Only those activities pertaining to the category of Extended-SNA have been included. (CSO 2000).

SAMPLE SIZE/SAMPLE SELECTION

The sample, on which this study is conducted, consisted of 100 housewives, time constraints did not permit a sizable selection of families to be included in the sample; Families were selected to represent a cross section of societies. Variables undertaken were age, family income, educational level of the housewives and number of children and elders present in the family. The survey was conducted in 20 localities in the city of Agra dominated by middle class families.

The survey was purposive and no household listing prior to the survey was carried out. Housewives from such families were randomly selected where household tasks are wholly or mainly shouldered by the housewives themselves and they are not employed outside the home.

The observations have been randomized at various times so that they can be representatives of all activities. Each family has been observed on three types of days – on a normal day, on a weekly variant and on an abnormal day *i.e.* festival, function party etc. A working day for women was considered of 14 hours, from 6 a.m. to 8 p.m.

Table 4
Activity wise Average per hour Market Rate

S.No.	*Activity*	*Per hour Average market rate (Rs.)*
1.	Child Development and caring	6
2.	Kitchen Management	9.5
3.	Home Management	17
4.	Clothing	5

The market wage selected was that of a substitute household worker. For calculating wages for each activity, a schedule was administered to 15 respondents so as to calculate the wages. Average possible wages were computed from the schedule. Activity wise per hour market rates has been given in the table 4.

RESPONDENTS PROFILE

1.	Total No. of Respondents	100
2.	Mean age of housewife	35.34 years
	(a) Below 40 or equal to 40	73.00
	(b) Above 40 but less than 60	27.00
3.	Average Family Size	4.9
4.	Average Number of Children	02.09
5.	Distribution of family by monthly income	
	(a) Below 5000	28
	(b) 5000 to 10,000	44
	(c) Above 10,000	28
6.	Distribution of family by Number of Children	
	(a) No Children	18
	(b) One Child	26
	(c) Two or more children	56
7.	Distribution of family by Number of elders Present	
	(a) No elder	70
	(b) One elder	16
	(c) Two elders	14
8.	Distribution of the families by the Housewife's level of Education	
	(a) Intermediate & Below	26
	(b) Graduate and above	74
9.	Distribution of families by Occupation Husband	
	(a) Service	55
	(b) Business	39
	(c) Profession	06

LIMITATIONS OF THE STUDY

Of course, there are some problems in the time use approach, for example,

1. Practically no one engages in any activity in isolation or in strict sequence. Many different tasks and the time spent on them tend to be simultaneous or to overlap; Due to differences in their efficiency of doing domestic work, housewives take different time to produce the same output or produce different quality of output with the same time, creating difficulties for imputation of their values, both in terms of labour input or production of output; Direct observation method is likely to overlook an important aspect, that is of double counting of time. This can result in an upward bias of the results.
2. Lack of awareness about proper timing; ignorance and inability to report two or more activities done simultaneously and unwillingness on the part of respondents to answer the question are other problem, which were faced by the investigator during the study. Direct observation made the subject conscious hence normal pattern of work might not be captured; Respondents might forget to mention irregular and short duration activities. Dual activities are often missed out in yesterday recall method. Study used the recall method and therefore the results are likely to suffer from memory bias.

RESULTS AND DISCUSSIONS

1. By assumption, a housewives' monthly total time allocation under all activities and all categories have been 14 hours a day (6.00 a.m. to 8.00 p.m.) and 420 hours a month but it exceeds the assumed time limit of 420 hours. This can be attributed to two reasons –
   (a) There is an element of overlapping in many activities which could not be segregated by the observer.
   (b) The housewives duties do not draw to a close at 8 p.m. as would in case of a marketed activity and continues even beyond the official working hours. Thus total working hours exceeded our assumed time limit.

"A study of Value Addition by the Housewives to the Family Income Through Extended-SNA Activities"

	Activity Classification	*child development & Caring*		*Kitchen Manage ment*		*Home Manage ment*		*Community service*		*Total*	
Category of house wives		Time Allocation (hours)	Value Addition (Rs.)	Time Allocation (hours)	Value Addition (Rs.)	Time Allocation (hours)	Value Addition (Rs.)	Time Allocation (hours)	Value Addition (Rs.)	Time Allocation (hours)	Value Addition (Rs.)
Total	All	123.46	1172.90	186.92	1121.5	97.27	1653.59	51.43	257.15	459.08	3442.8
		(26.89)	(34.06)	(40.71)	(32.57)	(21.18)	(48.03)	(11.20)	(7.46)		
By Age	Below 40	141.60	1345.2	187.96	1127.76	93.96	1597.32	50.31	25.55	473.83	3582.68
		(29.88)	(37.54)	(39.66)	(31.47)	(19.82)	(44.58)	(10.61)	(0.71)		
	Above 40+	61.45	583.8	184.13	1104.78	106.18	1805.60	54.27	271.55	406.03	2936.9
		(15.13)	(19.87)	(45.34)	(37.61)	(26.15)	(61.47)	(13.36)	(9.24)		
By Income	Upto 5000	106.47	1011.5	170.63	1023.8	98.29	1534.93	39.22	196.10	406.61	3053.12
		(26.18)	(33.13)	(41.96)	(33.53)	(24.17)	(50.27)	(9.64)	(6.42)		
	5000-10,000	101.66	965.80	184.42	1106.50	94.53	1607.01	53.54	2677	434.15	3215.91
		(23.41)	(30.03)	(42.47)	(34.40)	(21.77)	(49.97)	(12.33)	(83.24)		
	above 10,000	156.69	1488.60	207.03	1242.20	108.55	1845.35	60.55	302.75	532.82	4021.30
		(29.40)	(37.01)	(38.85)	(30.89)	(20.37)	(45.88)	(11.36)	(7.52)		
No. of elders present in the family	No. elders	116.51	1106.8	184.38	1104.80	95.83	1629.11	50.80	254.0	447.52	3345.0
		(26.03)	(33.08)	(41.02)	(33.02)	(21.41)	(48.70)	(11.35)	(7.59)		

Contd....

	Activity Classification	child development & Caring		Kitchen Management		Home Management		Community service		Total	
	one elder	138.08	1311.8	205.89	1235.30	109.76	1865.92	61.23	306.15	514.36	3852.7
		(26.84)	(34.04)	(40.02)	(32.06)	(21.33)	(48.43)	(11.20)	(7.9)		
	Two elders	136.63	1298	177.76	1066.60	90.55	1539.35	43.48	217.4	448.42	3407.40
		(30.46)	(38.09)	(39.64)	(31.03)	(20.19)	(45.17)	(9.69)	(6.38)		
No. of children present in the family	No child	58.86	559.20	202.40	1214.40	117.55	1998.35	59.55	297.75	438.36	3145.6
		(13.42)	(17.77)	(46.17)	(38.60)	(26.81)	(63.52)	(13.58)	(9.46)		
	One child	119.58	1136.0	187.48	1124.9	101.62	1727.54	55.55	277.75	464.23	3473.6
		(25.75)	(32.70)	(40.38)	(32.38)	(21.89)	(45.73)	(11.96)	(7.99)		
	Two or more children	133.49	1298.1	181.58	1089.4	98.81	679.79	46.84	234.20	450.72	3403.61
		(29.61)	(38.13)	(40.28)	(32.00)	(21.92)	(19.97)	(10.39)	(6.68)		
Education of house wives	Intermediate or below	102.35	972.3	201.17	1207.0	110.36	1876.12	59.89	299.45	473.77	3481.6
		(21.60)	(27.92)	(42.46)	(34.66)	(23.29)	(53.88)	(12.64)	(8.60)		
	Graduate or above	128.82	1223.8	181.85	1091.1	92.75	1576.75	48.53	242.65	451.95	341105
		(28.50)	(0.35)	(40.23)	(0.31)	(20.51)	(0.46)	(10.73)	(0.07)		

Note: Figures in parenthesis indicate per cent of the total.
Source: Primary Data

2. The maximum time of housewives is taken up by kitchen activities (40 per cent) and child development and caring (27 per cent) which amounts to 67 per cent of the total time allocation of housewives on domestic activities followed by household maintenance and community services.
   Out of the total value addition of rupees 3442.78, by housewives to the family income through Extended SNA activities, maximum contribution comes from child development and caring activities (34 per cent). Kitchen activities are the second income contributing activity. (32.6 per cent).
3. The time allocation according to age reveals that:
   (a) Women of both the groups under study spend maximum of their time at kitchen activities (39 per cent and 45 per cent respectively).
   (b) Women below 40 spent 30 per cent of their time on childcare while women above 40 spent most of their time on other activities such as home management, clothing, socializing etc. Thus, the younger women's contribution is more by Kitchen and caring activities; while regarding the activities, women of 40+ add more value as compared to their younger counterparts.
   (c) The value addition in absolute terms by housewives below 40 is greater (Rupees. 3582.60) than the value added by housewives of 40+ (Rs. 2936.9). The contribution in the form of child development and caring is greater for women below 40. (Rupees 1345); which is more than twice the contribution of women 40+ (Rupees 583.80).
4. Time allocation and value addition according to the family income reveals that—
   (a) Women of all income groups spend most of their time in kitchen related activities (42 per cent, 42 per cent and 39 per cent). A closer inspection reveals that women in higher income groups spend marginally less time (39 per cent) in kitchen as

compared to 42 per cent of lower income families. This may be attributed to the availability of sophisticated kitchen appliances.

(b) The findings lead us to conclude that women belonging to upper income group give more time to children and kitchen in spite of better availability of household appliances and outside help, which require greater supervision and maintenance.

(c) Contrary to the popular belief, study finds that housewives in upper income group contribute more (Rupees 4021.30) than women with lower family income (Rupees 3053). The contribution of lower family is only 67.4 per cent of their better off counterparts for child development activities and 82.4 per cent for kitchen related activities. For clothing and socializing activities, it is also less than the better off counterparts.

5. Time allocation according to the number of elders present in the families shows that:

(a) In families with two or more elders, the housewives contribute more time (30 per cent) in care giving than the family with one elder only (27 per cent).

(b) Under kitchen activity, much variation was not found (40-41 per cent). This may be because the elderly in the family share kitchen related activities. So that whatever time required due to the pressure of elders leveled off by their sharing.

(c) Housewife's contribution is greater in families with one elder (Rupees 3852/-) than the two elders' families (Rupees 3407/-), and lowest in no elder family (Rupees 3345). In one elders' family, the contribution of housewife is greater by 13 per cent as compared to that of a women with two elders family, it is due to that fact that housewife has to spend more time on caring, kitchen and socializing.

6. Time allocation according to number of children reveals that:
   (a) There is major variation regarding percentage of time spent on care giving in families with children. Families without child, 13 per cent of time is spent on caring but when there is one child, this time doubles to 26% and in case of two or more children, there is not much variation and it becomes only 29 per cent.
   (b) Women with no child family spends greater time on socializing (13 per cent) as against (10-11 per cent) by one, two or more children family. The housewife having no child contribute more by home management and community services.
   (c) The economic contribution of housewife having two or more children is less than the housewife who has only one child. The reasons is that playing of the children with siblings save the housewives time.
7. Time allocation according to educational level of housewives reveals that:
   (a) More educated women spend less time in kitchen (39 per cent) and more on care giving (29 per cent) *vis-a-vis* as compared to those with less education (42 per cent and 22 per cent respectively). It clearly indicates better time management and greater involvement in child development for educational women.
   (b) Comparing the value addition according to educational level of housewife, there is no significant difference between the two groups.
   (c) Activity wise contribution reveals that more educated women contribute more through child development (35.9) as they spend greater time on guidance and caring of children. In all other categories contributing to family income is greater for less educated women.
8. It is important to note that the rate per hour taken is the minimum rate admissible for the unskilled labour.

Had we taken wages for skilled labour this contribution would have increased manifold. In addition, there are various activities, which are neither visible nor accessible to the observer and as such as the caring, sharing, and sacrifices of the housewives in undertaking these activities.

SUGGESTIONS

On the basis of the experience of the present study and its findings, following suggestions can be put forward.

1. Domestic activities, because they are fully non-marketed, require social evaluation techniques similar to those used for other non-marketed activities like subsistence agriculture.
2. There is need to reconcile the inadequate system of macro data collection and measurement with various micro studies that seek to measure women's work. This calls for cooperative efforts of NGOs, Governments, researchers and professional institutions.
3. There is need for revision of concepts, definition of keywords, statistical classification, standardization of data to have better comparability.
4. Though there are difficulties in proper classification and valuation of domestic services, these are not impossible to deal with. This requires frequent sources of data collection, elaboration of statistical information, removal of male bias from study and wider awareness regarding women's work and economic activity.
5. National statistics on employment, mortality, morbidity etc. disaggregated by gender and timely and regular availability of socio-economic indicators on women should be ensured to provide the widest possible audience with accurate and full information on women's productive and reproductive responsibilities. Women can form 'self-help groups' and come forward for propagating and creating awareness about women's contribution to family income.

CONCLUSION

Policy makers have the tendency to define women exclusively in terms of their social roles and to ignore their economic roles. They have simply assumed that what men do is publicly important, measurable and subject to the influence of government policy, while what women do is seen as private, important only to the individuals involved, unmeasurable and subject to the influence of culture, rather than public policy. Such assumptions leads to definitions of work, of production, of household's decision-making, which make women's productive role as invisible in national and international statistics.

Recently, policy makers are becoming more aware that ignoring women's productive role is a serious distortion of reality, which reduces the efficiency as well as the equity of government programmes. They have been helped to reach this awareness by women themselves, who have become increasingly active on their own behalf; lobbying governments and insisting on accountability.

The present study is a humble effort to devise a method to not only make visible but also to highlight the enormous amount of unpaid work that women do that under girds and subsidizes all other kinds of work. Though there are difficulties in valuation of domestic services, but they are not impossible to deal with. Women must receive due place in economic and social sphere.

BIBLIOGRAPHY

Ahooja Patel Krishna (1995), *Women and Sustainable Development* – An International Dimension, Ashish Publishing House, New Delhi.

Ahooja Patel Krishna, Uma Devi. S., Tadas. G.A. (Eds) (1999), *Women and Development* – Har-Anand Publications, New Delhi.

Amsden, Alice H. (1980), *The Economics of Women and Work, St. Martins* Press, New York.

Boulding, E, (1997), The world of women; household patterns and women's occupation around the work. Women in the twentieth century, World, pp. 17-18.

Beneria, Lourder (1992), *Account for women's work* – The progress of two decades, World Development, Vol. 20, No. 11, 1992.

Bhattacharya, Sudhir, (1985), *On the Issues of under Enumeration of women's work in the Indian Data collection system.*

Bhattacharya, Sudhir, (1981), *Women's Activities in Rural India:* A study based on NSS 32nd Round (1977-78), NSSO Department of statistics, Govt. of India, June, 1981.

Boserup, E. (1970), *Women's Role in Economic Development,* Allen and Unwin, London.

Borooah, Romy & Cloud Kathleen (Eds) (1994), Capturing Complexity – An Interdisciplinary look at Women, Households and Development, Sage Publications, New Delhi.

Dixit Maitreya (Eds), (1998), *Women and Achievement,* Dynamics of Participation and Partnership, Kanishka Publishers, New Delhi.

Hawrylyshyne Oli (1976), *The value of Household Services:* A survey of Empirical Estimates, Review of Income and Wealth, 22, 1976.

International Labour Office, Geneva (1982), *"Women, work and Development"*, Unpaid Work in the Household.

ILO, Economically Active Population, *Estimates and Projections, 1950-2025,* Third Edition 1986.

ILO, Women in the World of Work, Statistical Analysis and Projections to the year 2000, Trends and Prospects ILO 1989.

Indian Council of Social Science Research (ICSSR) (1975), *Status of women in India,* Allied Publishers, New Delhi.

Jain Devaki, (1985), Domestic Work – *Its Implication for Enumeration on women's work and Employment;* Women, work and Society edited by K. Saradamoni, Calcutta.

Jain Devaki and Banerjee Nirmala (Eds) (1985), *Women in Poverty:* Tyranny of the Household, Shakti Book, Delhi.

Papola T.S. and Sharme A.N. (Eds) (1999), Gender and employment in India, Vikas Publishing House Pvt. Ltd., Delhi.

Palmor A. (1998), Gender of economics and the economics of Gender, working paper in economics' no. 15 university of west of England, Bristol.

Ramu G.N. (1989), Women, Work and Marriage in urban India – A study of Dual and Single Earner couple, Sage Publications, New Delhi.

Rao, A.S. & Pathak D.S. (Eds) (1996), Women in Economic Development – Indo-Canadian Perspective, Creative Book, New Delhi.

Sue Hatt (1997), Gender, work and labour Markets – Macmillan Press, London.

UNDP, Human Development Report – 1994.

Warde, A. and Hetherington K. (1993) – A changing domestic decision of labour? In work. Employment and society, Vol. 7. No. 2 pp. 23-45.

ENCYCLOPAEDIA

1. Degumarti Bhaskara Rao, Degumarti Pushpa Latha (Eds) (1998), International Encyclopaedia of women – Discovery Publishing House, New Delhi.
2. Jha Uma Shankar, Mehta Arti, Menon Latika (Eds) (1998) – Status of Indian women, (1998), Crisis and Conflict in Gender Issues Vol. 1, 2, 3, Kanishka Publishers, New Delhi.
3. Nelly. P. Stroniquist (Eds) (1998), Women in the Third World (An Encyclopaedia of Contemporary Issues).
4. Gupta, Mukta (Ed) (1998)– International Encyclopaedia of Women's Development, Vol. 2 Sarup and Sans, Delhi.

JOURNALS

1. Economic and Political Weekly, October 26, 1996.
2. Economic and Political Weekly, May 9, 1981.
3. Shram Shakti, A Journal of Women's studies, July 1983.
4. The Indian Economic Journal Vol. 45, April-June 1997, No. 4.
5. The Indian Journal of Labour Economics Vol. 35, No. 1, 1992.
6. Indian Journal of Gender studies, Vol. 6, No. 1, January-June 1999.

KEY TERMS AND NOTES

1. Census of India in its instructions manual observes that
   (a) : Work may be defined as participation in any economically productive activity. (Para 79).
   (b) : "A man or woman who is doing only household duties or making something only for domestic consumption (and not for sale) is not doing any work in Census terminology" (Census of India, 1961, Para 84).
2. SNA– System of National Accounting.
3. SNA Activities; those pertaining to system of national accounts.
4. Extended– SNA Activities– any service or work which is productive, "even if it does not have a monetary value". If any activity is of such character that it might be delegated to a paid worker, then that activity shall be deemed productive."
5. NON-SNA Activities– the activities neither considered as economic nor included in the SNA.
6. Third Person Principle– "If any activity is of such character that it might be delegated to a paid worker, then that activity shall be deemed productive."
7. Direct Observation– In this method, the investigator collects the time use pattern by being physically present with the respondent or around her often for the whole day.

16

INFLUENCE OF LITERACY AND SHG PARTICIPATION ON SOCIAL SUSTAINABILITY

K. Sudha Rani, G. Hussain Reddy** & K. G. Bharathi***

Weaving of congenial environs for an equitable social growth is the building of social sustainability. It demands open opportunities of development as well as empowerment of the weaker social components. A policy of social sustainability has to ensure sustainability of resources as well as the sustainability of the people wi.h the changing conditions of habitat, social setting and technological development. National development policy and the programmes devise ways of equitable distribution of avenues of growth, it introduces the appropriate closes of the growth incentives, offers the network of infrastructure and encourages collaboration and co-operation among the constituent cultural wings still there are some institutional bottle necks hinder the equitable growth of all cultural wings of Indian Society. The main crux of the problem lies in development of human resources and their capability building for better performance and protecting their interests against the social miscreants. The Government of India has launched a number of programmes for the promotion of skills,

* Associate Professor, Dept. of Adult & Continuing Education, S. V. University, Tirupati

** Project Assistants, Dept. of Adult & Continuing Education, S. V. University, Tirupati

abilities and components among the masses in various spheres. Thus the adult literacy programmes and SHGs came into existence as instruments of empowerment of people to enable them to be socially sustainable. In view of this the investigator has made an attempt to know the influence of literacy and SHG Participation on social sustainability . For the Present study, the influence of literacy and SHG

Participation on the 3 aspects namely, communication skills, decision-making capacity and awareness on, health, legal and developmental programmes which are the basic components so as to enable the people to attain social sustainability.

The objectives of the present study :

1. To study the influence of literacy and SHG participation on communication skills of the sample.
2. To identify the influence of literacy and SHG Participation on the involvement of the sample in decision-making
3. To know the influence of literacy and SHG Participation on the awareness of the sample on developmental programmes, legal and health aspects.

METHODOLOGY

The study was conducted in the Tirupati Rural and Tirupati Urban mandals of Chittoor District in Andhra Pradesh. 50 CEC Learners with out SHG Participation, 50 Illiterate SHG Participants and 50 literate SHG Participants were selected as the sample of the study. A schedule was devised by the investigator and administered to the sample and collected the data.

INFLUENCE OF LITERACY AND SHG PARTICIPATION ON COMMUNICATION SKILLS

Communication is the vehicle of knowledge. In the present world, one cannot dispense with communication. Communicating with others is an essential skill in family affairs, community relations, and business dealings. In spite of the increasing importance placed on communication skills, many individuals continue to struggle with this, unable to communicate their thoughts and ideas effectively. This inability makes it nearly impossible for them to complete effectively in the work place, and stands in the way of career progression. Even among the poor people if the communication skills are properly developed then they will be able to exchange their ideas with lot of confidence and authenticity. Good communication skills among the people are the basic and essential component which enables them to be socially sustainable. In this study an attempt has been made to study the influence of literacy and SHG participation on the communication skills and the findings are presented below.

Table 1
Percentages on Communication Skills Possessed by the Respondents

S. No.	Group	N	Poor %	Moderate %	Good %
1.	Literatures without SHG	50	19(38)	26(52)	5(10)
2.	SHG Illiterates	50	23(46)	18(36)	9(18)
3.	Literates in SHG's	50	15(30)	15(30)	20(40)

The percentages obtained by the responses shows that majority of the literate SHG participants possess with good communication skills than the other two groups. Poor communication skills among majority of the SHG illiterates were found. Majority of the literates without SHG Participation possess with moderate communication skills.

Table 2
Mean Value Scores on Communication Skills of the Sample in Rural and Urban Mandal

S. No	*Mandal*	*N*	*Mean*	*S.D.*	*T value*
1.	Rural	75	32.693	4.899	1.463 NS
2.	Urban	75	34.360	7.295	

The mean values in the above table shows that the respondents belonging to the urban mandal are having good communication skills than the respondents of rural mandal. The obtained 't' value indicates that there is no significant difference in the communication skills possessed by the two groups. Through the discussion with the rural respondents the investigator came to know that their participation in SHG meetings is low, they feel shy and the rural society being highly orthodox, their family members are not allowing them to come out and speak with the officials, in meetings etc. The investigator found a lot of potential and ability among the rural respondents also but the objection from the objection from their elders and husbands is becoming an obstacle to use it.

INFLUENCE OF LITERACY AND SHG PARTICIPATION ON PEOPLE'S AWARENESS

Awareness is the competence among the learners, which enables them to use their discretion in taking initiatives in the context of personnel, familial, economical, social, political and national issues for self, societal and national prosperity. An awareness has to be created so that they could identify and understand their present problems and adverse circumstances, could be able to identify the human and institutional resources available to solve any particular problem and cause of some specific problem enhance. Their scientific know-how required to control adverse circumstances and make consolidated efforts for complete redressal of problems. They should be aware of their duties and responsibilities. Each deprived and backward person should become aware to release his cresting problems, to know the benefits obtain from development and welfare facility.

In the present study the investigator has made an attempt to identify their awareness on legal, health aid developmental programs.

INFLUENCE OF LITERACY SHG PARTICIPATION ON LEGAL AWARENESS

The basic knowledge of law is essential for every citizen of the country. The intended beneficiaries. Usually do not know about these laws. They are innocent of their rights so crated, the laws remain sheer legislature exercises in fertility because these laws cannot be successfully implemented unless people know about the utility and can use legal mechanism to enforce them. Law can rule the people only when they are concretized to the legal rights and obligations and have where with all moral and material to use the redresser mechanism. Otherwise the rule and law become and remain only an academic cliché. Keeping this in view, an attempt has been made to identify the influence of literacy and SHG participation on the legal awareness of the people.

Table 3
Percentages on Legal Awareness Among the Respondents

S. No.	*Group*	*N*	*Poor*	*Moderate*	*Good*
1.	Literates without SHG	50	17(34)	16(32)	17(34)
2.	SHG Illiterates	50	18(36)	18(36)	14(28)
3.	Literates in SHG's	50	11(22)	18(36)	21(42)

The percentages obtained in the above table shows that majority of the literate SHG participants are more aware than the respondents of the other two groups. Majority of the respondents of illiterate SHG participants are less aware of the legal issues. The equal percentages of low, medium and high awareness among the respondents of literatures without SHG Participation were observed.

Table 4
Mean Value Scores on Legal Awareness of the Sample in Urban and Rural Mandals

S. No	*Mandal*	*N*	*Mean*	*S.D.*	*T value*
1.	Rural	75	8.533	5.476	5.610**
2.	Urban	75	12.813	3.698	

The findings of the above table reveals that legal awareness among urban respondents is higher than the rural respondents. The obtained 't' values indicate that there is significant difference in the legal awareness of the two groups. The laws that are being formulated to help the people can only be effective when they themselves are aware enough to take recourse to them. To the question on their response to the corruption and injustice, the SHG participants answered that they collectively take action to solve the problems. They said that they are now able to even fight for the atrocities against women. They have acquired a lot of confidence about their own ability to stand on their own feet.

INFLUENCE OF LITERACY SHG PARTICIPATION ON AWARENESS OF DEVELOPMENTAL PROGRAMMES

India is a second largest country in the world in terms of population and seventh in terms of area. Majority of its population are living in the rural areas. Hence it was rightly said that India lives in villages. The development of the country lies largely in the development of villages. After independence the Government of India has laid stress on the development of villages and has placed poverty alleviation and rural development on the national agenda. This has led to the launching of poverty alleviation and income generation programmes. However, not all these poverty alleviation programmes have been an ******* success because the beneficiaries are not able to utilize the gains because of the lack of awareness about the programmes.

People were quite unaware of the various welfare schemes launched by the government for them and were therefore denied whatever benefits could come their way. In order to understand their awareness about the development programmes and the extent of utilization by the sample, an enquiry was made and the findings were presented.

Table 5
Percentages on the Awareness of Developmental Programmes Among the Respondents

S. No.	*Group*	*N*	*Low %*	*Medium %*	*High %*
1.	Literates without SHG participation	50	14 28	16 32	20 40
2.	Illiterate SHG participants	50	14 28	21 44	15 30
3.	Literate SHG participation	50	12 24	18 36	20 40

Percentages obtained in the above table indicates that majority of the literates and literate SHG participants possess high awareness on developmental programmes. Awareness among the respondents of illiterate SHG participants was medium. Low awareness on developmental programmes among the percentage of the three groups was found. It shows that the literacy and SHG participation enhanced the awareness among the respondents.

Table 6
Mean Scores and t value on the Awareness of Developmental Programmes in Rural & Urban Mandal

S. No.	*Mandal*	*N*	*Mean*	*t value*
1.	Rural	75	2.547	
2.	Urban	75	4.040	4.443**

The obtained mean values indicates that the awareness on developmental programmes among the urban respondents was found to be high than the rural respondents. t value shows that there exists significant difference in the awareness of the three groups.

INFLUENCE OF LITERACY AND SHG PARTICIPATION ON THE AWARENESS OF HEALTH AND NUTRITION

One fundamental need of developing countries is to enhance skill over a wide range of critical problems concerning health, education, nutrition and population. A fair knowledge about health and nutrition is essential to maintain good health and to save from the diseases. Diseases caused by a faulty diet are common among the poor. Poor nutrition results in poor resistance to infections and greater incidence of diseases. People in general, particularly in rural areas and urban slums are not knowledgeable about health matters, such as the prevailing health problems in the community their prevention and control. An attempt has been made in order to know the influence of literacy and SHG Participation on the health awareness of the respondents as they are being provided with information on the health aspects in the continuing education centers and SHGS.

Table 7
Percentages on health awareness of the respondents

S. No.	*Group*	*N*	*Low*	*Medium*	*High*
1.	Literates without SHG	50	13(26)	17(34)	20(40)
2.	SHG Illiterates	50	15(30)	19(38)	16(32)
3.	Literates in SHG's	50	14(28)	14(28)	22(44)

The above table reveals that majority of the literates without SHG Participation and literate SHG Participants are more aware than the illiterate SHG Participants. Majority of the illiterate SHG Participants possess moderate awareness on health aspects.

Table 8
Mean Value Scores on the Health Awareness of the Sample in Rural and Urban Mandal

S. No	*Mandal*	*N*	*Mean*	*S.D.*	*T value*
1.	Rural	75	8.573	3.060	8.479**
2.	Urban	75	12.270	2.928	

Parents can afford to give proper nutritious food and health care only when they are more aware on the health aspects. The findings in the above table signify a lot of difference in the awareness of the rural and urban respondents. From the responses of the sample the investigators came to know that majority of the sample are not aware of the prevention and precautions to be taken in the occurrence of the burning diseases like AIDS, cancer etc. To the questions "what do you want to learn regarding to the health aspects", they replied that they want to know about the AIDS, Heart attacks, Diabetes, B.P. In both the mandals the respondents are aware of the nutritious diet and immunization. The respondents of the urban mandal said that the doctors, officers in the SHGs meetings, gave the health information. This is lacking in the rural areas.

INFLUENCE OF LITERACY AND SHG PARTICIPATION ON DECISION-MAKING CAPACITY OF THE PEOPLE

The decision-making is at the root of every human activity, which involves several stages to reach the final cut point. In rural families, a large number of decisions used to be of routine type and does not require much deliberations, but with the changing circumstances, the need for decision making is also increasing women were generally not involved in this social process even in the decisions pertaining to their own life and were considered neither knowledgeable nor competent for this task as they were confined within the four walls of the home. They are denied opportunities to participate in the decision-making process. As long as women would leave behind in the process of decision-making, it would be hard to get the democratic process started. In view of this the present study aims at identifying the decision-making capacity of the sample. The findings were presented below.

Table 9
Mean Scores on the Involvement of Respondents in Decision Making in Urban and Rural Mandals

S. No	Mandal	N	Mean	S.D.	T value
1.	Rural	75	25.520	4.234	4.535**
2.	Urban	75	31.640	5.253	

The obtained values in the above table indicate that the involvement of urban respondents in decision-making is higher than the involvement of rural respondents. There is significant difference in the decision-making capacity of the two groups. Form the responses of the sample it is clear that the involvement of rural respondent in decision-making on the community aspects is found to be low. They are limited to the decisions related to the children's education, purchase as provisions, cloths etc. Their husbands and elders in the family do not allow them to take the decisions on property purchase or sale, savings and political matters etc. However the urban respondents said that their family members would take their decisions into consideration on the crucial aspects also.

Table 10
Percentages on Decision-making Capacity of the Respondents

S. No.	*Group*	*N*	*Low*	*Moderate*	*High*
1.	Literatures without SHG	50	18(36)	18(36)	14(28)
2.	SHG Illiterates	50	12(24)	22(44)	16(32)
3.	Literates in SHG's	50	12(24)	17(32)	21(44)

The percentages in the above table indicates that involvement of the literate SHG Participants in decision making is higher than the other two groups. Majority of the illiterate SHG participant's involvement in decision-making is moderate. Equal percentages of moderate involvement in decision making among literates with out SHG Participation and illiterate SHG participants were found.

FINDINGS OF THE STUDY

1. Literate SHG participants possess good communication skills then illiterate SHG Participants and literates without SHG Participation. Lack of Opportunities among the CEC Learners to enrich their communication skills was observed. The investigator found that the illiteracy as an obstacle among illiterate SHG participants in communicating with officials.
2. Legal awareness among literate SHG participants was found to be high. It was low among illiterate SHG participants. The respondents of urban mandal are more aware than the rural respondents. The ability to solve the problems and to fight against corruption, injustice and discrimination was found among SHG participants. It was found to be low among CEC learners.
3. The respondents of the three groups are aware of nutritious diet and immunization. Awareness on the diseases, prevention and precautions was limited.

Literate SHG participants are more aware on health aspects than the other two groups of respondents. All of the respondents expressed the need of information on prevention and perceptional measures of different diseases. Acquisition of literacy and SHG participation led to better nutritional practices, in caring for family health.

4. The awareness on developmental programmes was high among literate SHG participants than the other two groups. The utilization is very low among all the respondents. They are demanding loans from the government. They did not even know about various welfare schemes launched by the government for them and denied whatever benefits could come their way. The investigator came to know from the responses that the literate SHG Participants are approaching the bankers and government officials. Illiterate SHG Participants are depending on the literates for this purpose. SHG participants are demanding and availing various amenities, which is lacking among CEC Learners due to lack of collective strength.
5. Involvement of SHG Participants in decision-making on home and community related aspects is high. It was found to be low among CEC learners. The involvement of the rural respondents is limited to household decisions. They said that their family members do not consider their decisions on political and economic matters. Majority of the respondents expressed that they have the ability to take the decisions but due to objection from their husbands they are not involved.
6. CEC Learners without SHG participation expressed the reasons for their low awareness on legal, health and developmental programmes is that the lack of access to information. Lack of collective strength is a serious roadblock in the way to solve the community problems expressed by the CEC learners. Non-utilization of the literacy skills was found among them, which may lead to relapse into illiteracy.

7. Mutual help and co-operation among the SHG Members is high. The information given in the meetings of SHGs enabled the learners to know the causes for this deprivation. The literate SHG participants said that literacy helped them a lot in the active participation of SHG activities.
8. Due to lack of literacy skills the illiterate SHG Participants are depending on the others in approaching banks and officials. They expressed the need of literacy in carrying out the SHG activities like saving scheme, getting loans etc.
9. The observations among CEC Learners without SHG Participation were positive change in attitude, increased awareness; decision-making capacity is limited to household activities and possessed with moderate communication skills.
10. Good communication skills, perceptive improvement in the confidence, increasing demand for amenities, gain in potential to act against social and economic injustice were observed among the literature SHG participants.
11. Moderate communication skills, awareness on legal, health and developmental programmes, dependence on literate and educated persons for savings of income, approaching banks, to get loans etc interest in community work were observed among the illiterate SHG participants.

From the above findings it is clear that literacy and SHG participation shows positive impact on the awareness-decision making and communication skills of the respondents. The literacy along with collective strength (SHG Participation) contributed much in promoting competence among the respondents and it was low among SHG Participants with out literacy and literates without SHG Participation.

SUGGESTIONS

Proper functioning of Continuing Education Centers (CEC) in order to help the learners to the literacy retention, to acquire information on various aspects of life. No programme can succeed unless the desire to learn is rooted in the conscience of the people. The investigator observed the desire for learning among the SHG Participation than CEC learners. Consciousness raising campaigns should be organized in the CECs.

As literacy is recognized as the instrument of social change and to meet the demand for literacy of the savings scheme in SHGs, compulsory literacy among the SHG members should be implemented.

Emphasis should be given to intensify the training programmes especially in rural areas on public relations, entrepreneurship development, finance management, marketing strategies, periodical meetings by the officials in the CECs and SHGs should be conducted to talk to the people and to bridge the gap between officials and the rural masses.

Their participation and utilization of the benefits of the developmental programmes is found to be low. They must be provided adequate information on the developmental programmes in the CECs and SHGs and to encourage them to participate in the programmes.

REFERENCES

R. Venkata Ravi Editor (2004), "Empowerment of People Gross Roots Strategies and Issues ", Kauishka Publishers, Distributors, New Delhi-110 002.

Sushama Sahay (1998), Women and Empowerment Approaches and Strategies, Discovery Publishing House, New Delhi-110 002.

P. Adinarayana Reddy, (2004), Literacy and Social Change, Sarup and Sons, New Delhi-110 002.

NABARD (2004), Banking with the poor Financing Selp-Help groups-Regional Office, Hyderabad.

Chaturvedi, S.C. (1969), "Impact of Social Education on the life and living of people in Certain Areas of U.P. Ph.D. Social Work, Lucknow University.

17

POPULATION AWARENESS OF SECONDARY SCHOOL TEACHERS: A CASE STUDY OF AJMER CITY

Laxmi Thakur

The population of the world has become 6.3 Billion approximately and still is increasing at the rate of 1.3 per cent per annum. Currently, the world population grows by 80 million per annum. Almost 99 per cent of natural increase occur in the less developed countries. The more developed countries as a group account for a mere 1.4 per cent of natural increase, although there is wide regional variation: Europe's population experiences a natural decrease of about 1.0 million per year, but the remaining countries and regions (Australia, Japan, New Zealand and North America) have a natural increase of about 2.1 million.

About 6.6 million people are added the world's population each month, equivalent to the population of Israel or Salvador. The increase each week, at 1.5 million is roughly equivalent to the population of Botswana. The number of people added annually to world population has been declining recently. Reaching its most recent peak of about 87 million around 1990. The number added each year has peaked a number of times in the past and has been strongly affected by changes in China's birth rate. China and India account for a total of more than one third (39%) of births worldwide. Global growth will continue to reflect changes in birth rates in such large countries.

The Population of earth started increasing with the knowledge of agriculture and according to Julian Sorrell Huxley, in that era the population increase was such that it doubled itself in 17,00 years approximately. Thus it became 2.5 corers in the Bronze Age (3000.BC) and then 7 crores in the iron age. About 2000 years ago by the year 1600 the total world population was 50 crores (half of the today's Indian population) which turned to 90 crores in 1800 and became a billion in the year 1830. On 11th July 1987, when we crossed five billion marks then the whole world was forced to give thought sincerely and tried to solve this problem at global level.

As far as India is concerned we have already crossed one billion mark on 12th may 2000 and still increasing at the rate of 1.7% per annum. At present we Indians are approximately 106 crores and contributing 1.65% of the world's population. By 2040, we will be 2 billion, which will be one fourth of the world's population. The population density in India is also increasing very rapidly. It was 216 person per square Km in 1981 and raised up to 324 person per square Km in 2001. In last twenty years (1981-2001) density has increased by 50% exactly. The situation is very alarming because we have only 2.24% of world's land area and 16.5% of world's population on it.

This rapidly growing population is hammering the human life in every field. In India and the countries like India, having unplanned population growth due to mass illiteracy, conservative traditions and customs, and basically the unawareness of these factors behind the population phenomena. Nearly half of the population of our country is below the age of 18 year. If we do not prepare them with the adequate knowledge through population education and awareness, we shall be defeating the purpose of our population policy, which is based on the democratic principle of voluntary participation of the individual in the population control programme. The young minds are more receptive to such ideas so that they can easily develop on healthy and favourable attitude for a small family. It becomes our duty to aware the people about population phenomena. Like all other problems, the problem of population growth begins in the minds and the seeds of its solutions must also be sown.

Awareness is a process, where the person comes to know about the new idea or practice. He or she has only some very general information about it and knows little about its usefulness limitation and applicability to him/her. The term "population awareness" refers to factual knowledge about population dynamics required to understand the nature and magnitude of the burden imposed by rapid population growth. Population awareness can develop the key concept of responsible and rational decision-making which involves further knowledge and understanding of the consequences of one's actions, which in turn links individual to the society, then to the nation and next to the world. Hence, an individual becomes an important element in the entire developmental process. If a teacher is aware about the phenomenon, he/she can make aware the young people at very early stage of their educational life, as the young minds are very receptive to the new ideas. Besides, teacher is considered responsible persons and society also respects him so people will listen them attentively. Family planning experts have also recognized that it is very difficult task to make aware the adult couples, because they are slow learners with the rigid values and beliefs. So, it becomes our moral duty too ware the people about this daunting problem. As it is assumed that a teacher is a good communicator and can very well deliver the ideas to other people. Keeping this in mind present study was carried out, by administrating awareness test among them.

OBJECTIVES OF THE STUDY

- To asses the degree of awareness among teachers towards population problem.
- To observe the difference among different groups of teachers, *i.e.* between the male-female teachers; government-private school teacher, post graduate-under graduate teacher; different age group teachers.
- To identify and pin point the weak areas of population awareness and suggest remedial measures to improve upon those areas.

SAMPLE OF THE STUDY

The sample for the study was selected from 65 schools of Ajmer City. In that 25 were government and 40 were private schools and all schools were of secondary level. Out of 65 schools four schools were selected, two of them were girls & two were of boys school. In both the categories of girls & boys one was private with English medium and another was government with Hindi medium. The sample was restricted to secondary school teachers only and in total 146 teachers was selected randomly for the present study.

TOOL USED

In the present study population education awareness test was administered on the secondary school children. The test items were classified in four major constituent component of population education. They are:

(i) Family size and family welfare
(ii) Responsible parenthood
(iii) Population chance and resource development
(iv) Population related beliefs and values.

The test, strive towards achieving the ultimate goal of population awareness among teachers by collecting evidences, on the degree of awareness on its numerous facets and dimensions.

RESULTS & DISCUSSION

The study was carried out according to plan and proper procedure. The raw data obtained through 'Population Education Awareness test' from secondary school teachers. The questionnaire is divided into four major area of population awareness. One of the important aims of the study has been to observe the level of awareness of secondary school teachers towards the problem of population. The result of the study is presented in two parts.

The first part consists of Table 1 to 4, which observes the level of awareness among secondary school teachers, with five different groups (*i.e.* male–female, Post graduate – Under graduate, Government-Private, English-Hindi medium teachers; Teachers of age group of 20-40 & 41-60). The second part depicts the difference of awareness on four different areas between the teachers of English-Hindi medium schools and these groups are divided into two another groups *i.e.* male-female which is further bifurcated into under graduate and post graduate sub groups. This part consists of Table 5 to 8.

The result shows the scores of respondents on Population Education Awareness Test. The total number of respondents was 146. Primarily scores have been divided into five sub-groups on the basis of gender, education, nature of school, medium of instruction and age of the respondents. In the gender group, 35 males and 111 females were selected. It was found that percentage of awareness was good in both the groups, but the female respondents were more aware than their counterparts. In the educational level group, out of the total 116 were post graduate and only 30 teachers were graduate. In both the groups scores were quite high *i.e.* 73.38% and 72.45% on Population awareness tests. The third group includes 68 government and 78 private school teachers, their mean scores on PEAT were 28.44 and 35.43 respectively and the percentage of private school was highest (84.35) among all the groups. Whereas, percentage of government school teachers was 67.71 only, it is the lowest percentage among all the groups (Table 1).

Table 1
Results obtained on Population Education Awareness Test (N–146)

S. No.	*Various Groups*		*Total number of respondents*	*Mean scores*	*Secured marks in Percentage*
1.	Gender	Male	35	29.22	69.57
		Female	111	31.03	73.88
2.	Educational Level	Post graduate	116	31.82	73.38
		Under graduate	30	30.43	72.45
3.	Nature of School	Government	68	28.44	67.71
		Private	78	35.43	84.35
4.	Medium of Instruction	English	49	34.10	81.19
		Hindi	97	29019	69.50
5.	Age of Respondents	21–40	65	31.77	75.64
		41–60	81	29056	70.38

In the fourth group of Respondents Teachers in English and Hindi medium are divided on the basis of language of instruction. Surprisingly enough, there was significant difference between these two groups. English medium teachers had secured very high percentage (81.19%) in comparison to teachers of Hindi medium (69.50%). The fifth group or respondents was divided on the basis of their age. The young group (21 to 40 years of age) comprises of 65 respondents who secured high percentage *i.e.* 75.64 in comparison to another group, which secured 70.38% in the age group of 41 to 60 years. It can be concluded that young group is more aware because the mass media and other methods of non-formal education are playing positive role in the level of awareness and the minds of young people are more receptive then older age people.

Table 2
t-value of Male & Female scores of English and Hindi respondents

Medium of School	*Gender*		*t-value*	*df*	*Significance*
Hindi	Male	N_1=20			
N=97		X_1=544	1.85	95	Not significant
		M_1=27.20			at 0.05 level.
	Female	N_2=77			
		X_2=2294			
		M_2=29.79			
English	Male	N_1=15			
N=49		X_1=497	1.41	47	Not significant
		M_1=31.99			at 0.05 level.
	Female	N_2=34			
		X_2=1152			
		M_2=33.88			
Total	Male	N_1=35			
N=146		X_1=1023	1.81	114	Not significant
		M_1=29.22			at 0.05 level.
	Female	N_2=111			
		X_2=3445			
		M_2=31.03			

Thus, it could be said that only education cannot play a significant role regarding population phenomenon. In this connection, population education is must to create an awareness among the masses. Here we can see from the table the young teachers are much more aware because now-a-days with the realization of population explosion formally or non-formally our educational and political system are providing some of the Population awareness among the people without influenced by caste, creed and colour.

This table depicts that male teachers and female teachers are alike in awareness because there is no significant difference in male and female respondents even when the medium of instruction was also different. So it can be concluded that the gender does not play any significant role so far as population awareness is concerned.

Table 3
t-value of Post Graduate and Under Graduate Teachers of Medium of School

Level of education	*Medium of school*		*t-value*	*df*	*Significance*
Postgraduate N=116	English	N_1=37 X_1=1273 M_1=34.40	1.69	114	Significant at 0.05 level.
	Hindi	N_2=79 X_2=2313 M_2=29.27			
Undergraduate N=30	English	N_1=12 X_1=361 M_1=30.58	0.933	28	Insignificant at 0.05 level.
	Hindi	N_2=18 X_2=525 M_2=29.16			
Total N=146	English	N_1=49 X_1=1671 M_1=34.10	2.14	114	Significant at 0.05 level.
	Hindi	N_2=97 X_2=2832 M_2=29.19			Insignificant at 0.01 level.

In the above table the language medium of the teacher is not playing any significant role in awareness. But there is difference in mean scores of Hindi and English medium teachers. Table 3 is showing that out of total sample only 49 teachers were of English medium, who secured higher mean score (34.10) than Hindi medium (29.19) teachers who were 97 in numbers. Level of education could not play any significant role in the performance of teachers of Hindi and English medium. When total sample was analyzed then it was found that there is significant difference among the performance of English and Hindi medium teachers at 0.05 levels whereas, this difference is insignificant at 0.01 levels.

So far as population awareness among teachers is concerned, it is found that there is a significant difference between the awareness of private and government school-teachers. The mean of total private teachers is 35.43 whereas, the mean of Government school-teachers is 28.44 only. This difference can be seen in the teachers of postgraduate but not

Table 4
t-value of scores of teachers from Government and Private Schools

Level of education	*Nature of school*		*t-value*	*df*	*Significance*
Postgraduate	Government	N_1=57			
N=116		X_1=1628	4.47	114	Significant difference at 0.01 levels.
		M_1=28.56			
	Private	N_2=59			
		X_2=1948			
		M_2=33.01			
Undergraduate	Government	N_1=11			
N=30		X_1=307	1.85	28	Not Significant at 0.05 level.
		M_1=27.90			
	Private	N_2=19			
		X_2=586			
		M_2=33.84			
Total	Government	N_1=68			
N=146		X_1=1934	5.95	114	Significant at 0.01 level.
		M_1=28.44			
	Private	N_2=78			
		X_2=2764			
		M_2=35.43			

in the undergraduate teachers. It may be because of number of government teachers in undergraduate category is very less *i.e.* eleven only. This small group of eleven respondents is not able to affect the large group, as a result the t-value is insignificant but holistically it can be concluded that teachers of private schools have performed better on population awareness test than teachers of government schools.

This part deals with the data obtained on questions pertaining to 'family welfare and family size'. Table shows that Hindi medium teachers had performed well (80.68%) in comparison to English teachers (71.28%). Surprisingly enough, in both the groups *i.e.* English as well as Hindi medium respondents Female undergraduate respondent secured highest scores, which proves that level of degree (PG & UG) does not have any influence on attitude regarding 'Family size and Family welfare.' So far as gender is concerned it has influence on teacher's awareness because in most the groups, Female's performance is better than males. If we take mean of all the four female groups, it comes 81.08% and means of all the four

Table 5

Awareness of Teachers Regarding Family size and Family Welfare

S. No.		*English (N=49)* Male (N=15) U.G. (N=3)	P.G. (N=12)	Female (N=34) U.G. (N=9)	P.G. (N=25)	Total	*Hindi (N=97)* Male (N=20) U.G. (N=8)	P.G. (N=12)	Female (N=77) U.G. (N=10)	P.G. (N=67)	Total
1.	No. of Questions(n)	15	15	15	15	15	15	15	15	15	15
2.	Maximum Scorer (nxN)	45	180	135	375	755	120	180	150	1005	1455
3.	Obtained Scorer (EX)	35	150	119	234	538	89	91	132	862	1174
4.	Mean Score EX/N	11.7	12.00	13.22	9.36	10.98	11.12	7.58	13.2	12.86	11.19
5.	Percentage (%)	77.77	83.30	88.15	62.40	71.28	74.13	50.55	88	85.77	80.68

male group comes 71.55%. It is very good sing of women development that they are more aware about Family Size & Family Welfare Programmes.

Table 6
Awareness of Teachers Regarding Responsible Parenthood

S. No.	*English (N=49)*					*Hindi (N=97)*				
	Male (N=15)		*Female (N=34)*			*Male (N=20)*		*Female (N=77)*		
	U.G. (N=3)	*P.G. (N=12)*	*U.G. (N=9)*	*P.G. (N=25)*	*Total*	*U.G. (N=8)*	*P.G. (N=12)*	*U.G. (N=10)*	*P.G. (N=67)*	*Total*
1. No. of Questions(n)	5	5	5	5	5	5	5	5	5	5
2. Maximum Scorer (nxN)	15	60	45	125	245	40	60	80	335	485
3. Obtained Score (EX)	12	51	43	108	214	23	27	47	291	388
4. Mean Score EXN	4.0	4.25	4.77	4.32	4.33	2.87	2.25	4.7	4.34	3.54
5. Percentage (%)	80	85.00	95.55	86.4	87.34	57.5	45	94	86.86	80

This table shows that the teachers of English and Hindi medium school have sound knowledge with regards to "responsible parenthood". The total means percentage of all the teachers is 83067, which is very high. So far as medium of instruction is concerned. English medium teachers have performed better (87.34%) than Hindi medium (80%). Here gender is also playing significant role because females are performing well as compared to their male counterparts. Significant difference can be in PG. Male female teachers of Hindi medium where males had scored only 45% and females have scored 86.9%. In English medium also UG females group is performing significantly better (95.55%) than UG male the same line Hindi medium. UG female had also responded with very high percentage (94%) with regard to responsible parenthoods.

Table 7 shows that the performances of English medium teachers are better (69.76%) in comparison to Hindi medium (63.0%). It we study results on the basis of gender again female's performance is better (66.38%) than males (59.49%). Holistically, performance on this aspect is neither very much strong nor very poor. If population education should have been imparted to these teachers when they were doing their degree courses than they would have been performed very well on this veriable particularly.

Table 7
Awareness of Teachers Regarding Population Change and Resource Development

S. No.		English (N=49)					Hindi (N=97)				
		Male (N=15)		Female (N=34)			Male (N=15)		Female (N=34)		
		U.G. (N=3)	P.G. (N=12)	U.G. (N=9)	P.G. (N=25)	Total	U.G. (N=8)	P.G. (N=12)	U.G. (N=10)	P.G. (N=67)	Total
1.	No. of Questions(n)	17	17	17	17	17	17	17	17	17	17
2.	Maximum Score (nM)	51	204	153	425	833	136	204	170	1139	1649
3.	Obtained Score (EX)	28	153	108	320	609	85	93	88	773	1039
4.	Mean Score Exn	9.33	12.75	12.0	12.8	12.22	10.62	7.75	8.8	11.53	9.68
5.	Percentage (%)	54.90	75	70.58	75.29	69.76	62.5	45.58	51.76	67.86	63.0

Table 8
Awareness of teachers regarding population related beliefs and practices

S. No.		English (N=49)					Hindi (N=97)				
		Male (N=15)		Female (N=34)			Male (N=20)		Female (N=77)		
		U.G. (N=3)	P.G. (N=12)	U.G. (N=9)	P.G. (N=25)	Total	U.G. (N=8)	P.G. (N=12)	U.G. (N=10)	P.G. (N=67)	Total
1.	No. of Questions(n)	5	5	5	5	5	5	5	5	5	5
2.	Maximum Scorer (nxN)	15	60	45	125	245	40	60	50	335	485
3.	Obtained Score (EX)	8	36	31	91	166	24	20	26	189	259
4.	Mean Score EXN	2.66	3.0	3.44	3.64	3.19	3.0	1.66	2.6	2.82	2.52
5.	Percentage (%)	53.33	60.0	68.88	72.8	67.75	60.0	33.33	52.6	56.41	53.40

Above table shows clearly indicates that males have not performed well on beliefs and practices related to population aspects specially male postgraduate teacher's performance is very poor *i.e.* 33% percentage. If we compare male female data, female postgraduate teachers of English medium have secured the highest scores on beliefs and practices related to population. Here it can be concluded that males must make aware about different aspects of population so that take proper decisions regarding their families and can impart this education to their students also.

CONCLUSION

The population of the world has become 6.4 Billion approximately and still is increasing at the rate of 1.3 percentage per annum. Currently, the world population grows by 80 million per annum. Almost 99 percentage of natural increase occurs in the less developed countries. India has already crossed one billion marks and still increasing at the rate of 1.7% per annum. At present we Indians are approximately 106 corers and contributing 16.5 percentage of the worlds population. The population density in India is also increasing very rapidly, it was 216 person per square Km in 1981 and raised up to 324 person per square Km in 2001. In last twenty years (1981-2001) density has increased by 50% exactly. The situation is very alarming because we have only 2.24% of words land area and 16.5% of world's population on it.

This rapidly growing population is hammering the human life in every field. It becomes our duty to aware the people about population phenomena. Like all other problems, the problem of population growth begins in the human minds and the seeds of its solutions must also be sown. Keeping this in view present study was carried out, by administrating awareness test among school teachers. The sample for the study was selected from 65 schools of Ajmer City. The samples were restricted to secondary school teachers only and in total 146 teachers were selected randomly for the present study. In the present study population education awareness test was administered on the secondary school children. The test items were classified in four major constituent component of population education.

Result of the study was divided into two major subgroups. There was significant difference between teachers of Hindi and English medium. English medium teachers had secured very high percentage in comparison to teachers of Hindi medium. Young group is more aware because the mass media and other methods of non-formal education are playing positive role in the level of awareness and the minds of young people are more receptive then older age people. In this connection, population education is must to create an awareness among the masses. Young teachers are much more aware in the present scenario, which indicates that our educational & political systems are providing population awareness among people either through formal education or through non-formal education.

The second part of result is showing that on all the four different areas of population awareness, women's performance is better then their counterparts. All these four areas has significant importance in human's life because when the whole world is facing problem of growing population and depleting resource, at that time at least our teachers should be made aware about the seriousness of problem. Our main aim should be to impart this knowledge to our youth to make them a responsible citizen.

RECOMMENDATIONS

- Education plays an important role in this direction, so education should be provided to every person especially to rural women.
- Since 'population awareness' emphasizes on the values also, and a teacher, or a communicator should play an important role to develop new ideas and values so that pace of its development can be accelerated.
- To make the people aware, media plays an important role, this media must be attractive, palatable and acceptable.
- Interesting street plays, puppet-shows, songs related to population, one-act plays, slogans (short and impressive), beautiful & meaningful posters, radio and Tele-plays about population problems, spot-painting competition, quiz-contest (with prize), exhibition etc. should be organized to create an awareness.
- If population awareness programme is to succeed one has to lay greater emphasis on processes where real learning takes place by bringing about a change in a learner in his understanding, values and attitudes. This

involves adoption of very effective methods and subtle means and techniques by a skilled and a dedicated person.

- 'Population awareness' programme must emphasize the dual role of a citizen that he is expected to play by following the small family norm in his own life and participating effectively in family welfare and other population programmes launched by the community.
- Making population awareness, a success, women should be given decision making power in fertility behaviour. Their status and dignity as an equal partner in the of process of development including decision making in social, cultural, economic and political fields will have to be augmented considerably.

REFERENCES

U.S. International Population policy (1993), An official Statement. *"Population and Development and Review"*, Vol. 1, No.2, pp. 403-406.

Recommendations of the European Population Conference (1993), "I opulation & Development Review", Vol.19, No.2, pp. 406-416.

'Science Summit' on world Population: A Joint Statement by 58 of the World's Scientific Academies (1994), *"Population and Development Review'*, Vol.20, No.1, pp 233-238.

The Tokyo Declaration on Population and Development (1994), *"Population Development Review"*, Vol.20, No.1, pp. 239-245.

Parakh, B.S. (1985), "Population Education: Interception to Institulisation", NCERT, New Delhi.

A.L.N. Sharma, B.S. Parakh, D. P. Jain, (1988), "Population Education Awareness Test, *National Population Education Project*, NCERT.

Shrivastava, N.L. (1973), "Attitudes of newly married males in Patna towards family formation", *Journal of family welfare*, 22(1) pp. 54-63.

United Nations World Report, (1990).

18

PARTICIPATORY COMMUNICATION IN AGRIBUSINESS: A DEVELOPMENT STRATEGY FOR HILL WOMEN OF UTTARANCHAL

Neelam Bhardwaj and S. K. Kashyap***

The former President of Tanzania, Julius Nyerere, clearly pointed out, People cannot be developed; they can only develop themselves. For a while it is possible for an outsider to build a man's home, an outsider cannot give the man pride and self-confidence in himself as a human being. Those things a man has to create in himself by his own actions. He develops himself by what he does; he develops himself by making his own decisions by increasing, the understanding of what he is doing, and why; by increasing his own knowledge and ability, and by his own full participation as an equal in the life of the community he lives in (Nyerere, 1973, 60).

Participatory Communication can become a inspiring force for development in a significant way and Video SEWA is a case. It's with Leelaben who was a vegetable vendor from slums of Ahmedabad and now she works as a part of the team of women of mixed background who produce very effective and popular video films for community education and awareness. They have produced over one hundred films very professionally leading to a new ray of hope among slum dwellers of Ahmedabad. From where has this spirit come?

*, ** Associate Professor, Agricultural Communication, G.B. Pant University of Agriculture & technology, Pantnagar- 263145, Uttaranchal, India

How can other women be guided on same track to take lead in enterprising professions? What role communication has to play in this adventure?

IN CONTEXT OF A STATE WHERE WOMEN HAVE THE STAKE

Uttaranchal, a state newly created on 9 November 2000 is in nascent state of development. It is bestowed with a diversified agro-climatic and socio-cultural mildew. It is dominated by hill region, which constitutes about 92.5% of the total land area. The Hill region of Uttaranchal with different agro-ecological and climatic conditions has integrated systems of farming, forestry, horticulture, livestock and off-farm activities. It has been observed that women contribution in agriculture is more than 80 per cent. The various farm activities performed by hill women are weeding, manuring, sowing, transplanting, harvesting, threshing, winnowing and post-harvest operations (AICRP Report, 1999). In addition to it, women perform various allied activities like collection of fodder, taking care of domestic animals, collection of fuel wood and doing major household activities. In spite of their major contribution in state economy their role is still subservient. They are lacking in accessibility resources and inability to fully exploit the natural agro-resources.

The agricultural policy of Uttaranchal aims at increased agricultural production and food security of the stage. Other than the traditional agricultural production, the state has ample scope in the horticultural crops like mango, litchi, stone fruits, nut fruits, pomegranate fruits, citrus fruits, strawberry, tea-production and processing, vegetable production, spices, potato, flower crops, herbal, medicinal and aromatics plants and seed production.

The policy of the state of Uttaranchal to make the agricultural vocations and technologies women-friendly and to manage the agricultural and natural resources on watershed basis for an integrated development gives importance to the present paper. Looking into the contributions made by the hill women in agriculture there is an emergent need for developing better entrepreneurial skills in agriculture sector. This requires training intervention that could make the women self-dependent and better user of existing natural resources.

Only proper, relevant and appropriate training strategy for the various skills necessary to perform well in agribusiness, which will ultimately result in better entrepreneurs, can do this. Training will act as an organized effort by which women can get knowledge and skill and develop proper attitude for any definite purpose. It is an integral part of the human resources development process and is concerned with providing learning experiences for women so that they may be ready to move into new directions. The hill women have scarcity of infrastructural resources in terms of land, irrigation water, technology and poor transportation. They have low investment capacity resulting in low productivity of crops and low exposure to mass media for better access to agriculture information. Communication has been viewed as an indispensable tool for development. International Commission has envisaged the fact that for the study of Communication Problems "Development strategies should incorporate communication policies as integral part in the diagnosis of selected priorities (MacBride, 1980). Participative communication can change hill women's perceptions towards self-determined change. It can foster development among community through collective action by making use of popular media and interpersonal skills. It has been concluded that action is more likely to be an outcome when people engage in dialogue and search together. The concept of dialogue action, introduced by Paulo Freire, is an exemplary role model of participatory communication, which was applied, by Atucha and Crone (1982) in an integrated education, health and family planning programme in Honduras. Nair and White (1987) outlined the achievement of communication with continuous interaction of sources over time 'to arrive at shared meaning'. The researchers concluded that the goals of the institutions involved ultimately coincided with the needs and interests of the communities.

GROUP MANAGEMENT

Population in hill village is comparatively less and scattered. Hill women are overburdened with agriculture and other domestic activities; they seldom find time to organize themselves for any collective action. The development communication/extension worker should facilitate the process of cooperative action by understanding and applying the concept of cognitive social capital. Uphoff (1999) proposed this concept, which referred to norms, values, attitudes and beliefs that predisposes people towards cooperation. The trainer has to would women behaviour by developing willingness among them for collective learning, shared sense making, conflict resolution and intentional reasoning for group decision-making. This requires inculcating trust among women members through simulation games and role playing methods. It will help them to understand the roles, rules, precedents, procedures and social networks, which facilitate cooperation and collective action.

This understanding with ultimate outcome of collective action can be gathered through participatory communication approached. The case of humid pampas of Argentina is an effective example.

The Humid pampas, the richest region of Argentina, was facing a terrible threat of soil erosion, spreading in large areas of its three central provinces. The National Institute for Agricultural Technology (INTA) known in the past for its aloofness as the official technical body, organizations in the region to participate in the land recovery programme. A multimedia communication project come up and had a very significant impact because it was participative.

LEADERSHIP SKILLS

Central to group activity is the leadership role for stabilizing the group and carrying out the responsibilities to the group. In Agribusiness, the leader has the varying responsibilities like decision-making, delegating the work, planning, harmonizing of their activities. Socio-metric technique and election method can be employed by the trainer to identify the leader among the women particularly in agribusiness.

The identified potential leader should be trained by the informal methods such as providing opportunities to observe, talk with and read about such personalities of the past and present who did exemplary tasks through innovative ways. The formal training through lecture method, discussions, workshop, apprenticeships can also be carried out. The trainer should clearly demarcate the content for which the women leaders require training. The trained women leaders should be deployed for the responsibility suitable to the agri-business requirement.

INFORMATION MANAGEMENT SKILLS

Information is the key component in the development process. Information is not only used as input for scientific research but also a national resource for entrepreneurial decision-making. Information management aims at harmonization of development goals, human resources and technologies. Hill women, who live in fragile eco-regions, are untouched with outside world due to poor access to latest technologies, trainings and exposure and other information sources. The trainer should develop training modules, manuals and other materials suitable for both the literate and illiterate women involved in agri-business operations.

In operations, the women contribute more in the hill area. The hope of generating prosperity in the hill area agri-business largely depends upon making their contributions more viable through strong linkage with the training organizations, banking and corporate sectors. Training organizations should also ensure additional support for credits, expert guidance for marketing information and media organizations for the commercial advantage. They should forge linkages with some of the organizations which are taking care of agri-business at the National level like NABARD, National Horticultural Board, National Dairy Development Board, and Indian Institute of Packaging, State Agricultural University can play a leading role through its established extension network. At present G.B. Pant University of Agriculture and Technology, Pantnagar is imparting need based trainings through two Krishi Vigyan Kendras and six Krishi Gyan Kendras spread all over the hill region. Women farmers can be specially trained and skilled in group management, finance and marketing management, post harvest operation and leadership skills. It is equally important that small Farmers Agri-business consortium be formed exclusively for women at the grass-root level, which will enable them to join the mainstream of free market economy.

The example of fishermen group of Philippines set a stage. In an experiment of Family Centre of the Asian Social Institute (FCASI), the FCASI workers, in partnership with the local people, undertake community organizing in fishing villages around Laguna de Bay and along parts of Manila Bay. It was observed that through participatory approach to media, the community, affected by specific problems, was challenged to think, to internalize and to come out with creative decisions and choices. Their experiences proved their capability, willingness and enthusiasm in these activities. For the fishermen participatory communication became a powerful tool for liberation from the traditional modes of thinking that serve as obstacles to social change.

REFERENCES

AICRP, Report, (1999), Resource Management of Farm families, Annual Report (1998-99). Department of Family Resource Management, College of Home Science, G.B. Pant University of Agriculture & Technology, Pantnagar.

Bhardwaj, N., Singh, A.K. and Arun, Kumar, S. (2002), Research Issues and strategies for Agri-business management, Kurukshetra, 50 (6).

UpHoff, N. (1999), Understanding social capital, learning from analysis of experience of participation, In Partha, D. and Serageldin, I (eds.). Social Capital A. Multifaceted perspective. The World Bank, Washington, D.C.

Nyerere, J. (1973). Freedom and development. Dar- Es- Salam., Tanzania, *Oxford University*, Press.

Deza, Alfonsco B. (1989), The Intercultural communication programme (ICP). Philippines Report, Manila, the Philippines, Asian Social Institute.

Atucha, Luis Maria Aller and Catherie, D. Crone (1982), A participatory methodology for integrating literacy and health education in Handuras' Convergence: and International Journal of Adult Education, 15 (2)., 70-81.

Nair, K.S. and Shirly, A. White (1987), Participation is the key to development communication. Media Development, 34 (3). 36-40.

19

SELF-HELP GROUPS AND POVERTY ALLEVIATION

D. Sunder Raj*

INTRODUCTION

Lack of institutional credit has been considered as one of the major constraints to the poor to come out of the vicious circle of poverty. Even after 50 years of independence there is no proper banking system to meet the credit needs of the poor. At the government level attempts like introduction of cooperatives followed by nationalization of commercial banks and opening up of regional rural banks were made with a view to reach the institutional credit to the weaker sections particularly the poor. However, all these efforts hardly helped the poor to have better access to institutional credit. Mainly because, the credit needs of the poor are small and urgent. As such the bankers do not take much interest to bank with the poor as this type of transaction do not provide them any profit. Moreover, bureaucrats and politicians impose from above these formal credit institutions with excessive intervention. Beside this formal rules and regulations and lack of traditional culture of credit management also kept the poor away from the formal credit institutions (Kumaran, K.P. 1997).

Providing affordable credit to the poor has been recognized as a prime component of development strategy from a long

* Junior Faculty, Council For Social Development, Southern Regional Centre, Rajendranagar, Hyderabad – 500 030.

time. Many schemes and resources have thus been devoted to the provision of credit targeted at the poor especially in the rural areas. Such credit is provided on subsidized terms (Shridharan, Damyanty; 1997). In order to give a new approach to rural finance, the NABARD had introduced the 'Self – Help Group (SHG)' in 1992, which is generally treated as finance to a tiny group. This new approach, in other words, is called 'Micro Finance' (Das Gupta, 1999).

Women have been long neglected in their role as beneficial of the process of development. Though they constitute a half of the population, their contribution to development in society is often undermined. However in recent times, gender has been increasingly viewed as a principle underlying the distribution of resources in the household and as well as in the society. Women's empowerment is more important because of the special problems that women face today. Gender bias in social, educational, economical and political fields is still manifest in many civilised societies of the world. Empowerment of women can serve as an essential input in development.

Women are marginalized over years at various stages right from the fetus to the funeral. Being agreed that women are the part and parcel of the humankind and human being is incomplete with out women, they are branded as second sex and are kept aside from reaching the front stage.

Economic progress in any country whether developed or underdeveloped could be achieved through social development. Empowering women contributes to social development. Women's contribution to national development is crucial. The process of economic development would be incomplete and lopsided unless women are fully involved in it. Emancipation of women is an essential pre-requisite for economic development and social progress of the nation (Gurumoorthy, 2000). The Self-Help Groups (SHGs) empower women and train them to take active part in the socio-economic progress of the nation.

Greater access and sustainable flow of credit is critical for empowerment of poor. The credit needs of the rural poor are determined by a compiled socio-economic milieu where it is dependence of the rural poor as moneylenders still continue in many areas, especially for meeting the emergent needs of rural poor. Under the circumstances, a non-formal agency for difficult to adopt project-lending approach as usually followed by banks and where the dividing line between credit for consumption and productive purposes is blurred. Despite rapid pace of expansion of financial system encompassing spheres of social and mass banking, the credit supply to the poor, in the form of SHG could emerge as promising partner to the formal credit system.

Economic impoverishment of poor is partly on account of their inability to control acute imbalances in income and consumption patterns in terms of both seasonality and magnitude when capital stock and other physical resources hardly provide succour. An investigation into indebtedness and debt redemption behaviour of poor households reveal struggle for smoothening of fluctuating cash flows. The conduct of credit repayment by most poor is a surrogate of their behaviour. In fact the loans extended by informal sector to poor are discounted future savings, so much so that many believe their saving habit only can propel their development.

THRIFT AND CREDIT GROUPS IN ANDHRA PRADESH

Self-help Groups are now gaining acceptance as an alternative system credit delivery, for meeting the credit needs especially to the people who are the poorest of poor generally comprising small/marginal farmers, landless agricultural labourers, rural artisans, women folk and other micro entrepreneurs. Greater access and sustainable flow of credit are important inputs for empowerment of poor. The credit needs of the rural poor are determined by a compiled socio-economic milieu where dependence of the rural poor on moneylenders still continue in many areas, especially for meeting the emergent needs. Under the circumstances, it is difficult for a non-formal agency to adopt project-lending approach as usually followed by banks and where the dividing line between credit for consumption and productive purposes is blurred. Despite rapid pace of expansion of financial system encompassing spheres of social and mass banking, the credit supply to the poor, in the form of SHG could emerge as promising partner to the formal credit system (Kumaran, 1997).

The Thrift and Credit Groups are mostly informal groups widely known as the Self-Help Groups (SHGs) whose members pool savings and relend within the group on rotational or need basis. Self-help groups are organized in the selected villages for economic and social development of the rural poor and women in particular. These groups have a common perception of need and impulse towards collective action.

According to Gurumurthy (2000), the SHG disburses micro credit to the rural women for the purpose of making them enterprising women and encouraging them to enter into entrepreneurial activities. Credit needs of the rural women are fulfilled totally through these SHGs. Self-help Groups enhance equality of status of women as participants, decision makers and beneficiaries in the democratic economic social and cultural spheres of life. Self-help Groups also encourage women to take active part in socio-economic progress of our nation.

Several development agencies have promoted and inspired formation of different kinds of thrift and credit groups in Andhra Pradesh to channelise the various poverty alleviation and social development programmes. These groups vary widely in terms of their membership, size, decision-making process methods of group action etc. The characteristics of different types of micro credit groups operating in the state are :

SELF MANAGED THRIFT AND CREDIT GROUPS

Self – Help Groups:

Self-Help Groups are small economically homogeneous and affinity groups of rural poor, voluntarily formed to save and mutually agree to contribute to a common fund to be lent to its members as per group decision. These groups are usually formed by Government or Non-governmental Organisations

(NGOs) with emphasis on both thrift and credit activities. The group through a consensual approach ıakes all financial decision.

Development of Women and Children in Rural Areas (DWCRA)

The Department of Rural Development under DWCRA forms Groups with maximum membership of 15 women in Rural Areas popularly known as DWCRA groups. Here again thrift is used as an entry point to weave women groups. Based on the thrift record, Government through District Rural Development Agencies (DRDA) releases maximum matching grant of Rs. 25,000 per group for enabling women groups to take up income generating activities. Under the programme, banks also extend credit facilities to such groups for meeting incremental fund requirements.

Podupulakshmi Groups

Podupulakshmi Groups are DWCRA groups functioning on lines of SHGs. Thrift is an entry point activity for these groups' members as micro loans based on the priorities decided by the group members. Government DRDAs have been extending matching grant assistance to such groups based on their thrift, credit and repayment records. The matching grant received from the Government is completely fanged with the group's corpus. Banks have also been extending further loan, enhancing group's overall fund base to enable internal lending of higher order for meeting both consumption and productive credit requirements of the members.

Avval Committees

Avval Committees are women thrift and credit groups formed in tribal areas of Adilabad District (A.P.) under the aegis of Integrated Tribal Development Agency (ITDA). These groups have rudimentary elements of SHGs. Sri Saraswati Grameena Bank took the initiative of restructuring and strengthening these groups on the lines of SHGs by extending need based financial assistance to the group while introducing the self management concepts in the field to thrift and credit activities.

SELF MANAGED NETWORKS

Mutually Aided Cooperative Societies (MACS)

Government of Andhra Pradesh has enacted the Andhra Pradesh Mutually Aided Cooperative Societies Act during 1995. The Act provided for voluntary formation of cooperatives as accountable, competitive self-reliant business enterprises based on thrift, self-help and mutual aid. They are owned, managed and controlled by members for their economic and social betterment. Several coalitions and networks of women SHGs have institutionalized themselves under the new enactment. Under this, the members are generally woven into small groups to ensure group responsibility, endorse loan transactions, and provide moral security for repayment of loans and participation of individual members in every activity of the society. The small groups are federated at village level in the form of mahila mandals where fund collection and loan disbursements are made in a decentralized manner with the financial decision making vested with the local leadership. However, in the event of fund deficit/surplus, the local mahila mandals look upon the central MACS for transference/deployment of financial resources.

Women Groups of Working Women's Forum:

Women groups of membership not exceeding ten are formed by Chennai based voluntary agency in a few parts of Andhra Pradesh. These groups are given intensive training to advocate and manage social, political and economic issues pertaining to rural women. The women members are extended small loans for taking up household industrial activities backed by personal surety of the leader concerned, while the leader's loan itself is guaranteed by the system the leader based on her organizing potential can graduate to organizer level for promoting several such groups. The groups formed by the working women's forum are federated to Indian Cooperative Network of women which is a cooperative owned and managed by member women.

EXTERNALLY MANAGED THRIFT AND CREDIT GROUPS

Grameen Groups

Grameen replicating agencies forms these groups. Under this system, five persons are formed into a group with thrift as entry point. The group is given intensive training in credit management and group management. They are put through a Group Recognition Test before they become eligible to access credit for income generating activities. The credit terms like quantum of loan, interest rate, repayment period etc., are determined by the credit agencies. The loaning is done on staggered basis 2:2:1 with the leader of the group secures each loan. However, the group is empowered to priorities the persons to be covered in the initial loaning.

Rashtriya Mahila Kosh (RMK) Groups:

Though there is no such nomenclature as RMK Groups, they are essentially those groups promoted by NGOs which have accessed assistance from Rashtriya Mahila Kosh, a fund set up by Government of India for assisting women for undertaking income generating activities. The RMK has formulated a set of schemes for NGOs for on lending to SHGs. The schemes delineate the type of activities eligible for finance, quantum of finance, interest rates and repayment terms. In practice, credit is directly extended to individual women in-group mode on the recommendation of group leaders.

ACTIVITY MANAGEMENT GROUPS

Anganwadi Groups

Anganwadi Groups are women groups formed by Department of Women & Child Welfare at habitation level for implementing their health, nutrition and literacy programmes for rural women. These women are encouraged to take up income generating activities for which micro loans are extended for setting up individual or group enterprises.

Joint Forest Management (JFM) Groups

The village community in notified forest areas is formed into Vana Samarakshana Samithis (VSS) or Joint Forest Management Groups to protect and conserve forest wealth. The Group activity is the important core concept of Joint Forest Management. Government of Andhra Pradesh and Madhya Pradesh have chosen SHG route for social mobilization under the programme. Further, the village community is expected to forsake part of their income from forest-based activities and instead take up alternative income generating activities. Inculcation of thrift and credit habit in such groups will go a long way in sustaining their income levels.

Watershed Groups:

The farmers in micro watershed area are formed into groups for implementing technology package for watershed development with intervention of facilitating agency, normally an NGO. While on farm development activities are funded through grant support, these groups have also been availing micro loans from formal credit agencies under the various Government sponsored programmes for raising crops, animal husbandry, non-farm activities etc. A few of such group have also been formed with thrift as entry point activity.

SELF-HELP GROUPS AND PARTICIPATION

Gender discrimination is a universal phenomenon. Both inside and outside the house, women are excluded form positions of power. They are denied the opportunities to participate in decision-making process. The primary challenge facing women today is to increase their participation and become actively involved in decision (Chandra 1997). Participation has two dimensions-quantitative and qualitative. People's participation in terms of numbers has no meaning. Today there is a need for change from quantitative to qualitative. Active participation in social, economic and political spheres would help in enhancing process of decision-making empowerment and it will also give women the desired self respect and social dignity and these of course, are the pre-requisites of empowerment. Very rightly Karl (1995) expressed that, "increased participation of women in decision-making at all levels will help to "adjust" the goals pursued through development".

Participation is the point where women are taking decisions alongwith men equally. To reach this level, mobilization is necessary. By organizing themselves and working collectively, women will be empowered and gain increased representation which would lead to increase empowerment and ultimately greater control. Participation of women in SHGs makes a significant impact on their empowerment, both in social and economic aspects. Participation helps, women come out in open to discuss their problems. It also helps to bring awareness among rural women about savings, education, health, environment, cleanliness, family welfare, social forestry, etc. and make them self-reliant.

Development programmes of different types (employment provision, income generation, awareness creation etc), have been designed and implemented aiming at enhancing the socio-economic condition of the downtrodden. Many programmes do not succeed as every one accepts, is that people are not given a role to play in identifying analyzing and prioritizing their needs and finding ways and means to solve their problems. People's voice is often ignored. Participatory approach must be introduced at all stages, if we are really concerned with peoples' empowerment. As this approach brings the people to the focus in the project activities, the result would certainly be fruitful and rewarding for the people as well as for the implementing agency (Tamilmani, 2002).

The Copenhagen Declaration on Social Development and as well as the Beijing Declaration of Fourth World Conference on women both of 1995 recognised the need to enhance the participation and leadership roles of women in political, civil, economic, social and cultural life and in the development process. The informal groups of women significantly improve women's participation both from economic and social aspects.

There is a greater potential for the group approach in future while conceptualising and implementing any programme for the poor, particularly women.

SELF-HELP GROUPS AND EMPOWERMENT:

Women's empowerment is synonymous with the achievement of equality and equal mind-ness in society. Women's empowerment will result in traditional female values being more respected in the society. The empowerment of women through SHGs would lead to benefits not only to the individual woman and women groups but also for the family and community as a whole through collective action for development. They assume the role of decision makers in major and deciding aspects of the family and village.

The Self-Help Groups (SHGs) or the Thrift and Credit Groups are mostly informal groups whose members pool savings and re-lend within the group on rotational or need basis. Self-help groups are organized in the selected villages for economic and social development of the rural poor particularly women. The Self-Help Group is a viable alternative to achieve the objectives of rural development and to get community participation in all rural development programmes. In all stages of economic and social activities involvement of women becomes essential. SHGs encourage women to take active part in the socio-economic progress of our nation.

According to Suguna (2001), "empowerment is a process of awareness and capacity building leading to greater participation to greater decision-making power and control, and transformation action". Empowerment of women means developing them as more aware individuals who are socially developed, politically active, economically productive and independent and are able to make informed choices and intelligent decisions in matters that affect them and their nation.

The multi-dimensional process of empowerment requires awareness, access to education and training, participation in decision-making and politics and the mobilization of women for economic self-reliance. The micro-credit movement in India is gathering momentum as women at the grassroots organize themselves into SHGs (Sudha Rani *et. al.*, 2002).

Self-help Groups are now gaining acceptance as an alternative system credit delivery, for meeting the credit needs especially to the people who are the poorest of poor generally comprising small/marginal farmers, landless agricultural labourers, rural artisans, women folk and other micro entrepreneurs.

Empowerment can serve as a powerful instrument for women to achieve upward social and economic mobility and achieve power and status in society. It is a source of mobility, equality and emancipation, both at the individual and at the societal level. Gender development constitutes an important part of development in this context. It is important in this respect to bring women into the mainstream of development so that society benefits from the women empowerment.

Attempts to empower women, with the formation of local women's collectives intended to foster new opportunities for women to gain economic and political power are ultimately expected to become self-sustaining, self-governing and self reliant.

Development of SHGs in India reveals that the existing formal financial institutions have failed to provide finances to landless marginalized and disadvantaged groups. SHGs encourage savings and promote income generating activities through small loans. The experiences available in the country and elsewhere suggest that SHGs are sustainable, have explicability, stimulate savings, and in the process help borrowers to come out of vicious circle of poverty (V.M. Rao, 2002).

SELF HELP GROUPS AND POVERTY ALLEVIATION:

Poverty alleviation has been the primary concern of development planners since long. Poverty alleviation efforts mainly through state driven credit intervention produced only sub-optional results. The real break-through came when efforts to fight poverty emanated from within with in civil society. The new people centered paradigm has broadened the scope of anti-poverty policies and gave a special role to credit, particularly micro finance in the overall poverty eradication process. It is a recognized fact, today that the relationship between finance and poverty is a complex one. Beside, a few experiments under South Asia poverty alleviation programme implemented under aegis of UNDP have demonstrated the credit could play a role in financing the provision to basic needs, especially in the areas of low-cost housing, water supply and sanitation and health services. In other words, the process of empowerment envisages allowing people to create necessary conditions to mitigate socio-economic exclusion more effectively.

Empowerment of poor, particularly approach and social mobilization are the possible process for eradicating poverty. Poverty can be effectively eradicated only when the poor start contributing to the growth process through their active involvement. Voluntary organization, community-based self-help groups and local governmental organizations have a substantial role to play (Sivasubramanian, 1999).

Women are critical actors in the process of moving their families out of poverty. According to Agarwal, Deepti (2001), women need to be viewed not as beneficiaries but as active participants in the process of development and change. Empowerment of women can be effectively achieve if poor women could organize into groups– for community participation as well as for assertion of their rights in various services related to their economic and social well being. Simultaneously micro-credit and SHGs are also key elements for the empowerment of the rural women and help them to improve their living conditions and acquire small capital assets. A systematic strategy seeking to change societal attitudes for women, improve women's self-perception, create an enabling policy, institutional and legal environment and faster economic empowerment through mobilization, thrift, easy credit, up gradation of services and improved income generation opportunities are essential for emancipation of women. Satya Sundaram (2001), opines organizing the poor is crucial for their upliftment. They do not have crucial inputs like credit, it is here, empowerment of women assumes importance. SHGs have emerged, in order to help the rural poor particularly women, in securing inputs like credit and other services.

According to Dodkey (1999), SHGs have been found an effective and economic means of ensuring access of credit to the poor and vulnerable sections of the society, as the translations cost is much less and because of the constant and effective supervision the loan is properly utilized and repayments are prompt and excellent. Thus SHGs are the solution to accelerate the socio-economic development of the rural poor in India.

It is here the importance of the women and potentiality are exhibited, where a few women together are rewriting the fate of themselves and families. Women power is known when she participates in all development matters. Participation in SHG have emboldened women financially and mentally has set to the opening of closed minds and improving the quality of life and their social status. The impact of women participation on social front could be assessed mainly in terms of improvement in literacy level, health, quality of life and standard of living.

The possible out come through group approach / SHGs at individual level are self-employment/ assured wage employment through they year, sustainable livelihoods, improved health and education, enhanced social dignity and better status of women/girl child etc. And at the community level self-managed and self-reliant, inclusive role in gram panchayats, all children are in schools and social equality etc. The informal groups of women significantly improve women's participation both from economic and social aspects.

Self-Help Group also leads to women empowerment, which would simultaneously lead to the benefits, not only to the individual woman and women groups but also for the family and community as a whole through collective action for development. They assume the role of decision makers in major and deciding aspects of the family and village. Women's empowerment is synonymous with the achievement of equality and equal mindness in society. Women's empowerment will result in traditional female values being more respected in the society.

SOME ILLUSTRATIONS

In these days of globalisation, liberalisation and 'reforms', where profitability and 'viability' of operations are the only consideration, an organization 'Share Micro fin' promoting self-help groups is providing itself to a successful phenomenon. With 500 employees, it has disbursed over Rs. 75 crores to poor women. The strategy is simple. Women clients are allowed access to small loans of Rs. 4,000 to Rs. 10,000 and seasonal loans of Rs. 3000 to Rs. 5000. This could be as little as few hundred depending on the need of the client and the proposal. The impact has been positive with income increase ranging from Rs. 30 to Rs. 250 a day. And most important, they have proven that such operations are viable, with repayments being 100 per cent (Vikaram Reddy. P., 2001).

Bindu Mahila Sangam:

Nizamabad district has just 13,728 SHGs with women membership of a little over 1.7 lakh and 700 odd groups were involved in the skill development programme. Bindu Mahila Sangam of Srirangam village in Nizamabad Mandal formed in 1996 saved Rs. 17,000 got a revolving fund of Rs. 25,000 and Rs. 80,000 under the NABARD linkage scheme. The 10-member group has an equal number of buffaloes and sells milk earning Rs. 1,000 to Rs. 1,500 per month each member. Besides, they were also able to purchase four bovines each with the extra income.

Rudramma Mahila Sangam:

The Rudramma Mahila Sangam of Yedpally village has 10 members all making leaf plates for holding sweets, tiffins, meals and so on with the help of a pressing machine got Rs. 10,000 as income in just tow months.

Durga Mahila Sangam:

Mrs. Survana of Durga group has been in the national limelight when she met UN Secretary General, Mr. Kofi Annan. She has the good fortune of interacting and presented him with one of the soft toys, her group makes. Quite amazingly, this group has sold Rs. 2 lakh worth of goods at the industrial exhibition held in January 2001 at Hyderabad (Geetanath. V. 2001).

Mansingh Baba Mahila Sangam:

Women (Lambada) of this group make 'Banjara' garments and assorted ornaments made of German silver. Subhadra, a member says, "through SHG we are able to get the necessary capital for making more such material". The group makes a cool profit of Rs. 3,500 per month.

CONCLUSION

Women are being increasingly seen as an important index of the social health of nation. . If 50 per cent of the population cannot participate fully in the growth process, economic growth and social development would be difficult. Women have to be encouraged to participate in country's development process itself. It is not just an ideal for a welfare state but imperative for the growth of an economy. There is growing emphasis on human resource development on one hand, several economic variables like income, employment and health status etc. on the other.

The failure of formal sector credit to address the needs of the poor has led to alternatives, which build upon existing traditional embryonic institutions common in our society. These traditional groups provide an organizational framework, which facilitate self-reliance in access to credit. Self-help Groups are now gaining acceptance as an alternative system credit delivery, for meeting the credit needs especially to the people who are the poorest of poor generally comprising small/marginal farmers, landless agricultural labourers, rural artisans, women folk and other micro entrepreneurs.

The impact of women participation on social front could be assessed mainly in terms of improvement in literacy level, health, quality of life and standard of living. It is here the importance of the women and potentiality are exhibited, where a few women together are rewriting the fate of themselves and families. Women power is known when she participates in all development matters. Participation in Self Help Groups have emboldened women financially and mentally, which has set to the opening of closed minds and improving the quality of life and their social status.

Qualitative Indicators for Empowerment

The Draft country paper– India for the Fourth world conference on women, Beijing, 1995 proposed the following qualitative and quantitative indicators for evaluating women's empowerment.

- Increase in self esteem
- Increase in knowledge and awareness levels on issues affecting the community, such as, women's health nutrition, reproductive rights, legal rights, literacy etc.
- Change in the women role and responsibility in the family and community.
- Visible increase or decrease in levels of domestic violence and other forms of violence perpetrated on the women and girl child.
- Change in social and other customs – e.g. Child marriage, dowry, discrimination against widows etc.
- Visible changes in women's participation in attending public meetings, training programmes.
- Increase in bargaining/negotiating power of the women as an individual as well as in collectives.
- Formation of cohesive women's groups/collective at village district and state levels.
- Positive changes in social attitudes amongst the community members
- Recognition of women's economic contribution within and outside the household.
- Women's decision-making over her work, income and expenditure in her control or is she still subservient to male members in the family.

Quantitative Indicators of Empowerment

- Demographic trends like- maternal mortality rates, fertility rates, sex ration, life expectancy at birth, average age of marriage.

- Numbers of women participating in different development programmes
- Greater access and control over community resources governmental schemes.
- Visible change in health nutritional status, changes in literacy
- Participation levels of women in political process at the local level.

REFERENCES

Shridharan, Damyanty; (1997), "Encourage Self-Help Groups", Social Welfare, Vol. 44, No. 7.

Doodkey, M.D., (1999), "Sustaining Rural Women", Social Welfare, Vol. 45, No. 12.

Das Gupta A., (1999), "Rural Banking for Women", Social Welfare, Vol. 45, No. 12.

Gurumoorthy, T.T., (2000), "Self-Help Groups Empower Rural Women", Kurukshetra, Vol. 48, No. 5.

Gosh, Suddasattwa; (2000), "Design Issues in Micro Credit", RBI Occasional Papers, Vol. 21, No. 1.

Kumaran, K.P., (1997), "Self-Help Groups: An Alternative to Institutional Credit to the Poor : A Case Study in Andhra Pradesh", Journal of Rural Development, Vol. 16, No. 3.

Laxmi R., (2000), "Micro Finance : The New Development Paradigm for Poor Rural Women", Kurukshetra, Vol. 48, No. 13.

Geetanath V., (2001), "SHGs doing Wonders for Women", The Hindu, April 3.

Vikram Reddy P., (2001), "Microfinance catching up among rural poor", The Hindu, April, 2.

Sivasubramanian, M.N., (1999), "Credit Based Poverty Alleviation Programme : Innovative Approach", Kurukshetra, Vol. 48, No. 2.

Agarwal, Deepti, (2001), "Empowerment of Rural Women in India", Social Welfare, Vol. 48, No. 4.

Satya Sundaran, I., (2001), "Self-Help Groups : Challenges and Opportunities", Social Welfare, Vol. 48, No. 4.

Chandra, (1997), " Women and Empowerment" *Indian Journal of Public Administration*, Vol. XLIII, No. 3,

Karl, Marilee, (1995), "Women and Empowerment Participation and Decision-making", Zed Books Ltd, London and New Jersey.

Suguna, B. (2001), "Women's Empowerment: Concept and Framework", *Social Welfare,* Vol. 48, No. 9.

Lalitha, N & B S Nagarajan; (2002) "Self-Help Groups in Rural Development", *Dominant Publishers & Distributors,* New Delhi.

Dr. K. Sudha Rani, Uma Devi & Surendra;(2002), "SHGs, Micro-Credit and Empowerment", *Social Welfare,* Vol. 48, No. 11, February.

V. M. Rao, (2002), "Women Self Help Groups : Profiles from Andhra Pradesh & Karnataka", *Kurukshetra,* Vol. 50, No. 6, April.

Tamilmani, (2002) " People-centred Development Projects through PRA", *Kurukshetra,* Vol. 50, No. 3, January.

Annexure:

Table 1
District Wise Self-Help Groups in Andhra Pradesh
(Total groups as on September 2000)

Sl. No	*Districts*	*DWCRA*	*SHG*	*TOTAL*
1	Adilabad	8119	2599	10718
2	Ananthapur	9958	8528	18486
3	Chittoor	7286	6638	13924
4	Cuddapah	3941	4573	8514
5	East Godavari	7714	34420	42134
6	Guntur	5628	10778	16406
7	Karimnagar	4604	17225	21829
8	Khammam	5620	4130	9750
9	Krishna	6259	13741	20000
10	Kurnool	3849	8977	12826
11	Medak	4940	11958	15491
12	Mahaboobnagar	6011	10877	16888
13	Nalgonda	3583	11967	15550
14	Nellore	9036	5182	14218
15	Nizamabad	4897	4520	9417
16	Prakasam	7708	8657	16365
17	Ranga Reddy	6717	3869	10586
18	Srikakulam	3153	12258	15409
19	Visakhapatnam	3099	7970	11069
20	Vizianagaram	2955	6941	9896
21	Warangal	3729	12526	16254
22	West Godavari	5309	8533	13842
	Total	124115	216864	339572

Source: Commissioner, Rural Development, Government of Andhra Pradesh

20

POPULATION EXPLOSION VS. ENVIRONMENTAL DEGRADATION

*K. Vijaya Kumar**

INTRODUCTION

Nothing is constant on this earth, as everything constantly moves towards either a progressive or regressive direction. All living beings expect better life which helps to make new creations and explorations of new quality of life. For example, man is a dynamic being, who constantly thinks for new ventures and reacts as per the situation; whether of climate or weather change according to season. When a person does not react as per the situation or the condition, it indicates that the society is decaying. Actually, the change may occur in two ways: the first one for survival and the other one for social recognition. Man protects himself, builds systems to fulfill his needs and aspirations, and tries his best to get social identity or recognition. In fact, old ideas have exhausted their utility and have reached a saturation point. The strategy for growth has essentially remained unchanged, which is not the right approach to development, as such approach will only rebuild the same past, but cannot build a new future.

Technological and scientific advancement pose a great challenge to the human race. This type of progress not only opens new vistas, new aspirations and new ways of living but

* Associate Professor of Sociology, School of Distance Education, Andhra University.

also leads to population explosion and consequent environmental degradation.

POPULATION GROWTH

Though various efforts are being made for better progress and development of the society in all fields of life, same is being nullified by the speedily growing population. Even if man is dynamic and can react as per the demands and needs of the society, the situation is not at all controlable due to population explosion. Therefore, "there is a link between development and population explosion". Unless the 'population bomb' is diffused, all efforts are unless and normless society will prevail in future. For the better future of the nation, population control is the need of the hour. Some of the negative aspects of population explosion, as also some dangers are discussed, keeping in view the better future of mankind.

With the observation of the past four decades covering the years of 1951-1991, the population drastically grew upto the peak from 360 millions in 1951 to 1003 million in 1991. If the same trend goes on till the middle of the 21st Century, the population will likely to reach 1500 millions. Even then, it would be growing at a reauced rate of half-a-per cent per annum. The population of China is likely to be stabilized around 1,146 millions by 2035. It appears, therefore, that the population of India is likely to outgrow the population of Chine by around 2030. The relation between population growth and environmental degradation is felt worldwide.

ENVIRONMENTAL PROTECTION – THE NEED OF THE 21ST CENTURY

Environmentalism is a movement to preserve the quality and continuity of life on earth. The 19th century was the century of industrialisation. It was only in the 20th century that awareness of ecology of environment and the havoc that industrialisation and modern ways of life had caused it, all of which became a major concern all over the world.

There is a large-scale degradation of forests, with soil erosion as a threatening factor in the country. Today, there are about 48 million forest dwellers in India living within or in the vicinity of foıests. For them forests have continued to be an important source of livelihood and means of survival. Forests in India, happen to cover a fifth of the land area. When satellite imagery revealed that the country was losing on an average 1.3 million hectares of forests per year, that the quantity of top soil lost due to the degradation and destruction of forests was equivalent to the loss of 30 to 50 million tonnes of foodgrain in a year, that dams were silting at a much faster rate due to the run off from deforested hillsides, the Government realized the need of the day to reconsider the forest policy and the rights of the people to forests. Social Forestry, Joint forest management are some of the buzz words of most people's movements agitating on environmental issues, and that people should be allowed to have a say development decisions, from large dams to afforestation projects (The Hindu, Survey of Environment, 1992). The Environmental Problems would be multiplied by the middle of the 21st century on par with population explosion.

Pollution is caused by waste generated from different sources – urban, agricultural and industrial sectors. It is estimated that municipal sewage accounts for 80 per cent of polluting effluents in our country. Here comes the need of environmental education to people. As many think, industry is not the major culprit for environmental degradation. Against 750 million cubic metres of industrial of effluents, nearly 3,650 million cubic metres of sewage flows into our rivers. With the increasing urban slums, the problem of pollution will be much more rampant. Creating all round awareness to the problems and consequences of waste whether in the domain of public health, aesthetic quality or natural resource management should take priority. Mass environmental education programmes should be launched.

After World War-II, there was a growing concern about pollution, dwindling of energy resources and dangers of pesticides and radiation. Concern for environment often conflicts with the vested interests of land-owners, developers and industrialists (with ignorance on the part of illiterate farmers) and the defence interests of major nuclear powers.

Pressure of Population and its Adverse Effects (1951-2021)

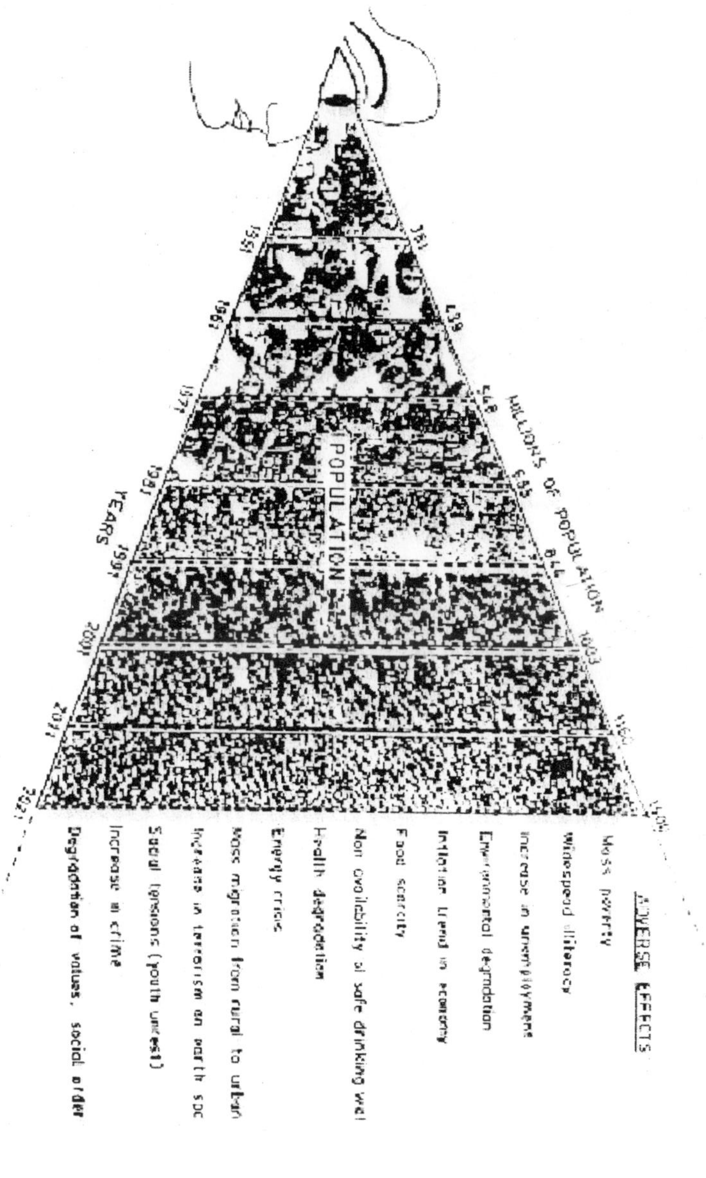

There are many voluntary organisations which continue to lobby and litigate for preserving and trying to extend environmental safeguards. Chiefly among them are:

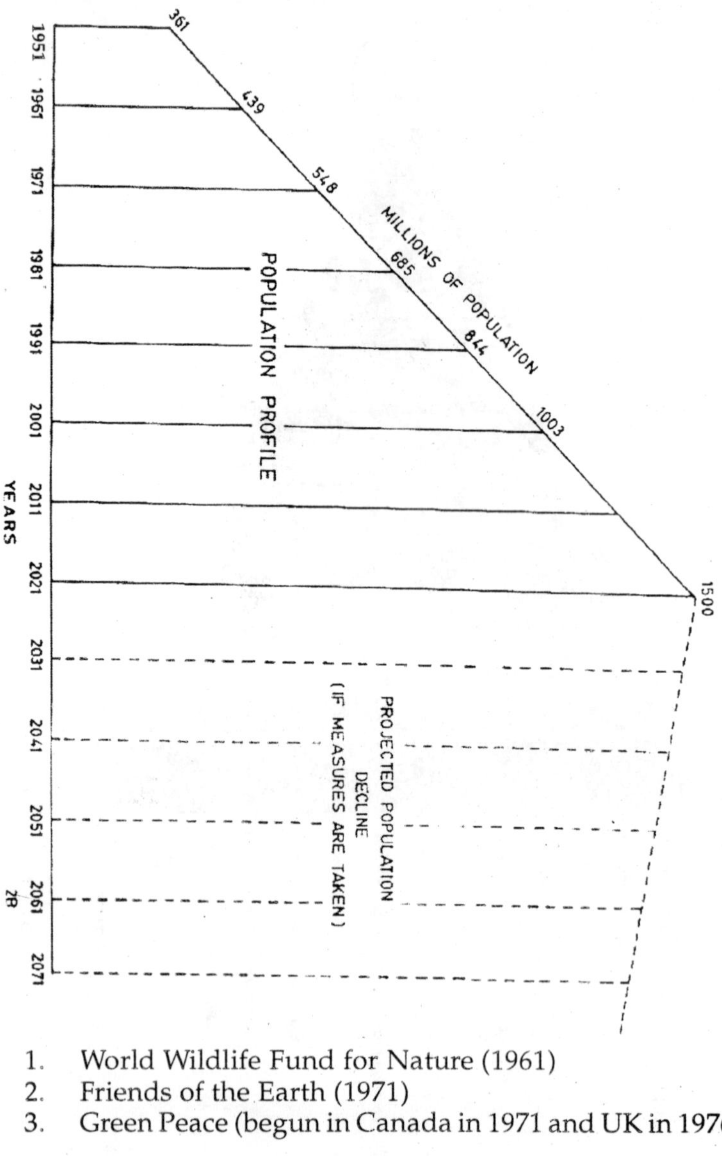

1. World Wildlife Fund for Nature (1961)
2. Friends of the Earth (1971)
3. Green Peace (begun in Canada in 1971 and UK in 1976)

4. The Royal Society for the Protection of Birds (1904, Europe's largest conservation pressure group).
5. United Nations major conservation projects.

CONSTITUTIONAL MEASURES

Article 48A of the Indian Constitution mentions: "The State shall endeavour to protect and improve the environment and to safeguard the forests and wildlife of the country."

Article 51A of the Constitution further stipulates that "it shall be the duty of every citizen of India to protect and improve the natural environment and to have compassion for living creatures."

Although the term 'environment' has not been defined in the Constitution, in could be interpreted in a broad manner as the quality of physical-natural environment; the air we breath; the water we drink and use for recreation; the land we cultivate, mine and build on; and wildness we seek to enjoy today and to preserve for future generations, covering the entire spectrum of measures to be considered to prevent environmental degradation.

HUMAN SOCIETY ENDANGERED

Human society faces disaster by the year 2050, if it does not change to a more life-sustaining technology, according to Dr. Carl Sagan.

The global environment will be worsening and, by 2050 A.D., there will be drought all over the planet, conflict over water resources and massive flooding of coastal cities and for all natural resources.

MAJOR ENVIRONMENTAL ISSUES:

Global warming: Recently, climatologists have produced evidence that could act as a natural thermostat that keeps temperatures of ocean surfaces from raising above a certain point. Global warming can cause radical changes in the large-scale circulation of huge rivers and of air that creates and defines regional climates.

Ozone hole: The life-protecting ozone in the high atmosphere has weakened by upto five per cent since 1978 under the influence of chlorofluoro carbons or (CFCs).

Ozone depletion: Fossil fuel burning will lead to increasing Hydrocarbons and decreasing oxygen levels. Oxygen is the vital gas which is needed by all kinds of life in this living world. The ozone layer acts like a shield for incoming short wavelengths of ultraviolet radiations. If the ozone layer is disturbed, there will be many ill effects on the biosphere.

Regarding environmental degradation, the eminent journalist and writer, Kushwant Singh suggest that the universities should not award a degree to any student unless he or she plants at least a dozen saplings. He further suggests that there should be a revolution for population control and protection of environment in the country.

It is the high time to increase awareness mainly on two aspects (1) rapid growth of population and its negative reflections of the quality of environment and the quality of human life and for sustaining the economic and social progress of a country. The Government policy on population and environment and Forest should widely be published especially in major groups including the NGOs, farmers and other communities and directly involving them in the process of identification, formulation and implementation of environmental programmes. The important role of mass media is also necessary for promoting public awareness over population, National Conservation strategy and Environment and development.

In recent years, due to population pressure, advancement of technology and developmental activities, advancement of bio-diversity in the country is fast dwindling inspite of several legislative measures undertaken.

The impact of people on the environment depends on their numbers and on their level of consumption (including the use of renewable and non-renewable resources). Both expand independently and both lead to increasing pressure on the environment as a supplier of resources and as a repository of wastes (WHO, 1992).

The living conditions of millions of urban and rural poor are such that pose threat to their health and in the long run, have potentially catastrophic social consequences. In spite of effectively implementing poverty alleviation and family planning programmes, the magnitude of poverty problems in India are still quite staggering. The latest year for which the data are available and the absolute number of poor did not decline much over this period of 20 years. There were 21 million poor in 1973-74 and 320 million in 1993-94; in the rural areas, the corresponding number was 261 million and 244 million.

India, the second most populous country in the world, has no more than 2.5 per cent of global land but is the home of 1/6th of the world's population living in a resource-poor country with a high population density. In one way or the other, the efforts are being made to improve per capita income, availability of food, clothing, education and employment as well as enhancement of the quality of life and prevention of environmental deterioration. Nonetheless, there is a potential threat posed by rapid population growth, which swallows all efforts and further mitigating the social and economic progress so far made.

However, environmental concerns are being integrated with development through mandatory clearance of projects based on environmental impact assessment. The negative reflections on rapid growth of population in the context of the degradation of environmental quality, affects physical, social and economic progress of a country.

As such, increasing the growth of population presents special problems related to air and water pollution, degradation of common property resources, threat to biological diversity, solid waste disposal and sanitation, besides increased deforestation, industrialisation, urbanisation, transportation and input-intensive agriculture, which happen to be some of the other major causes of environmental problems being faced by the country.

SUMMARY

The relationship between population growth and environmental degradation is felt worldwide. Though various efforts are being made for better progress and development of the society in all fields of life, same is being nullified by the rapidly growing population. Even if man is dynamic and can react as per the demands and needs of the society, the situation is not at all controlable due to population explosion. Therefore there is link between development and population explosion. Unless the 'population bomb' is diffused, all efforts are useless and norm-less society will prevail in future. Hence every citizen should be taught about the negative reflections on rapid growth of population in the contest of the degradation of environmental quality especially large-scale degradation of forest with soil erosion, hazards of pollution dwindling of energy resources and natural resources which are all threatening factors" in the country. Air, water and land are the basic amenities of life, over population and rapid utilisation of these has given rise to degradation of environmental quality leading to physical, social and economic problems and health hazards.

REFERENCES

Ashish Bose, India's quest for population stabilisation progress, pitfalls and policy options, Demography India.

The state of India's environment, The Centre for Science and Environment, 1984.

Population Atlas India, Census of India, 1991.

Our planet, our health, W.H.O., 1992.

The Hindu Survey of Environment, 1992.

Jaidev Sharma, Defuse population Bomb, current topics March, 1993.

Kushwant Singh, Speech at Assembly Hall, Visakhapatnam on 27th April, 1993.

Nabhi's Compilation of Ninth Five Year Plan 1997-2002.

21

CHILD LABOUR IN INDIA: AN ANTHROPOLOGICAL PERSPECTIVE

*P. H. Mohammad**

The issue of child labour has attained an enormous focus in the recent past. Thanks to the deliberations and discussions held, in the context of World Trade Organization (WTO), on relationship between international trade and labour standards Child Labour has been identified as a vulnerable phenomenon in the society. These deliberations (Which were basically driven by the concern over the adverse impact of a deepening recession on children, resulted due to the debt crisis and structural adjustment programmes), have heightened the attention to the plight of the children and galvanized global action in their favour (Rasheed, 2000). Thus a global momentum is sponsored with a sequence of developments such as (i) The child survival on development campaign (launched by UNICEF and embrassed by a high power global alliance); and (ii) Adoption of the convention, by the UN general assembly in 1989, on the rights of the child, (driven by the international children's NGO community).

This Global Campaign against child labour has reached its peak when 71 Heads of State or Governments and 88 ministerial delegates jointly adopted a world declaration on the survival, protection and development of children on 30 September 1990.

* Associate Fellow, Council for Development, Hyderabad, hothur17@yahoo.com.

Also a plan of action was drafted at the UN sponsored World Summit for Children (WSC). Accordingly seven major goals relating to survival, health, nutrition, education and protection of children, are identified and envisaged to fulfill the same by the year 2000.

These trends demonstrating tremendous appeal for the child cause, worldwide, have lot of implications to Indian society. Due to neglect of primary education India harbors the largest number of child labourers of the world (Dev 2001). Particularly, "the rural areas of India are home to large numbers of children who remain outside the portals of school, either earning a small wage to supplement the family income as workers in fields, quarries, brick-kilns, cottage industries or petty business, or what is even more common, as unseen hands– unpaid and unacknowledged– that facilitate the work of adult men and women" (Nira ramachandran 2002).

A cursory glance at the statistics relating to child labour reveal that, of the 230 million children in the age group of 5 – 14[1], only around 61 per cent attend school, the number of working children in the country are 11.3 million (census of India, 1991). Other estimates place the number of child workers much higher. A study (Chaudhri, 1996) has estimated, using both Census and NSS data, the number of working children in country at 12.7 million in 1991. Thus, the total child labourers in the country are estimated to be about 230 million when estimated using the 1981 proportions.

Several view points analyzing the causes for rampant child labourers in India, have been emerged since the phenomena being identified as the evil, by the various International and National Conventions. These perspectives contemplating the reasons for child labour in India have mostly been relegated the economic reasons as the causes for child labour. They have analysed the child labour causes in terms of economic factors such as poverty, unemployment, trade, wage markets, high costs of education etc. (Basu 1998; Basu and Pham 1998; Jacoby and Skofias 1997; and Grote *et. al.* 1998). But what is lacking in the literature on the reasons for the child labourers in the country is the understanding of the issue from anthropological and sociological perspectives. In this regard, the present article attempts to entail a focus on the sociological reasons for child labour in India.

As observed by Mehta and Jaswal (1996) "The prevalence of child labour has been more or less in all periods of time, though varied in its nature and dimension, depending on the existing socio-economic structure of society. In the past, child labour has been a part of the social organization in which all members pooled their labour to produce for the subsistence and survival. This was particularly true of rural subsistence farming where the work of the child formed part of the labour necessary for the reproduction of the system and value of labour taken as part of child's socialization for reproduction of the labour power. Child labour in the different periods has a chequered history and presents a vivid account of child's sad plight."

CHILD LABOUR AND SOCIALIZATION

It is argued that the normative pattern which existed in the traditional Indian society has provided the legal sanctity to the institution of employing the children into workforce. The child work was conceived to be an integral part of socialization process which converts the child into an adult or the earning member of the household. So when viewed child labour as a socialization process that occupies a key position in brining the child into mainstream, it gives us the scope to relate all the work/ activities that the child associate with, are part of their training process which is needed to prepare them for future endeavors. Similarly in traditional India, the society was scattered according to traditional occupational communities where each caste was identified with a particular occupation and where the entire family members contributed to the household economy. In this context, every child work contributing to household moral economy was termed to be part of the training process. Hence, in traditional India, the main curriculum was consisted of educating about the techniques and dimensions of the traditional occupation belonging to the particular caste/ community and to convert the individual into a responsible person in the society. This training was very essential for rendering hard work (*shrama*) which is essential for attaining *moksha* (liberation from life and death), an essential element of the *Purusharthas*[2] following the Hindu philosophy. Therefore, the perfection of individual was depended upon the training one received since the childhood. Thus, the child labour and child education in traditional Indian society were quite intertwined.

There are interesting theories explaining the existence of social positions and occupational structures that gave rise to typical social institutions which promoted child labour in an institutional form, in traditional Indian society. Two such important institutions have been extensively quoted in the literature on the theories of Indian society – Jajmani system and hereditary specialization of occupations.

JAJMANI SYSTEM

Dumont states that, "it has become common practice to apply the term 'the Jajmani system' to the system corresponding to the prestations and counter-prestations by which the castes as whole bound together in the village, and which is more or less universal in India. To a large extent it is a question of natural as apposed to monetary economy. It is also a question of the closed economy of the Indian village in which essential goods and especially services are found, or used to be found, either on the spot or in the immediate vicinity: this fact corresponds, therefore, to what has long been called the 'village community', in the economic sense of the phrase." (1988:97).

Dumont further explains the Jajmani system in the following terms, "what is the principle behind what is called the Jajmani system? In the first place it makes use of hereditary personal relationships to express the division of labour: each family has a family of specialists at its disposal for each specialized task. Secondly, it regulates prestations and counter-prestations in a way which accords with custom: for the usual tasks, repayment is in kind: it is not made individually for each particular prestation but is spread over the whole year, as is natural for a permanent relationship in an agricultural setting:

a little food may be provided each day, and there is always the right to a fixed quantity of grain at harvest time, and finally there are obligatory presents (often of money) on the occasion of the main festivals of the year and, above all, at the major family ceremonies, which are advantageous occasions for the Praja of the house. A fact which underlines the limited but effective solidarity which is thus set up between "Jaiman and Praja is that in many regions those who are considered the main servants of the village enjoy an allotment of land from a communal fund set apart by their patrons" (Dumont 1988;98-99).

HEREDITARY SPECIALIZATION

According to this, "the caste system comprises the specialization and interdependence of the constituent groups. Specialization entails separation between these groups, but it is oriented towards the needs of the whole. This relationship to the whole, which must be repeatedly emphasized, links the division of labour with hierarchy. It also sharply distinguishes the Indian form of the social division of labour from the modern economic form, which is oriented towards individual profit and in which, at least in theory, the market is left to regulate the whole". (Dumont 1998:92).

Epstein narrated about this arrangement as it existed in her study village, Wangala, as following, "Gold smiths, Blacksmiths, Carpenters, Potters, Washermen and barbers were the hereditary wangala craftsmen castes known for their specialized skills in their respective crafts. Their number was small and they were largely dependents on peasants for their livelihood. Functionaries also owned small areas of agricultural lands which they cultivated themselves. They were respected for their skills and craftsmanship and enjoyed higher status and some privileges when compared to the Scheduled Castes. Functionaries provided peasants with goods and services, in return for which they received annual payments mostly in kind in the form of food grains during harvest times. They lived side by side with the peasants in the main streets of the wangala" (1988:44).

These two popular institutions existed in Indian society give us the scope to find the roots of the present form of child labour when viewed from the broader anthropological/ sociological perspective. What is pertinent to note here is that these particular institutions have facilitated for the rampant child labourers to persist in Indian society. Because, as referred,

1. Training as an integral component imbibed in traditional occupational structure as the instrument used for attaining individual's growth has motivated the family to subscribe the child for the work in the very tender age.
2. The vertical division of labour existed as a social rule in the society and the duly accorded household labour following the Jajmani system and the hereditary specialization of occupations has legitimized the children employing immensely in the workforce.

CHILD LABOUR IN THE CONTEXT OF CHANGE

The occupational structure in India has undergone severe alterations, compared to past, as a result of contacts with foreigners. Several reasons are accorded for a change to be resulted in any occupation. For example, as viewed by Abbott, "Chains of effect in the system of professions begin sometimes in external events, sometimes within the professions themselves. Tasks can be created or destroyed by changes in technology and organizations. New groups can emerge through client differentiation or through the forces leading to enclosure. There are also forces within professions that strengthen or weaken jurisdictions – the development of new knowledge and skill and the structural changes like professionalization and organizational development" (1988:111). In view of this, the context is raised to reckon the reasons for change in occupational structure in India and their impact on child labourers as presented in the following.

Western Education

This is one of the most important factors which has shown the utmost influence on the traditional Indian society and to initiate change in the value system. The education system was redefined with a strict formal learning method as against the traditional form of non-formal education which was basically acquired through socialization process. As a result, the child work which was felt as an essential element to train the children in their respective occupation techniques was de-linked from the mainstream of the society. In the words of Srinivas (1996:192-193) "New economic opportunities came into existence as a result of the establishment of law and order, removal of internal customs barriers, and the extension of communications linking, first, the different parts of the country into a single economy and, second, the country with the world outside. The building of railways, digging of canals and roads, introduction of such plantation crops as indigo, Tea, Cotton, Coffee and Jute, and the growth of towns and factories, provided employment for thousands all over the country. However, for an Indian to take advantage of the better-paid and more prestigeful occupations such as the higher level of the administration and commerce, and the professions, English education was indispensable. The new opportunities, at least at the higher levels, were usually taken advantage of by the high castes, resulting in a considerable overlap between the traditional and new elites. This had the twin effect of increasing the cultural and ideological distance between the high and low castes, as well as making the new opportunities doubly desirable. In the first place, they were well paid and prestigeful, and in the second, only the high castes had access to them.

Diversification of Economic Opportunities

Similarly, the diversification of rural economy which was resulted by the exposure of indigenous socio-economic systems to the western ones has demanded the individual to train in the non-traditional activities where hereditary specialization has lost its importance. But at the same time, the process of diversification of economic opportunities has failed to provide all kinds of livelihood systems that create space for catering to the needs of the families which were retrenched from traditional occupations. Hence there was a lag between the resultant economic opportunities and the demand from the workforce. Aι this juncture people who entered into new professions first have started concentrating the resources in their hands and filling the posts on the basis of primordial attachments than giving priority to qualified. As a result, people from certain social categories were left with jobless and thus succumb to join under the landlords for no wages or low wages where the children also were promoted into workforce for the want of survival. Besides, the remaining working population from the villages was forced to migrate to the towns and cities and to take up the works in the tea shops, factories, hazardous industries, rag picking, begging, etc. The children became the victims of all these developments as they were forced to contribute their share to the household economy.

Agricultural Revolution

The revolution in agricultural also added its owes for the rampant child labourers in the country as it emerged as the new area for the child labour employment. To cater the growing needs of agricultural sector with the systematic irrigation facilities, the demand for labour was increased and thus the children who were employed in handworks – weaving and oil pressing, etc. were accommodated in agriculture sector as agriculture labourers.

Change and Modernization

The new opportunities which were resulted due to change and modernization, brought new demand for child labourers as the new professions (which were caste-free occupations) came up. Hotels, quarrying, mining, automobile industry, slate making, diamond cutting, etc., are some of the new professions emerged outside the caste attachment. These were added to several new occupations, opened up in the village itself in due course of time. For example, well – boring and repairing of pumps, cycles, televisions and radio; agents for cattle feed cakes and seeds; operating larger and smaller grain mills where the scope for child employment was increased.

Srinivas stated that, European missionary effort was a significant factor in the modernization of India. Spurred by an evangelizing zeal, missionaries highlighted the evils of indigenous society (1996:192). Srinivas further states that the missionary onslaught was particularly significant in as much as it threw the new, western-oriented Indian elite on the defensive and made them address themselves to the immense task of reforming their society and reinterpreting their religion (P. 193). Missionaries were also active in humanitarian work and education. They ran hospitals, Orphanages and schools, concentrating their attention on the poor and lowly, that is, untouchables and others from the low caste, tribal folk living in remote areas, and women behind the purdah. They stimulated the growth of regional literatures by setting up printing presses, cutting types for various Indian scripts, printing books and founding journals, writing dictionaries and grammars, and translating classics in the regional tongues into English (P. 193).

These changes resulted in Indian society are reflected in some of the studies undertaken demonstrating the changes in Indian society. They have highlighted the erosion of traditional occupational pattern in India. Mayer (1996) observed that "Of the artisans, only the Carpenters have continued their trade to a significant extent – of the sixteen adult males, four are full-time carpenters in the village and three more work in Dewas; the rest are tailors, a mason, a mechanic, etc. None of the Blacksmiths practices his trade in the village. The tanners no longer tan hides for sale in Dewas. Only one Potter knows how to make pots, the rest either make bricks (an ancillary traditional work) or do other work. There is only one full-time barber, two more of the thirteen adult Barbers working part-time. And the Drummer says he works only if he has no daily labour, since the latter pays him more than the usual honorium for drumming. Thus a minority of artisan males follow their traditional callings. For alms–takers the situation is similar. The village priest, a Brahman and some of the Naths and to a lesser extent the Bairagi priest continue their ministrations, but most men are in other work. Again, only three families of pinjaris are cotton carders and mattress makers. The Goat herds now farm for a living, the village's goat herd being led by a pinjara and many other castes having a few animals. Of the nine Tailors, only two are practicing, their sons having taken up work when this was better paid than tailoring – a decision that some now regret".

Besides the studies focusing on changes in Indian society, some have demonstrated the reasons for these changes resulted in the Indian society. Epstein in her study in a village in south India has observed that "Education is the key factor influencing economic and social changes." She observed that, in her study village, 'Wangala', people did not realize the importance of education in the earlier years of the post-independence period. Therefore, they were not keen to send their children to school. The overall literacy noted in the village was very low and educational facilities were inadequate. In those days, villagers failed to appreciate the importance of education. Most villagers considered education less important than agriculture or other allied activities. It was generally believed that only Brahmins who possess little or no lands should be educated and seek employment. Lack of awareness, poverty, ignorance and inadequate educational facilities were the main factors responsible for the earlier education backwardness in 'wangala'. An increased interest in education was a slow and phased process.

The change against the traditional system in the Indian village was studied by Baily. In his words, "Less frequently, and on some areas, a few low castes had access to new trading or employment opportunities. Bailey mentions how the prohibition policy of the government of Bengal (of which Orissa was then a part) resulted in relative prosperity for the Ganjam and Boad Distilleries (1957:160-161). Oilmen (Telis) all over eastern India benefited from the enlarged market for trade in oil and pressed oil seeds brought about by improved communication and population growth (1957). The Noniyas of eastern Uttar Pradesh, Kolis of the Surat Coast in Gujarat and members of several other groups also benefited from the new employment opportunities resulting from railway, road, and canal construction. In all such cases, the wealthier families or sections became possessed of a desire to move up in the caste hierarchy by acquiring the symbols and ritual of the higher castes.

CONCLUSION

The issue of child labour has mostly been identified with the economic reasons thus letting aside the socio-cultural factors that have led to the emergence of rampant number of child labourers particularly when considered in the Indian context. Hence there has been literature pointing at the problem around the economic reasons only. Also, the measures combating the problem of child labour also are mainly relating to tackle the poverty as the solution to reduce child labourers in the society. In this regard it is argued in this paper, that the phenomena like child labour should be studied in the context of traditional social institutions which promoted and legitimized it. The aspects like sensitization of the parents, children, government departments and other Civil Society partners are yet to be taken a serious shape as the strategies to combat the problem. It is necessary to sensitize the society about certain evil tendencies (such as the jajmani system and the hereditary specialization of occupations) which existed in the traditional Indian society and provided legal sanctity for employing child labour as highlighted in the above discussion. Because, this kind of education would make the society to understand the issue more deeply and instill among the partners, the spirit of bringing a child labour-free society. Besides, training should be adapted as a tool to make the masses and other stake holders aware of the debate undertaken against child labour in India and outside also.

NOTES

1. A child in the age group of 5-14, who undertake paid work is defined as a child labourer.
2. Hinduism talks of four goals of life which human-beings ought to pursue. If *moksha* (liberation from life and death) is the ultimate goal of a person, the wish for a long span of life on this earth is

his immediate desire. The harmony between the two aims is unfolded in the theory of *purusharthas*. There are believed to be four purusharthas or aims of life; *artha, kama, dharma and moksha*. *Artha* (wealth) refers to acquisition and enjoyment of wealth; kama (satisfaction of biological desire) refers to the satisfaction of sex drives and temporal interests and aesthetic urges; dharma (right conduct) refers to the acceptance of the prescribed discipline and obligations in social, religious and cultural realms; and moksha refers to the ideal of spiritual realization. While the first three goals are all external to man and therefore attainable (*sadhya* or means), the last one is immanent in him and it has only to be given a chance for achievement (*sidha*). Hinduism does not deny the pursuit of any of these goals to any individual in because of his low status ascribed by birth.

REFERENCES

Abbott, Andrew (1988), The System of Professions – An Essay on the Division of Expert Labour. Chicago: The University of Chicago Press.

Bailey, F.G. (1957), Caste and the Economic Frontier.

Manchester: Manchester University Press.

Basu, K (1998), Child Labour; Causes Consequences and Cure, with Remarks in international standards". Journal of Economic Literature.

Basu, K. and Pham H. Van (1998), "the Economics of child labour". American Economic Review, Vol. 88.

Census of India, 1991.

Chaudhri, D.P. (1996), A Dynamic Profile of child labour in India, 1951–1991. Child Labour Action and Support Project, ILO, New Delhi, Quoted in Ramachandran, Nira (2002).

Dev, S. Mahendra (2002), Child Labour in India: Dimensions, Determinants and Policies. in 'Economics of child labour' edited by Kannan, K.P. (2001) New Delhi: Deep and Deep Publications Pvt. Ltd.

Dumont (1988), Homo hierarchies the caste system and its implications, Delhi OUP 1998.

Grote, U., Basu A. and Weinhold, D. (1998), Child Labour and the International Policy Debate, ZEF discussion paper on Development policy. Quoted in Dev, S. Mahendra (2002).

Jacoby, Hanan and Skoufias (1997), "Risk, Financial Markets and Human Capital in a Developing Country" Review of Economic studies, Vol. 64, pp. 311–35.

Massiin, Lionel (2002), New Delhi Institute for Human Development and United Nations World Food Programme.

Mayer, Adrian (1996), Caste in Indian Village: Change and Continuity 1954-1992. in 'Caste Today' edited by C.J. Fuller. Delhi: Oxford University Press (SOAS Studies on South Indian Understandings and Perspectives).

Mehta, P.L. and Jaswal, S.S. (1996), Child Labour and the Law: Myth and Reality of Welfare Measures. New Delhi; Deep and Deep Publications.

Nieuwenhuys, O. (1999), Children's Life Worlds: Gender, Welfare and Labour in the Developing world. New Delhi: Social Science Press:

Ramachandran, Nira, (2002), Introducing the concept in "Coming to Grips with Rural Child Work – A Food Security Approach edited by Ramachandran, Nira and Massiin, Lionel (2002). New Delhi: Institute for Human Development and United Nations World Food Programme.

Srinivas (1996), Mobility in the Caste System, in Singer, Milton and Bernard S. Cohn (1996) edited "Structure and Change in Indian Society. Jaipur: Rawat Publications).

22

NGOs IN INDIA: SOME OBSERVATIONS

*M. Venkataramana**

INTRODUCTION

After Independence, we have completed 50 years of planned development process. Since the top to down approach has failed in getting the expected results, more emphasis was laid on micro level planning. Looking into the results it was observed by the Government that peoples participation should be the prime concern and mere concentration of economic growth will not help in obtaining the desired results in development. The planned development has both success and failures. According to Ferrington and Bebbington (1993), looking from social and human development point of view, the odds seem to be highly in favour of failures rather than success. So, Nitya Nanda (2000) mentions that it is in this context, the attention is increasingly turning towards the NGOs as a vehicle for development. According to Francis (1993) NGOs are in a highly advantageous position to enlist the participation of people as they are at the disposal of the people and their duty hours are not time bound. Nor are they governed by rigid set of rules and regulations as found in the bureaucratic administrative set up and are flexible in their approach towards human development about several

* Junior Faculty, Council for Social Development, Southern Regional Office, Hyderabad–500 048.

Note: The author thanks Dr. K.S. Bhat, Regional Director, Council for Social Development, Hyderabad for his cooperation and encouragement in writing this article.

ways and means to enlist the participation of rural masses. As NGOs are growing as third sector of development their role is very important for the people of our country. The present article is based on secondary data and field observations in few parts of our country.

MEANING OF NGO

NGO is a quite loose and ambiguous term. It refers to a wide variety of non-profit organizations. NGOs are non-governmental, organised collectives with a purpose. "Organised encompasses wide range of structures from informal, unstructured associations and groups to highly structured and formalized collectives (Vanita Viswanath : 1993). As Mexime Weisgran (1977) notes in her study in India on Rajasthan NGOs, it is the term used rather loosely to refer to any organization that is not a direct division of national government.

According to Rajasekhar (2000), the term NGO is negative in the sense it seeks to give a meaning that NGOs possess the characteristics/features not possessed by the Government. The following four characters make the NGOs as distinct organizations: (1) voluntary formation, (2) working towards development and amelioration of suffering, (3) working with non-self serving aims, and (4) relative independence. However according to R.K. Murthy and Nitya Rao (1997), the NGOs have to work within the parameters of Government legislations and policies formulated for NGOs.

The present NGOs are an outcome of the experiences of voluntarism. Little history on this will help us to understand the present status of NGOs.

HISTORY

According to Roussean (French Philospher), "Doing good to fellow beings without motive in part of the gregarious instinct of man" (Jagadananda : 2001). The term NGOs is from west. In India they are called voluntary organizations. All the NGOs are not voluntary organizations. As K. K. Mukherjee describes the origin of formalized voluntary action can be traced back to the informal voluntary efforts which found their initial support from religion and consequently from the social institutional structure. The activities of Christian missionaries, mainly in the areas of health and education in remote villages and hill areas and their approach to human problems evoked a defensive reaction among the Hindus. This reaction motivated persons like Raja Rammohan Roy, Iswarchandra Vidyasagar and many others to take up various social reform issues (Mukherjee : 2001). Saroj Pachauri (1994) mentions that Gandhi's will for voluntary work during 1920s and 1930s for the upliftment of rural poor and the Scheduled Castes drew large number of committed persons to work for the disadvantaged community and this marked the beginning of Sarvodaya Movement. The national stream of NGOs got momentum in 1930s and 1940s, increased in number during 1950s and 1960s for relief and rehabilitation. During 1970s the NGOs worked on equity, social justice, community participation and integral development during 1980s on empowerment, consciensation and participation of people in development programmes.

As diversification of activities increased and the NGOs are multiplied in their number, it is difficult to classify exactly the types of NGOs. However, some discussion was made below based on the available literature. The role of the NGO depends on the activity which the NGO takes up and the type of NGO.

TYPES OF NGOs

D. Rajasekhar (1999) divided NGOs into four types :

(1) Operational or Grassroot NGOs
(2) Support NGOs
(3) Umbrella or Network NGOs
(4) Funding NGOs

Joel S.G.R. Bhose (2003) classified NGOs into 8 types–

(1) Charity NGOs
(2) Relief and Rehabilitation NGOs
(3) Service Providing NGOs
(4) Economic Development NGOs
(5) Social Development NGOs
(6) Empowerment NGOs

(7) Network NGOs
(8) Support NGOs

In practice, the roles of NGOs are mixed and heterogeneous. The NGOs be at grassroot level, mandal or block level, state level, national or international level.

Some statistical data on NGOs will help us in understanding their growth in our country.

STATISTICS

For many decades NGOs have been active in implementing development projects. According to World Bank, NGOs in India spend US $ 520 million a year, a figure representing a full quarter of the foreign aid India receives annually (Dharmarajan : 2001).

- India has 1.18 million non-profit organizations. 53 per cent work in rural areas, 47 per cent are urban.
- Nearly half of the NGOs in India are unregistered. Maharashtra is highest on registered organizations : 74% Tamil Nadu, the lowest : 47%.
- Out of the 20 million persons involved in the NGO sector, 85 per cent are volunteers and the rest are paid employees.
- Out of the NGOs 26.3 % are engaged in religious activities, 21.3 % are doing community service, 20.4 are in education activity, 17.9 % are in sports/culture, 6.6 are engaged in health, while 7.5 are engaged in other activities.
- 75 million households (40.7 per cent of total households in India) give for a charitable cause.
- Nationwide, only 7.4 per cent of total receipt are foreign funds, contrary to popular perception.
- Nationwide estimates of total receipts of NGOs for 1999-2000 were Rs. 17,922 crore. 51% of the funds are self-generated, 29 % are from Grants, 12.9 % are Donations, while 7.1% are through loans (Down to Earth : 2003).

ROLE OF NGOs

Depending on the objectives and area of operation specific roles will be created by the NGOs. Their role starts from motivation of people in identifying their needs and finally ends in completion of project and with follow up. The National Commission on Urbanization 1988 mentioned in their report that often governments and their agencies are unable to appreciate the wide variety of roles that NGOs can play at different levels like (a) assisting the weak in obtaining service and the state in effectively delivering them, (b) providing professional services in research, project formulation and implementation, (c) monitoring effects of developmental actions, (d) highlighting their contradictions, (e) advocating causes, (f) protecting and upholding values, (g) organizing people to actualize their potential and strengths and ascertain their rights, (h) strengthening democratic values and institutions, (i) facilitating participatory processes through education and intermediation. The watchdog role, the intermediary role, the innovator role and the service provider role are predominant in the list of priorities of NGOs. The newly conceived role it appears is that of deliverer of government sponsored services and implementer of Government sponsored welfare and development schemes.

DEFICIENCIES

Apart from the merits, some of the NGOs are facing certain deficiencies while performing their roles. D.R. Sachdeva (2000) gave a list of deficiencies in his book Social Welfare Administration in India. (1) Lack of dedicated leadership, (2) concentration of leadership in elderly persons, (3) Monopolization and interlocking of leadership, (4) Deterioration of services, (5) Failure to enlist popular participation, (5) Isolation, (6) Financial Scarcity, (7) Absence of erstwhile pioneering spirit, (8) Misuse and misappropriation of funds, (9) Inadequacy of trained personnel, (10) Absence of common Forum and Coordination, (11) Erosion of old virtues, (12) Set-back to their autonomy.

For most of the unemployed youth, starting an NGO is a self-employment activity. They start with an eye camp or a short service programme. Later they have to search for funds. Unless there is three years of proper functioning, no NGO can expect any grant from any funding agency. Under the assumption that some grant will come, some NGOs are starting some activity and expecting continuation, some NGOs are taking up an activity with given grant. This ends up with stopping of work due to paucity of funds. The other deficiencies are - (1) Lack of data base from the area of operation, (2) Lack of technical skills, (3), Improper preparation of project proposals, (4) Dependency on middlemen, (5) Lack of qualified people in the NGOs starting from proposed to report writing.

Dependency on political parties for funds, more political intervention also weakens the role of NGOs. According to Sujit Kumar Paul & Kakali Paul, very few NGOs presently taken the issue of sustainable rural development very seriously and trying to disseminate the idea of sustainable agricultural development and sustainable rural development to the grassroot level. But their area of action is limited and several restrictions and impositions are acting as hindrance to their independent activities. Specially in West Bengal, the NGOs could not function as well as compared to other provinces in India. Their scope to work has been limited and restricted and their entry to rural development got obstructed mainly for the establishment of Panchayat as a strong institution through regular election during the last two decades. As Panchayat tremendous public support, little need was there to opt for NGO. Moreover the clash of ideology between NGOs and Panchayat and their preconceived idea about NGOs role hampered to a large extent the collaborative work as well as participation of NGOs in the development process. But now the situation is changing.

SUGGESTIONS

The following are some suggestions from the above discussion.

The NGOs should clearly know their roles much before starting the programme and while implementing the programme. Otherwise, it leads to suspicion in the public which leads to problems even for the existence of the NGO.

For a better role of NGOs in rural development. Joel S.G.R. Bose (2003) has made the following suggestions– (1) Facilitating role and working catalysts, (2) Explore more and more local funding, (3) NGOs should realize that people are truly their masters, (4) Empowering the people involve them in evaluation and impact assessment, (5) People require capacities and not subsidies, (6) Good to have qualified hands and proper payment according to their capacity and capability, (7) Networking, (8) Avoid duplication & intervention of two or more NGOs, (9) Reduce their overhead charges, say 10%, (10) Coordination and linkage between administrative staff and field staff, (11) People centered intervention, (12) Application of common sense despite the well designed objectives and well articulated strategies.

Apart from these, the other suggestions that can be made are as follows -

(1) Data base should be created in the area of operation.
(2) Baseline survey should be conducted in the field area.
(3) Thorough knowledge of field situation is necessary for NGOs.
(4) Ability to mould the data according to the needs of funding agencies.
(5) Improve knowledge in proposal and report writing.
(6) Equip with participatory methods for identification of needs, planning, implementation, etc.
(7) Proper networking with other NGOs.
(8) Every NGO should have a frame of objectives in which it should work but the objectives should not change according to funds. After working in a specified area for some time from the objectives the NGOs should identify related new issues. Then there will be continuity of programmes with some consistency. This may be compared to the tree diagram in Participatory Methods.
(9) Proper documentation of the works done is also essential for NGOs.
(10) Trained persons should be appointed by the NGOs or the staff should be trained as NGOs work is now not a charity. It is going upto giving advise to planners. Minimum research knowledge is necessary for NGOs.

According to Neil Webster, "Donor funded projects with government institutions as partners were increasingly asking for NGO involvement. One consequence has been that the role of NGOs has been increasingly defined by other institutional actors for whom the NGOs local status is but one of several factors shaping the design of policy manifesting itself in the form of country strategy papers, sector programmes and individual project interventions" (D. Rajasekhar : 1999).

The well established NGOs have the above to a main extent. But the newly started NGOs and developing NGOs at grass root level are lacking the above by which their sustainability is becoming a problem.

Updating the knowledge, training in latest developments, involving in Conferences, Seminars, etc., publicity of the work done either in the form of brochure, report or media will also help the NGOs in strongly establishing themselves by which they can perform well in their activity.

REFERENCES

Bhose Joel S.G.R, 2003, *NGOs and Rural Development : Theory and Practice*, New Delhi : Concept Publishing Company.

David C. Korten, 1990, *"Getting to the 21st Century – Voluntary Action and Global Agenda*, USA, Kumarian Press, in Ranjani, K. Moorthi and Nitya Rao 1997 : *Indian NGOs and their Capacity Enhancement in 1990s*, New Delhi, EES, in Lalita N. 2004, *Rural Development in India : Emerging Issues and Trends*, Vol. 2, New Delhi : Dominant Publishers and Distributors.

Down to Earth, 2003, "Profit's the non-Word About non-profit organizations (NPOs), also thought non-governmental", Society for Participatory Research in Asia and Institute for Policy Studies, John's Hopkins University, USA, P. 60.

Dharmarajan Shivani, 2001, *NGOs as Prime Movers : Social Action for Social Development*, New Delhi : Kanishka Publishers.

Farrington J., and A. Babbington with K. Wells and D. Lewis 1993 : 'Reluctant Partners? NGOs, the State and Sustainable Development', London : Routledge in Nanda Nitya, 2000, "The Emerging Role of NGOs in Rural Development of India", *Social Change*, Vol. 30, No. 3 & 4, September-December, P. 36-43.

Francis C., 1993, "Rural Development, People's Participation and the Role of NGOs", *Journal of Rural Development*, Vol. 12, No. 2, P. 208.

Jagadananda, 2001, "Volunteerism : Current Scene and Prospects", *Yojana*, Vol. 45, December, P. 18-20.

Misra, Yatish, 2002, *Empowering People : Grassroot Organizations and Rural Development*, New Delhi, Kanishka Publishers.

Mukherjee K.K., 2001, "Volunteerism in India : Some Perspectives", *Yojana*, Vol. 45, December, P. 5&6.

Mencher Joan, 1999, "NGOs : Are they a Force for Change", *Economic and Political Weekly*, Vol. XXXIV, No. 30, July 24-30, P. 2081.

Murthy R.K., and Nitya Rao 1997, Indian NGOs, Poverty Alleviation and their Capacity Enhancement in the 1990s. An Institutional and Social Relations Perspective, New Delhi FES in Rajasekhar D., 2000, "Non-Governmental Organizations in India : Opportunities and Challenges", *Journal of Rural Development*, Vol. 19, No. 2,, P. 249-275.

National Commission on Urbanization, 1988, "People's Participation", *Report of the National Commission on Urbanization*, Vol. II, August, P. 312 & 313.

Nanda Nitya, 2000, "The Emerging Role of NGOs in Rural Development of India", *Social Change*, Vol. 30, No. 3 & 4, September-December, P. 36-43.

Paul Sujit Kumar & Paul Kakali, 2003, "Role of Panchayats and NGOs towards Sustainable Rural Development", *Yojana*, Vol. 47, No. 6, June, P. 21.

Pachauri Saroj, 1994, *Reaching India's Poor : Non-Governmental Approaches to Community Health*, New Delhi : Sage Publications.

Rajasekhar D., 2000, "Non-Governmental Organizations in India : Opportunities and Challenges", *Journal of Rural Development*, Vol. 19, No. 2,, P. 249-275.

Rajasekhar D. (Ed.) 1999, *Decentralised Government and NGOs Issues, Strategies and Ways Forward*, New Delhi : Concept Publishing Company.

Sachdeva D.R. 2003, *Social Welfare Administration in India*, Allahabad, Kitab Mahal.

Viswanath Vanitha, 1993 : *NGOs and Women's Development in Rural South India : A Comparative Analysis*, New Delhi : Visttar Publications.

Webster Neil, 1999, "NGOs and Local Government; Democratization of Local Development" in D. Rajasekhar (Ed.) : *Decentralised Government and NGOs Issues, Strategies and Ways Forward,* New Delhi : Concept Publishing Company.

Wiesgrau, Maxine, 1977 : Interpreting Development : Local Histories, Local Strategies (Lanham, New York), University Press of America Inc.

23

THE ROLE OF GOVERNMENT & NON-GOVERNMENTAL AGENCIES IN GOVERNANCE: A PERSPECTIVE

B. S. Vasudeva Rao &*
*M.V.S.S. Prakasa Rao***

India as developing country faces today, the greatest challenges in the sphere of socio-economic development, education, health and welfare of the masses. The population growth, regional disparities in development and widening rural-urban disparities, increasing rate of unemployment and underemployment and many development and welfare related issues have influence on the level of development and quality of life. In this context governance is significant to give a shape and direction for the desired level of socio-economic well-being of the society and also to achieve the same.

The good governance reflects in the goals and objectives of a government. More so in development policies and programmes and manner of their execution for achieving desired level of development. Above all, the general perception of the people about the functioning and government and of its

* Associate Professor, Dept. of Adult & Continuing Education, Andhra University, Visakhapatnam –530003.
e-mail: bsvasudevarao_au@Rediffmail.com

** Associate Professor, Dept. of Adult & Continuing Education, Andhra University, Visakhapatnam –530003.
e-mail: bsvasudevarao_au@Rediffmail.com

various agencies towards the performance in the sphere of development and welfare. It is also important to have decentralization of power functioning and resources so as to achieve, even grassroots level development and for performance-orientation.

The central and state governments followed an approach with positive discrimination and making special efforts by several programmes for elimination of poverty, developing disadvantaged groups, developing backward areas, protecting the rights of the child, raising the literacy levels, improving access to health care, empowering the women by increasing gender sensitivity, and ensuring equal opportunity for all sections of the society.

GOVERNANCE IN ANDHRA PRADESH

The Government of Andhra Pradesh has set itself an ambitious goal to achieve for the overall development of the state in all aspects. By 2020, the State will achieve a level of development that provides its people an opportunities to achieve prosperity and wellbeing and enjoy a high quality of life. The perspective plan is known as "VISION 2020" that envisages to achieve by 2020, every individual in Andhra Pradesh will be able to lead a comfortable life, filled with opportunities to learn, develop skills, and earn a livelihood. It is also aimed that with massive Poverty eradication efforts existing level of inequalities is expected to disappear. Disadvantaged groups-scheduled castes, scheduled tribes, backward classes, and children will be empowered and provided with various opportunities to achieve development by systematically harness their full potential.

The State Government aimed at to transform itself and quickly adopt a new role under "good governance" approach from being primarily a controller of the economy, it must become a facilitator and catalyst of its growth.

The State has increased allocation of budget for education and health, and embarked on a programme to achieve universal primary education and strengthen primary health care. Much emphasis laid on the systematic development of human resource that would form basis for the overall development.

The Government of Andhra Pradesh has set mission with set of strategies to fulfill the goals of Vision 2020. They are :

- Eradicate poverty and take care of its old, infirm, and genuinely needy.
- Enable its people to learn, earn and lead health and productive lives.
- Promote small families for a healthy and wealthy society.
- Empower and support its women and girls to fulfill their roles as equal shapers with men of the economy society.
- The aim to become the "Education Capital of India" by building 15 to 20 unique educational institutions in the state.
- Create the resources its people will need, such as capital and infrastructure, to transform their own futures.
- Make its government simple, transparent, accountable and responsive.
- The Government will pursue specific strategies to remove disparities between different categories of its people and between different regions of the state.
- Ensure that its people continue to have a strong voice and role in the governance of their state.

At the same time in the process of decentralization, government machinery got reoriented to be responsive to the needy and people oriented in many aspects of development administration. As part of the decentralized Community Initiatives Non-Governmental organizations have emerged to address the development issues based on a participatory holistic approach.

CONCEPT OF NON-GOVERNMENTAL ORGANIZATION (NGO)

The Non-Governmental organizations could also be sponsored by the government. The NGOs are known for their people-oriented by virtues of human touch, dedication, flexibility, self-reliance and nearness to the community. The Christian missionaries are playing vital role in this area. Other voluntary agencies and the movements namely Shantiniketan, Gandhian Movement, Chipco Mvs, Narmada Bachao Andolan are known for their contribution in bridging the gap between the rural and urban services by way of setting up educational, health and environmental services in different parts of the country.

Aiming at self-reliance of the people. Non-Governmental organization generally adopt a localized, but holistic approach to rural development and plan to organize their programmes in such a way as to cover all aspects of rural life. Mostly, activities of the NGOs are need based and also to solve local problems.

Based on the approaches they adopt and the priority they give, NGOs have been classified into seven categories by J.B. Singh. They are:

(1) ***Charity:***	Giving food, clothing, medicine, alms, in cash and in kind, land, building etc.
(2) ***Welfare:***	Providing facilities for education, health, drinking, water, roads, communication etc.
(3) ***Relief:***	Responding to immediate needs arising out of natural calamities like floods, drought, earthquakes and manmade calamities like refugee, ravages of water, etc.
(4) ***Rehabilitation:***	Continuing and taking up steps to the work in areas struck by calamities and starting activities that are durable in nature.
(5) ***Services:***	Building up infrastructure in the neglected backward areas.
(6) ***Development***	Socio-economic development
(7) ***Development of Human Beings:***	Conscious raising, awareness, raising, organizing, recording of priorities, to suit social justice, opening up of opportunities to the oppressed and the exploited.

THE ROLE OF NON-GOVERNMENTAL ORGANIZATIONS

In the contemporary era, NGOs and voluntary organizations play the multiple role as the promoters of development, catalysts for socio-economic and political changes as motivators for popular participation in influencing public policy and public opinion. They engage themselves in conscientization, play a role in enforcement of law and social legislation and also act as a vital link between the people and the government.

Creating awareness among the rural masses about their basic rights to services is an important role played by the NGO and voluntary agencies. Generation of awareness led to a situation in which demand their rights has made the local delivery system more responsive to the needs of the poor especially in the rural India. As an awareness creating agency, the NGO can:

- Supplement the government efforts so as to offer the rural poor choices and alternatives.
- Be the eyes and ears of the people at the village level.
- Adopt simple, innovative, flexible and inexpensive means with its limited resources to reach a large number with less overheads and with greater community participation and make communities as self-reliant as possible.
- Disseminate information and Activate the delivery system and to make it effective at the village level in respond to the felt needs of the poorest of the poor.
- Show how village level local resources could be used that include human resources, skills and local knowledge, grossly underutilized at present, could be used for their own development.
- To train a cadre of grassroots workers who would become professional in their field of work.
- To mobilize financial resources from within the community with a viewing making communities stand on their own feet.
- To mobilize and organize the poor and generate awareness to demand quality services and impose a

community system of accountability on the performance of village level of government functionaries.

DEVELOPMENT-NEED OF THE HOUR

In the process of development of the rural areas poor is emerging as the main target of all development efforts. Development is seen as process of change to be set in motion and guided towards the objective of eradicating hunger, disease, injustice, exploitation and related ills that afflict vast sections of the rural population. It is possible that technology transfer would have influence in terms of increased efficiency and effectiveness in the process of development. It demands the active participation of all the people for whom a programme or project is conceived. Participation of People has become an important input in rural development. Participation of people not to take benefits, but also to own the development process. There are several bottlenecks in achieving participatory development. There are cases of success but we need a cautious move to reap the benefit in its real sense.

EDUCATION

Education in the State will be strengthened to achieve two aims.

1. Universal access to primary education and skill-building and primary education will be strengthened by providing more schools, managing them, better and making teaching more effective.
2. In parallel, secondary and higher education will be augmented, mainly through the provision of courses specifically aimed at equipping students with skills that cater to the needs of the industry and society.

HEALTH

In respect to health, the State Government will focus on providing universal access to primary healthcare; enhancing secondary and tertiary healthcare and providing affordable access to these service; and strengthening disease preventions programmes.

The government will ensure a greater focus on decentralized and responsive administration by local government and participation by the community. The State Government will enable this shift in power and responsibility by providing active technical, resource, and policy support to local governments.

WOMEN

Women are the vital human infrastructure and their empowerment economic, educational, social and political – would hasten the pace of social development. Investing in women's "capabilities" and empowering them to achieve their "choices" and "opportunities" is the surest way to contribute to economic growth and overall development.

A women plays a key role in providing a home environment, safe drinking water, health diet, etc. The mother is responsible for physical, mental and social development of the child.

Women in villages are confined to their families and to helping take care of their cattle, village farming or gardening.

Recent studies highlight that women in India are major produces of food in terms of value, volume and number of hours worked. Nearly 63 per cent of all economically active men are engaged in agriculture as compared to 90 per cent women.

CHILD LABOUR

Child labour is an inevitable consequence of the economic forces operating at the family level. As long as poverty continues to exist it would be difficult to eliminate it. Any attempt to abolish it through legal recourse would, under the circumstances, not be practical since this would put already poor families under acute economic stress. In this situation, the only alternative that is left is to ban child labour in hazardous areas and to regulate and ameliorate the conditions of work in others areas. This assessment of the child labour areas. This assessment of the child labour situation is one which many governments including India have adopted.

GIRL CHILD

Years of neglect and discrimination against girl child cannot be turned around in a day. However, careful planning on the part of the government to raise educational level across the country with cooperation of the civil society will result in the empowerment of women.

DECENTRALIZED INSTITUTIONS : GOVERNMENT AND VOLUNTARY AGENCIES

From the beginning of the 1990s, there seems to be a positive change in the outlook towards decentralized institutions. In the emerging scenarios both panchayats and voluntary agencies, have a crucial role to play and can work together effectively if they view each others as partners rather than contenders in the process of decentralization and development.

CONCLUSIONS

For achieving value based governance, there is need to rectify certain areas in both government and non-governmental organizations like corruption, enlisting the support of non-official bodies, need to implement ideas generated on administrative reforms, need to change political climate, need to democratize and vitalize, Panchayat Raj Institutions.

GOVERNMENTAL AGENCIES

- The social-economic of good governance briefly enumerated in the Directive Principles of State Policy which have been mentioned in Vision 2020 document are yet to be realized even after half-century of freedom.
- Plethora of rules, regulations, forms and formalities have only increased the role and importance of the lower bureaucracy and the misery of the people.
- Swaraj appeared to have turned a blind eye to the many problems people face daily with the administration. Debureaucratization of administration at the grassroots is need of the hour to give relief to the people from over-regulation and over-administration.

- Our administration is sinking in its own sins and needs to be rescued through rational and administrative measures and patriotic leadership rising above party politics.

VOLUNTARY ORGANIZATIONS/NON-GOVERNMENTAL ORGANIZATIONS

Of course the weakness and deficiencies of voluntary organizations are not the same for all type of voluntary organization. They differ from organization to organization, region to region. However, some common problems can be enlisted and discussed which are applicable in general to all most all the voluntary organizations. Some of the main constraints are :

- **Absence of Erstwhile Sprite of Volunteerism:** The basic characteristic of a voluntary organization is volunteerism. Voluntary organization worked as pioneers in early days but the enthusiasm seems to have faded these days.
- **Lack of Dedicated Leadership:** Leadership qualities of the learners in voluntary organizations determine the quality and condition of the services rendered by any voluntary organization.
- **Lack of Funds:** Most of the voluntary organizations suffer from paucity of funds. Government does not give cent per cent grants in aid for numerous programmes.
- **Inadequate Trained Personnel:** It is believed that the personnel working in voluntary organizations may be of different kind. The main requirements of the personnel working in such organizations is a sense of dedication and commitment and interest in the social services.
- **Lack of Coordination:** The absence of coordination, council of voluntary organizations existing at local, state and national level to the common problems such as overlapping, duplication, non-coordination, etc.

- **Deterioration of Quality of Services:** Day by day the quality of services of the voluntary organizations is deteriorating.
- **Misuse of Funds:** It is the matter of fact that some unscrupulous elements have made fortunes by floating organization for their personal gains and managing grants from the government.
- **Lack of Public Participation:** Voluntary organizations are meant to provide opportunities to citizens for democratic participation but they have not been able to fulfill this obligation due to the method and manner in which they function, and failed to attract people, interested in constructive work and develop channels for people's enthusiastic participation.
- **Monopolization of Leadership:** It has been observed that there is a growing tendency towards monopolization and interlocking of leadership at the top level of voluntary action groups and organizations as is reflected in the same person being the president in one organization, secretary in the other, treasurer in the third and a member of the executive in the fourth.

The new value system will have to grow through opportunities for working together. It cannot come by preaching it has to come from actual experience and by sharing experience together through work. This is exceedingly important. And unfortunately, we have given little thought to learning by doing. The committed involvement of functionaries and active participation of masses only give value for good governance.

REFERENCES

Enlightened Citizenship, Rama Krishna Mission, New Delhi, December 1985.

Health Services with a Difference : Prajapita Brahma Kumari Iswariya Viswa Vidyalaya, International Headquarters, Mount Abu, India.

Journals of Yojana, Kurukshetra, and the News Daily like Hindu, Eenadu, Weekly like Employment News, India Today etc.

Non-Governmental Organizations in Development, (Case Study of Sadpur District), B.T. Lawrence, Rawat Publications, Jaipur and New Delhi, 1999.

Non-Governmental Organizations in Development : *Theory and Practice, Edited by Noorjahan Bava,* Kanishka Publications, Distributors, New Delhi-110 002.

Reaching Health to the Poor, Source Book on *District Health Management, T. Sundara Rama, Harh Mander, R. Srinivas Murthy,* Alok Sukhla, Voluntary Health Association of India, New Delhi, 1996.

Satya Sai Education in Human Values, *Discourses of Sri Satya Sai Baba,* Complied by Loraine Burrows, Prasanti Nilayam, Anantapur District, Andhra Pradesh, India, January, 1999.

Vision 2020, Swarnandhra Pradesh, Draft Vision 2020 Document, Government of Andhra Pradesh, India, January, 1999.

Voluntary Action and Gandhian Approach, *A Study of the Voluntary Movement in India,* D.K. Oza, National Bank Trust, India, 1991.

24

ADOPTION OF UN CONVENTION ON THE RIGHTS OF THE CHILD, 1989 AND CHILD LABOUR IN INDIA

P. Hazarika *

INTRODUCTION

Children belonging to poor and destitute families are the most vulnerable section of the society anywhere in the world. For, they suffer in malnutrition, health problem, insecurity of life, vitamin deficiency, mental and physical debility etc. Besides, some of them are put into work or forced to work by their parents as to tide over the financial crises. Thus, many children become family bread earner at their school going age, suffer torture and get abused at the hands of their users. Apart the employer, the parents become the first exploiter of children. Being abused by their employer/ parents many children turn out to be the professional criminal, involve in anti-social activity, spoil their own lives, and bring trouble to the families they belong to. Thus, an important section of the futurity become mentally crippled, physically sick and morally spoiled.

Such an untold tragedy of millions of children have been focused by the ILO, UNICEF and Human Rights Commissions. In South Asia (India, Bangladesh, Pakistan, Nepal, Sri Lanka, Bhutan and Maldavis) over 40 million children are out of primary schools. India shares over 28 million. 41% Indian school going children are dropping out before reaching the grade-V.

* Faculty Member, Demow College, Demow Sivanagar District, Assam.

Such not-school attending children either join the workforce or they are compelled to work hard labour at early ages due to economic necessity of the household. Those who stay at home as nonworker and non-student too have to suffer a lot either due to malnutrition, poverty and hunger, health problem and torture at home. The tragedy of such minor children cannot be described unless the children in the streets and in slum areas of the cities are confronted by a self.

In order to rescue such poor children from ocean of tears UN General Assembly adopted the Convention on the Rights of the Child (CRC) in 1989. It came into force in 1990.

The convention (CRC, 1989) seeks to lay down the minimum standard for survival, protection and development of all children. The United Nations' CRC, 1989 is an update of the ILO's 1924 Geneva declaration and that of resolution taken in 1959 in the UN General Assembly. In 1959 UN recognized the children's rights in the "Universal Declaration of the Human Rights". Thus, the CRC, 1989, is the restatement of the earlier declarations. The peculiarity is that CRC, 1989 recognises the need for specific attention to protect and promote the rights of the children, to support their growth and development for becoming worthy citizens of the world. It also represents international commitment to entitle the childhood special care and assistance, right to live, survival and development and protection against all forms of discrimination or punishment.

India has made a commitment in 1992 before the international community to implement and realise the objectives of CRC, 1989.

WHY HAS INDIA ADOPTED IT?

India was a founder member of the ILO in 1919. Since then, India has been implementing certain ILO & U.N. adopted conventions. In latter period, since 1945 ILO had come to be an inseparable organ of the UN. So, ILO's adopted conventions too have come to be known as UN conventions. Till to date India has adopted only 5 (five) international conventions recommended by the UN and its agencies.

These are–

1. Convention NO.	:	5, Year 1919-called, Minimum age convention.
2. Convention No.	:	15, Year 1921, Minimum age convention (Trimmers and stockers)
3. Convention No.	:	29, Year 1930, Forced labour convention.
4. Convention No.	:	123, Year 1965, Minimum age (underground work) convention.
5. Convention No. (NA)	:	Year 1989, Convention on the Rights of the child.

India's adoption of and commitment to CRC, 1989 was precipitated by some other international developments.

(i) ILO declared the year of 1979 as the International Year of the Child. So, under public pressure government of India had to setup the Gurupadaswami Committee in 1979 to submit its report on child labour in India.

(ii) Under the banner of UN a world summit for children was held in 1990. Heads of the governments/states of 159 countries attended the summit and endorsed the convention on the rights of the child, 1989. They signed a declaration on survival, protection and development of children. This came to be known as world declaration, 1990. The heads of the governments/states also signed a plan of action for implementing the world declaration. The CRC 1989 thus came into force from 1990 onward. Out of 159 countries, India was one of the signatories of the world declaration and its plan of action as well.

(iii) The Declaration, (1990) signed, *inter alia*, articulates a series of children's rights, among others, compulsory and free primary education for all are the main.

(iv) CRC, 1989 has become popular, either due to its relevance and necessity and/or world pressure. This convention has been ratified by 191 countries over the world.

(v) Declaration of human rights was made and was adopted by UN in 1948. In the history of human civilization, it for the first time acknowledged the human rights as a global responsibility. India under the Human Rights Act, had to set up National Human Rights Commission in 1992 and under the same government, had to recognise the human rights to children.

For, the first article of the Universal Declaration of Human Rights (1948) runs as follows:

All human beings are born free and equal in dignity and rights. They are endowed with reason and conscience and should act towards one another in a spirit of brotherhood." In fact, in total of its 30 articles equality of man, their freedom and rights have been established in a global order.

(vi) Surveys made by ILO and UNICEF and their activities for the betterment of children community in India exposed the miserable conditions of Indian children. The exuberant verbosity of government in fighting the miseries, poverty and hunger away and the realities in the country were exposed to the world.

THE IMPORTANT ARTICLES OF THE CRC

In the UN Convention on the rights of the child there are 10 principles and 54 articles. Throughout these articles the rights of the child and responsibility of parents and state have been articulated. Some important articles and their themes are as such–

Aritcle-1 : Every person below 18 years of age shall be considered as child.

Article-32 : A child has right to be protected from economic exploitation and any work which is (i) likely to be hazardous, (ii) interfering with child's education, (iii) harmful to child's health or physical, mental, spiritual, moral or social development.

Article-33 : Requiring state parties to take measures to prevent use of children in drug production and trading of drugs.
Article-34 : Requiring protection against sexual exploitation.
Article-35 : Prevention of abduction, sale and trading of children for any purposes.
Article-36 : Requiring protection against all sorts of exploitation which are prejudicial for child's welfare.
Article-38 : Granting child's right to education.
Article-39 : Providing measures to promote the physical, psychological recovery and social integration of child victims.

The responsibility of parents and the state have been enunciated particularly in Articles, 24,27 and 39. Parents and government have the joint responsibility in making a child into a fuller and perfect man and ensure her/him no exploitation during childhood.

WHAT CAN GOVERNMENT OR SOCIETY DO?

In Thailand school drop-out is very high. So, the Provincial Labour Welfare and Protection Office and the Provincial Primary Education Office of the Srisaket Province have jointly started an awareness raising project. The objective is to retain the children at school upto completion of their secondary education and stop child labour. The project has mobilized teachers and school administrators for this purpose. A total of 22 schools with higher school dropout rates participated in the campaign among teachers and children. The Ministry of Education has developed the school curriculum in the provinces where school dropout rate is high. The outcome of the project is that most children have completed education upto secondary level.

In the United Republic of Tanzania many children among farmers and shepherd families start working during their early childhood. This is an obstacle to their entry into and completion of primary school. So, government of Tanzania has launched a programme to bring children from poor families into school and pre-empt their participation into work before completion of primary education. The project has succeeded in generating enthusiasm for school among children, parents and teachers.

In Philippines a Multi Grade Education Programme (by the Department of Education, Culture and Sports) was initiated in 1995 in cooperation with NGO and started setting up school for the poor only. Monthly workshops are organised for teachers to sustain their continuing professional development and to wean away the problem of isolation while working in single-teacher schools. Here, the Alternative Learning System for Continuing Education (ALS-CEP), a bureau-provides education facilities to the over-age children who have been out of school.

Fe Y Algeria (Faith and joy) is an education project in Peru. It is also working in Guatemala. Peru is in west of Latin America and Guatemala is in middle America, near at Mexico. Faith and joy Algeria is a popular education movement association, – works for specific groups of children, youth and women belonging to poor communities. The programme includes education for work, formal education, distance education, literary and micro-enterprise training. This action plan has made remarkable success in abolition of child labour.

In Bangladesh, "Jatio Sramik League" provides vocational training for the young children who are out of school. It was started long back in 1969. There are now 4 instructors who work for and with 300 children. Casa de la Esperanza is an NGO working with street children in Panama. DLG (De Lass Gul) welfare programme in Pakistan is working for vocational training, literacy and promotion of education of poor children who are disadvantaged, dropouts and out of school. DLG is an NGO. In Nepal, Cheli-Beti programme has been launched to address the special needs of girls, for, girl's are married off early and put to work in husband's house but deprived of education. Moreover a bonded labour system known as 'kammaya' is prevalent in Nepal. Many NGOs have used the C-B- programme to educate the out of school children in NEPAL PANI (National Children's Patronage), a government programme of Costa Rica is being executed for street children and children in informal sectors in Costa Rica.

In India, 'Mukti Ashram' is working at New Delhi. It is linked with SACCS (South Asian Coalition against Child Servitude). It has rehabilitated over 1600 children since 1990. The objective of it is to fight against bondage. Most children 6-7 age group are lured away, kidnapped from native village and taken to work place in industries, mines, construction sites, hotels, agricultural sector, hundred miles away. They are confined to toil day in, day out without wages or cash. They are freed by Mukti Ashram, an NGO of its own style. CREDA (Centre for Rural Education & Development Action) has been working in Mirzapur – Bhadohi carpet manufacturing belt of U.P. It has been struggling to set free the bonded children in the factories. This and surrounding areas contribute 80% of India's total carpet production, most of which are exported. CREDA has contributed significantly to decline the child workers in carpet looms.

In M.P. Eklabya, an NGO, has made a gigantic success in universalising the primary and secondary education. It is the biggest NGO in India. It is providing alternative to child labour practices.

In Assam-Gyan-Bigyan Samimittee, is faring well in lower Assam in reducing the school dropouts, 'Posowa' collection of poem by Ms Rangila Medhi is an evidence of its success. ICCW (Indian Council for Child Welfare) Assam state branch has been working for street and destitute children since 1967. ICCW provides non-formal education, vocational training, supplementary nutrition, health cheek-up to deprived and disadvantaged children. It runs – 6 (six) street children centres at Paltan Bazar, Santipur (Bharalumukh), Noonmati (Mathgoria), Aryanagar (Charapbhati), Sivanagar (Hengerabari) & Bhatpara (Hatigaon). Rural Multimedia Publicity and Promotion, an NGO of Golaghat, has been run under Sri Abdul Motin to provide orientation training on prevention of HIV/AIDS in the society. AHRC (Assam Human Rights Commission, 1996) is also popularising the rights of the child through seminar, delivering lectures, casting T.V.

programmes, undertaking project study on state of the children, etc. But, Assam still owns over 3.4 million (in 2001 AD) not school attending children.

Under developed countries (UDCs) of ecumen areas including India have been experiencing a complex child labour problem because of their high fertility, large number of siblings, orthodoxical social attitude, self-defeating legislations, lethargy and laxity in implementing a strict population control policy. UDCs, as they are economically poor and socially backward, the academics fall in a quagmire in sorting out the reasons of child labour practices. So, many argues, in an UDC, like India with a vast geographical area, large population, unique socio-economic conditions and democratic government, abolition of child labour system is quite impossible in a decade or/so.

Counter views are also important to note. Say, how long can we wait poverty to be banished first? In fact, for abolition of child labour in India, for that matter other UDCs cannot wait poverty to be banished and social change to be experienced first. During 18th and 19th centuries most of the developed countries in Europe experienced child labour problem of high magnitude confounded by economic and social backwardness. Only because of their determination, courage and dedication they could abolish child labour system, have attained high social standard and have had the development experience. India can also attain such a stage by abolishing the child labour practices, eliminating excessive population by adopting CRC, 1989.

India shares 28.08% child labourers in 1971 of the total child labour force of Asia, in 1981 it decreased to 19.96%, & in 1991 it has increased to 40.79%. By 2001 A.D. and thereafter, India's % share may not fall further due mainly to inefficiency of child labour elimination projects and programmes, unabated population growth and inter regional migration of child labourers.

The Table 1 also exposes the child labour position of India. In fact the magnitude of child labour in the country is soaring high. The factors working behind are– non-poor development expenditure and programmes, non-reduction of poverty but rapid growth of human population in the country. As such, the size of child labour force of India in 2015 has been projected to be 60 million compa.ed to 33 million in 2001 A.D.

Table 1
Magnitude of Child Population, Non-workers Non-Students and Child Labour in India 1951-2015

Year	*Total Child Population 0-14 age group*	*Child population in 5-14 age group*	*Non-workers & Non-Students 5-14 age group*	*Child labourers Main+Marginal workers (5-14)*
1951	1338,80,440	866,11,750	497,00,129	133,87,144
1961	1800,82,782	1139,80,144	649,14,609	144,69,775
1971	2303,94,772	1507,78,259	894,82,123	107,53,985
1981	2631,07,053	1795,97,245	895,41,313	136,40,873
1991	2969,36,090	2033,00,112	971,68,306	231,61,013
2001	3397,74,600	2360,60,100	1012,91,000	339,99,220
2015	5072,56,430	2954,97,700	1077,15,000	604,28,950

Source: Research Project taken up by Dr. P. Hazarika on Child Labour in Assam

HOW CAN ACTION PLAN BE STARTED IN INDIA?

Considering the 18th century's phenomena of advanced countries and tne cross-current situation of India the following measures can be taken up for early abolition of child labour in the country.

(i) NGOs and VOs of the country (figures at over half a thousand) can be addressed to rehabilitate the child labourers and the child labour owning h/hs in penury. Such Non-governmental organisations showing interest and contributing significantly in rehabilitation of child labour and child labour abolition mission can be encouraged to work more by extending financial aid to top ten/twenty organisations in the country in recognition of their dedications. NGOs and VOs can collect the orphans and Orphan child labourers and get them nurtured in 'SOS' villages. They can set up "Home for underprivileged children" as has been done in Scotland with a view to educating and bringing up children of poor and ailing parents.

(ii) Compulsory education to all children is the alternative instrument of reducing the magnitude of child labour. Convention of the Rights of the Child (CRC), 1989 declared by the UN and accepted by the government of India in 1990 is on right direction for ending up the child labour practices in the country in near future. So, grown up youths, the college and university students, with or without forming NGOs can educate the over-age children and those who are not fortunate to have formal education. Through a weekly drive they can ensure to send the dropouts and not school going children to attend the school at local/village level.

In addition to providing non-formal education on regular basis, the school dropouts and the averaged children can be imparted vocational training, population education to understand the futility of getting early married, disadvantage of having large number of siblings and the social responsibility in a country.

(iii) In India panchayats can play a vital role in abolition of child labour and in controlling the population explosion. For, economic development has its own development limit, and it is not the lasting solution to the present day child labour problem. It is high time that each Panchayat delineates its geographical and administrative area, surveys its resources available and finds the strengths, weaknesses and strategy of development.

Similarly, each panchayat can make h/h survey compiling information of number of h/hs, average family size per h/h, identify the child labour owning h/hs and the magnitude of child labour in the panchayat area. From such a survey, the panchayat authority could sort out the type of existing child labourers and their assumed activities. A little observation can help the panchayat to find out the reasons of going in for child labour and the solutions there of.

The types of child labourers observed in the country are orphan child labourers, rag pickers, street beggars, child labourers belonging to ailing or disabled parents or economically poor and destitute families, child labourers caused by school dropout and child labourers belonging to poor families but having adult workers and working parents.

A panchayat can provide wage-work/ employment/ better earning facilities to adult workers and working parents of the child labour owning h/hs and asking them to withdraw their children can be put in 'SOS' villages and/or in the 'Homes for Underprivileged Children' as would be developed by the NGOs. Child labourers belonging to poor and ailing parents can be given free and compulsory education and vocational training by keeping them in 'Underpriviledged Children's Home' till they become 14 or 18 years. Out of the fund of Welfare Schemes, a Panchayat can give stipend to such children for attending the school, while their parents can be provided old age security/pension and or old age shelter.

But, parents defying to send their children to school in spite of their ability and advantages needs to be punished forcing them to pay penalty equal to adult wage rate per month or be given opt to go in for rigorous imprisonment.

(iv) Considering the land scarcity, habitation problem and limitation of the natural resources within the panchayat area, a panchayat needs to act as watchdog on immigration to its area and adopt a clear family size control policy. One such policy that can be thought of is as such– "a couple having first child shall have full social security, second child shall have no guarantee and the third child shall entail heavy penalty." As regards, compelling the parents sending their wards to school up to complete 18 years of their age and not to exceed two child norm certain coercion is a must. The amount of penalty rate per month can be made heavier and the sibling norm much more strict in case of currently immigrating families, whose fertility rate and family size both are evidently high. Decrease in population size and increase in resource must empower a panchayat to share more benefit and vice-versa. Others need not share the misfortune or deliberate mistakes committed by the people of a panchayat. In fact a panchayat can be (and needs to be) asked to be self-reliant and manage its problems with the people living there in. This cannot only relief the governments from financial burden, environment management risk and waste of money on family welfare head, but also can CRC, 1989 get implemented.

Logic runs, if China can control population explosion limiting the children norm for a married couple, and European countries can abolish child labour within one or two decades, then why not India can do the same? For the young academics the answer is positive. Yes, India can do it.

INDEX

A

S